Bridging the Americas:

The Literature of
Paule Marshall,
Toni Morrison,
and Gayl Jones

# Bridging the Americas:

## The Literature of Paule Marshall, Toni Morrison, and Gayl Jones

### STELAMARIS COSER

TEMPLE UNIVERSITY PRESS

Philadelphia

Temple University Press, Philadelphia 19122

Published 1995

Excerpts from *Song for Anninho* by Gayl Jones are reprinted by permission of Lotus Press, Inc.

Excerpt from "A Weekend in Austin: A Poet, the People, and the KKK" in *See No Evil: Prefaces, Essays, & Accounts 1976–1983* by Ntozake Shange. Published by Momo's Press.

Excerpts from "Bocas: A Daughter's Geography" in *A Daughter's Geography* by Ntozake Shange. Published by St. Martin's Press, Inc.

The paper used in this publication meets the minimum requirements of American National Standard for Information Sciences—Permanence of Paper for Printed Library Materials, ⊗ ANSI Z39.48-1984

Printed in the United States of America

**Library of Congress Cataloging-in-Publication Data**

Coser, Stelamaris, 1948–
    Bridging the Americas : the literature of Paule Marshall, Toni
Morrison, and Gayl Jones / Stelamaris Coser.
      p.  cm.
    Includes index.
    ISBN 1–56639–266–7(acid-free) — ISBN 1–56639–267–5
(paper : acid-free)
      1. American fiction—Afro-American authors—History and criticism.
2. Women and literature—United States—History—20th century.
3. American fiction—20th century—History and criticism.
4. Marshall, Paule, 1929–    —Criticism and interpretation.
5. Morrison, Toni—Criticism and interpretation.  6. Jones, Gayl—
Criticism and interpretation.  7. Caribbean Area—In literature.
8. Afro-Americans in literature.  9. Sex role in literature.
10. Brazil—In literature.  I. Title.
PS153.N5C73  1994
813'.54099287'08996073—dc20
                                     94–30421
                                         CIP

# CONTENTS

Acknowledgments    vii

Preface    ix

1. Stepping-Stones between the Americas: The Works of
   Paule Marshall, Toni Morrison, and Gayl Jones    1

2. From the Natives' Point of View:
   The Ethnographic Novels of Paule Marshall    27

3. The Redefinition of American Geography and History:
   Toni Morrison's *Song of Solomon* and *Tar Baby*    81

4. The Dry Wombs of Black Women: Memories of
   Brazilian Slavery in *Corregidora* and *Song for Anninho*    120

5. No Final Chord: The Music
   of Morrison, Jones, and Marshall    164

Notes    175

Index    217

# ACKNOWLEDGMENTS

I am deeply indebted to a number of people and institutions that have in one way or another contributed to the completion of this project: family and friends, colleagues and staff at both the University of Minnesota and the Universidade Federal do Espirito Santo (UFES), and the Conselho Nacional de Desenvolvimento Científico e Tecnológico (CNPq) in Brazil. This work would not have been possible without the funding from UFES and CNPq and the invaluable support of my Brazilian university throughout my doctoral program in 1987–1991. I also thank my colleagues in the Department of Languages and Letters at UFES for allowing me time and conditions to revise my dissertation and for adding their suggestions, bibliographical references, and helping hands. I particularly thank Mirtis Caser and Solange Bonn for their constant solidarity.

The interdisciplinary orientation of my project has much to do with the critical openness in the various departments constituting the field of American Studies at the University of Minnesota. I am indebted to Clarke Chambers, Stuart Schwartz, Prabhakara Jha, David W. Noble, John Wright, Joanna O'Connell, Gayle G. Yates, and George Lipsitz, professors who shared with me their experience and expertise and nudged me on with their example and encouragement. I am especially thankful to David, John, Joanna, Gayle, and George for their careful reading and response to my work. As my major adviser, George Lipsitz gave me friendly and competent guidance through the intricacies of cultural politics and contemporary theory;

I am thankful for his orientation and for the stimulating example of his own scholarship. Providential help with sources for my research came from Patricia Turner, bibliographer for humanities and social sciences at Wilson Library. It was a privilege to discuss my work with all of these people throughout the writing process.

I am indebted to colleagues and friends who shared their thoughts with me and helped me with their insights, particularly Jun Xing, Roberta Hill Whiteman (Bobbie), and Arlene and Luiz Diaz. Providential computer assistance came from my friends Beth Gama and Wes Olson. These and other people inside and outside the academy provided me with a much-needed multicultural community in the United States. Constant support came from my "sister" Charlayne Myers and from my "American Mom and Dad" Charlotte and Wayne Owens, whose family I joined as a foreign exchange student in 1966, and I thank them all.

Finally, I thank my parents, Orlando and Delourdes Coser, as well as my brothers and sisters for always being there for me. My deepest gratitude goes to my daughter, Marilia. She always supported me through the years even when that meant separation and *saudade*. Without her love, her companionship, and her patience, my work would not have been completed. I dedicate this book to her.

# PREFACE

This book examines some inter-American characteristics in work developed over the last four decades by black women writers from the United States. Even as the recent "renaissance" of literature by black women suggests parallel developments with the so-called boom of Latin American writers, novels such as *The Chosen Place, the Timeless People*, by Paule Marshall; *Song of Solomon*, by Toni Morrison; and *Corregidora*, by Gayl Jones also represent an affirmation, unprecedented in U.S. literature, of a sense of proximity and commonality between the Americas, particularly the shared heritage of colonialism and racism in the coasts and fields of the "extended Caribbean." The continental stretch thus baptized by Immanuel Wallerstein borders the Atlantic Ocean from Maryland in the United States to Rio de Janeiro in Brazil, with the Caribbean as its nodal point.

The storytelling of Morrison, Jones, and Marshall explores and expands that space and construes inter-American links in several different ways. The links may occur through intertextuality, mainly with the work of Gabriel García Márquez and Carlos Fuentes; by making an effective intervention in the ongoing debate over the history of gender and race relations in the *New World*; by exposing postcolonial domination within and between American nation-states; and above all, by illuminating the African roots of the Americas. The works of Morrison, Marshall, and Jones assume an innovatively "American" perspective and break a long tradition of estrangement and suspicion between a whiter "Anglo-America" and the multicolored "Nuestra America" idealized by José Martí. They now present the two hemispheres as equally multicolored and equally white-dominated. Their stories bridge individual and collective forms of resistance and sociocultural and ideological processes in Brazil, the Caribbean, and the United States. Political boundaries between nation-states still signal separation and difference, but identities and histories overlap and crisscross over and beyond those limits.

In addition to the combined focus on race, class, and gender, the articulation of a multicultural and polyglot inter-Americanness assumes special significance in a decade—the 1990s, five hundred years after Christopher Columbus named the continent—that calls forth a dynamic reinterpretation of *New World* myths, traditions, and conflicts. In their personal and literary histories, Paule Marshall, Toni Morrison, and Gayl Jones emphasize their black womanhood and their U.S. citizenship. But they are also American citizens in a larger way, having transgressed traditional boundaries and established enclaves. Their interracial, inter-American, intertextual stories, crossing the borders of fact and fiction, stand out as truly American literature.

Bridging the Americas: | The Literature of
Paule Marshall,
Toni Morrison,
and Gayl Jones

The Americas in the Works of
Paule Marshall, Toni Morrison, and Gayl Jones

# 1

## Stepping-Stones between the Americas: The Works of Paule Marshall, Toni Morrison, and Gayl Jones

The islands of the Caribbean—"steppingstones that might have been placed there long ago by some giant race to span the distance between the Americas, North and South."
—Paule Marshall,
*The Chosen Place, the Timeless People*

Contemporary black women writers in the United States have interrogated issues of history, culture, and literature related to the Americas. The connections drawn in their fiction between the United States, the Caribbean, and Latin America introduce a new cosmopolitanism and internationalism to U.S. literature. By thinking of America as one continent with a common history and by challenging dominant hierarchies of race, class, and gender, black women writers pose important challenges for readers and critics in general. They have made significant contributions to their own nation's literature and culture by bringing inside its borders sensibilities and concerns familiar to the "Third World" below the southern borders of the United States.[1]

The Caribbean and Brazil are choices for setting and reference points in *Tar Baby*, by Toni Morrison; *Corregidora* and *Song of Anninho*, by Gayl Jones; and *The Chosen Place, the Timeless People* (among several other works), by Paule Marshall. In spite of these writers' differences in style and perspective, the history of the African diaspora in the *New World* binds together the imaginative worlds they have created in fiction. Toni Morrison's novel *Song of Solomon*, although not directly connected with the larger America in geographical and historical aspects, is intertextually related to Gabriel García Márquez's novel *One Hundred Years of Solitude.* Style and imagery in Gayl Jones's works likewise respond to her reading of Carlos Fuentes. Incorporating geographical, historical, or literary spaces of the Caribbean and Latin America into their works, Morrison and Jones have drawn on the concept of literature as agent of social transformation, articulated by, among others, Latin American novelists García Márquez and Fuentes. Morrison and Jones have also acknowledged that they share with their Latin American colleagues a model of writing as storytelling, grounded in folk traditions and beliefs. They create a literary inter-space (*entre-lugar*) between the discourses of the Americas, a contaminated area of exchange.[2]

At the same time that Jones and Morrison permit a new reading of their works by this intertextual movement, they also graft onto Latin American novels the gaze of black women in the United States. Two of the most important phenomena in the post-1960s literary scene thus come together: the new visibility of writings by black women and the unprecedented popularity of Latin American novelists in the publishing industry and academic circles of the United States. By overstepping conventional closures of nationality, race, and gender, Morrison, Jones, and Marshall rewrite the boundaries between the American hemispheres on the basis of shared cultural, social, and economic relationships and common cultural roots in Africa.

The polyglot and multicultural texts of these writers reinvigorate and also subvert the literature of the United States. Long before Toni Morrison was awarded the Nobel Prize for literature in 1993, she and Marshall and Jones had been receiving extensive critical attention for their important role in the imaginative writing of black culture and history from the perspectives of black women. As an additional reading, this book constitutes an interrogation of the inter-American quality of their narratives. The three women help to blur the dividing line between the "advanced" society of North America and the neocolonial structure of the Caribbean (Anglo or otherwise) and Latin America by dealing with the complex and contradictory realities of mixed racial heritage in the Caribbean, the United States, and Brazil. The importance of their novels on an inter-American level is twofold. At the same time that they give visibility to and recognize bonds with the Southern Hemisphere, pulling together memories and experiences, they also inscribe their gender and race in the literature of the United States and of the continent. Avoiding essentialisms, they reinterpret gender and ethnicity in the process of remembering and writing Africa in the Caribbean, in the United States, in Brazil, and in the whole continent of America.

The islands of the Caribbean mark the birth of America. "Steppingstones" linking North and South, they are a continuing symbol for the meeting of different "cultural tributaries," as well as the initial place of displacement and domination of native peoples and Africans in the *New World*. Historian Gordon K. Lewis points out that it was in the Caribbean "sugar islands" that "the agrosocial system of slavery developed in its fullest and most harsh form."[3] Immanuel Wallerstein uses the term *extended Caribbean* to identify those societies developed on the basis of cotton, sugar, or coffee plantations that were supported by slave labor. Although such societies and the Caribbean islands as a whole resist simplistic generalizations regarding their sociocultural formation and development, Wallerstein's concept seems appropriate as a "unifying alibi" for a discussion of novels by Marshall, Morrison, and Jones.[4]

In Paule Marshall's *The Chosen Place, the Timeless People* and Toni Morrison's *Tar Baby*, the Caribbean islands continue to perform their historical and carnivalesque roles as the original and central space where "creolisations and assimilations and syncretisms were negotiated" in the *New World*.[5] These novels, along with Gayl Jones's novel *Corregidora* and her long narrative poem *Song for Anninho*, are set in areas within the extended Caribbean, interconnecting them and branching out along the routes of migration of African descendants into the largest cities of the United States and Europe. The stories focus on the struggles and negotiations within a continental "Afroamerica" throughout its long and complex processes of constructing cultural identity in the *New World*.[6]

The works of Jones, Marshall, and Morrison tell tales of sorrow and bitterness blended with sounds of music and joy, expressing the mixed colors and conflicting emotions of the American continent. In the attempt to define their own place and identity as black women in the United States, these writers cross centuries and lands and write a larger American narrative. Even as they record the process of reconstructing identity through black protagonists and their specific communities, they illuminate forms of resistance by groups oppressed in the neocolonial structure persisting today in the Caribbean–Latin

American region and among marginalized groups in the United States.

By so doing, their works also transgress conventional boundaries of genre and discipline. Morrison writes poetic fiction, Jones resorts to narrative poetry, and all three writers explore a mixture of auto-biography, collective history, and ethnography. Much as in modern interpretive ethnography, they weave facts out of the memories of people, stories told and retold in their homes, rites of song and dance, dreams and incantations. Much as in history, they describe racial and sexual exploitation, economic destitution, and racial seg-regation in the struggles of modern urban life as well as of colonial times. Although the texts are creative and imaginary, they grow out of individual and collective experience and are fueled with materials that have long been of interest to anthropologists and historians of comparative slavery in the Americas.[7]

Through close reading of specific works by Morrison, Marshall, and Jones, I propose to examine the various ways in which their storytelling constructs inter-American bridges. These can be formed through intertextuality, through their intervention in the historical debate over gender and race relations in the *New World*, through the ethnographic representation of black culture and the affirmation of African roots, or through the exploration of postcolonial relations of power in and between nation-states of the American continent.

## The Meaning of America

The cultural approximation of the different Americas is a new under-taking. Extremely asymmetrical levels of development and power, as well as conflicting "national interest" priorities, have complicated and delayed the prospects of a true dialogue between the hemi-spheres. While the United States is a necessary reference point in Latin American–Caribbean identity and history, whether as model or antagonist, Latin America has usually been denied any importance in the North except in Cold War strategic maneuvering and economic expansionism. The United States reinvented "America" the country as a continent in and of itself, in history books and in popular under-standing. According to historian David W. Noble, the word *America* is used here to "mean a single nation, the United States," revealing a deep commitment "to isolating our national culture."[8]

Rapid and successful capitalist development, political and technological achievements, and attending politics of racism and expansionism in the United States contrast markedly with the slower growth of the more economically isolated and racially heterogeneous populations of the rest of the continent, contributing to solidifying the "American" rhetoric and widening the gulf between "Anglos" and "Latinos." The perception of sharp differences separating the two cultural hemispheres has often been reinforced in Latin American critiques and in the work of the so-called Latin Americanists. Among them is anthropologist Charles Wagley, who traces the cultural barrier to the persistence of two fundamentally different "culture spheres" derived from "distinctive adaptations" to the *New World*. Quite contrastive "mother countries" supplied North and South America with "the basic social and cultural institutions." On the one hand was the "Protestant, neo-capitalistic, and bourgeois" northern Europe; on the other hand, the "Catholic, semi-feudalistic, and aristocratic-oriented" southern realm. Historian Richard Morse, another Latin Americanist, believes that the U.S. difficulty in relating to Latin America has to do with "economic and military asymmetries," as well as a parochial universalization of hegemonic U.S. values and categories. Such categories could not grasp the interweaving of Creole, American Indian, and African cultures of the Southern Hemisphere or the "heterodox world views" in the "multiple ethics" flourishing there. Mexican writer Octavio Paz has long portrayed Mexico and the United States as "two distinct versions of Western civilization," separated not only by their different social, economic, and historical developments but principally by abstract, fluid cultural aspects that cannot be easily measured.[9]

In the United States, stereotypes of "the other Americans" from below the border are part of the colonial heritage and often conflate with similar simplifications, ambiguities, and oppositions in images of African descendants or Native Americans. The "troublesome border" that exists between Mexico and the United States is similar to the line drawn between races and ethnicities within the latter country, particularly between whites on one side and blacks and Indians on the other.[10] The inherited stereotypes of Indians and Africans in the dominant culture of the United States intertwine with perceptions of the Caribbean and Latin America, areas where the percentage of "peoples of color" was usually greater than the European population during colonial times and tends to remain so today (except for Argentina, Uruguay, and the southern part of Brazil).

5

In the Hollywood imaginary, Latin America has been paradoxically synonymous with paradise and hell, nature and sin, attraction and repulsion. Ignorant and greasy bandits from Mexican deserts alternate with sensual, dark women on sunny beaches. In either case, the superior character of the North American white man is ascertained as he defeats the beast and conquers the beauty, thus gaining symbolic control over the continent. Even when Latinos are intentionally portrayed more positively, as in the movie *Flying Down to Rio* (1933), they are still represented as different and alien, incomprehensible to the gaze of the Anglo eye. "What have these South Americans got below the equator that we haven't?" wonder blonde girls gasping at the seductive games of a dark Brazilian woman in that film.[11]

The representation of the Caribbean islands and Brazil as havens for passion and "dark" mistresses recalls the colonialist pattern of mating outside marriage, established by the colonizers and solidified by the upper classes.[12] The movie industry has thus voiced and reinforced a difference from barbarism and sensuality that has been constructed by the white European since antiquity and that turned particularly problematic and contradictory in the age of "colonial encounters" in the *New World.* The repugnant Mexican "greaser" in early Hollywood stories is Caliban/cannibal/Carib/Caribbean, the same word and image of the "native," corrupted and carried down in major European texts and first immortalized by William Shakespeare's *The Tempest.*[13]

Latin Americans and black people in the United States share a similarly uneasy relation to "white America." The process of negotiation and construction of their identities often takes the form of a reactive response to white European traditions and principles. In most of Spanish America, wars of independence coincided with antislavery movements. Many newborn nations constructed themselves as mixed or mestizo to affirm their antagonism to the white colonizer. The ideology of an America of mixed races was established as early as 1819, when Simon Bolívar, the celebrated "liberator" of Spanish America, affirmed the dream of social syncretism to distinguish the newborn nations from the Spanish rulers who had decimated the majority of the Indian population. In Venezuela, for instance, Bolívar exhorted the congress to accept the country's mixed origins and the fact that Venezuelans "are neither European nor North American."[14]

By contrast, the anti-colonial pride and the nationalist ideologies of *mestizaje* do not preclude discrimination within Latin America against people of African descent. Bolívar was a Venezuelan from the *criollo* elite of Caracas and shared its fear of a black rebellion. His America may have been mixed but was required to remain under the power and control of the white upper class. Several decades would intervene before Cuban revolutionaries incorporated African color and heritage into their definition of nation, rewriting the dream and facing similar paradoxes.

In the case of Cuba, the abolition of slavery and independence from Spain were closely linked to anti-imperialist feelings regarding the domination of the United States.[15] The contrast between two Americas with clashing worldviews became even more focused. The Cuban poet and revolutionary hero José Martí (1853–1895) responded to the outside threat by underlining the difference between a white and racist Anglo-America and "Nuestra America," which he defined as non-Western. For Martí, the multifaceted space lying "from Rio Bravo to Patagonia" was marked by both a combination of cultures and a history of multiple exploitations. "Our America" was not an integral part of "the West" because of its racial, cultural, and social mixture and its peripheral and dependent status in relation to advanced capitalism.

A major leader in the struggle for the belated independence of Cuba and the abolition of slavery in the country, Martí sustained hope in a plurality of voices and colors joined together by the dream of the nation: "a Cuban is more than white, more than mulatto, more than black." Pride and faith in their own *patria* should draw white Creoles away from the racism of the "despotic and perverse colonizer" and also convince grieving Negroes, "the most oppressed Cubans," to forgive and trust. Recognizing the violent past and the persistent colonial shadow in the republican moment, Martí was nevertheless optimistic about the radical shift toward equality after the revolution of 1868.[16]

The association between the revolutionary struggle for independence, still taking place in Cuba and Puerto Rico at the end of the nineteenth century, and the unique geographical location of the islands gave the Caribbean (as Paule Marshall would later recognize) a special role in the development of American history. According to Martí, it had a "greater mission made obligatory by the times, and by its position at the crossroads of the world."[17] In political and economic affairs, the extended Caribbean occupies the paradoxical position of being both peripheral and central to the dominant interests of North America. As Barbara Christian ironically remarks, the Caribbean islands have always been an insignificant periphery of the United States but at the same time "intensely important," since "U.S. troops were continually invading one island or another."[18]

A combined ideology of racial integration and anti-imperialist resistance continues to pervade the political and intellectual leadership of Cuba and other parts of Latin America and the Caribbean, and is often evident in writings and interviews by such novelists as Mexican Carlos Fuentes and Colombian Gabriel García Márquez. For Latin Americans as for black writers in the United States, "Anglo-America" remains a constant counterpoint of difference and power.[19]

The reinvented inter-American dialogue in the novels of Morrison, Marshall, and Jones invites a revision of the term *America* and its hyphenated derivations. When "outsiders" from within (such as these black writers) and Americans from without (Caribbean and Latin Americans) join together in a cultural coalition, the question of (un)naming the descendants of African peoples acquires new complexity.[20] In the United States, terms used to identify African descendants and the offspring of racially mixed unions have undergone numerous changes since slavery, an indication of early impositions and later negotiations between these people and the dominant white culture. The latest sign of renaming as a way of reinventing the self and the culture came with Jesse Jackson's public move toward the adoption of "African American" as the new ethnic-racial category in 1989. According to John Wright, "the discussion over what to call themselves reflects a continuous debate over black people's place in American society," a place still uncertain and problematic.[21] That space is in a constant process of negotiation, and the shifting terms have to do with both the dominant ideology of the country and the strategies imagined by African descendants to assert their identities.

The continental implications of the use of "American" or any of its hyphenated variants, however, have not been sufficiently considered in that debate. The terms *Afro-American* and *African American*, if applied only to U.S. citizens, carry "quasi-imperialistic overtones," according to Elisa Larkin Nascimento. The use is "inherited from the tendency of the U.S. as a whole to label itself 'America,' thus appropriating the entire continent to its hegemonic self." As a black scholar and activist who has lived in the United States, Nigeria, and

Brazil, Nascimento argues for a true Afro-American coalition that must revise "natural" neocolonial assumptions and reflect "the fact that Afro-Americans come from Colombia, Costa Rica, Peru, Brazil and the United States alike."[22] U.S. anthropologist Melville Herskovits, well known for his studies of black families and African retentions in parts of the American continent, in 1945 proposed a similar agenda for the creation of intercontinental disciplines within Afro-American studies, "treating of peoples living in North, South and Central America, the Caribbean, and Africa."[23] If contemporary critical theory, particularly when focusing on emancipatory forms of narrative, wants to separate itself from what Henry Louis Gates, Jr. calls "the abusive Western practices of deflation through misnaming," the question remains central and inconclusive.[24]

The Harlem Renaissance writer Langston Hughes once declared in a poem, "I, too, am America."[25] Today, the voices of women, of Chicanos, of Latinos in general, of all the people marginalized in the ideal WASP nation join voices coming from throughout the continent to claim the same right and recognition. A new renaissance in writing by black women has taken place in the United States as a development of the civil rights and feminist movements of the 1960s and 1970s. Prominent within it, the literature of Gayl Jones, Toni Morrison, and Paule Marshall gives voice to the experience and history of black women.[26] At the same time, by willing to associate with narrative strategies and ideological concerns expressed by Latin American male writers, these women avoid the reductionism of an exclusively black female narrative. Self-segregation in a peripheral and idealized tower would only help reproduce essentialist mistakes of both mainstream and feminist criticism.[27] My reading of Morrison, Jones, and Marshall investigates their creation of this inter-space between genders, races, nations, and hemispheres.

## Women of Color and the Remapping of America

The possibility of change in North–South relations, according to Mexican writer Octavio Paz, comes out of the liberation movements that took root in the United States in the 1970s, "the rebellion of Blacks and Chicanos, of women and the young, of artists and intellectuals." As the "conscience of the nation" began to show an unprecedented willingness to "speak with themselves, with their own otherness," the potential for a real dialogue with Mexico and Latin America increased.[28] In fact, after establishing the visibility of their specific ethnic identities, women writers of color have supported commonality and solidarity among different ethnicities, a connection usually prevented by the rigid racial demarcations inherited from the dominant culture. In criticism, poetry, and fiction, these women seek to overstep boundaries, divisions, and antagonisms that they have faced in their lives. The discovery of bonds within the country has expanded to an awareness of similar cultural memories and social struggles in the "Third World" space of Latin America and the Caribbean.

In her critique of "mainstream" feminism, U.S. black critic Barbara Smith articulates a coalition of women of color under a Third World umbrella, bringing together "Native American, Asian American, Latina and Afro American women in the United States, and indigenous peoples of Third World countries." Rejecting a narrow, white, apolitical kind of feminism, Smith argues for "a multi-issued approach to politics . . . a multi-issued strategy for challenging women's oppression" that would combine related struggles of race, class, and gender. Even as she challenges the white control of the feminist agenda, she reflects on the difficulties presented by multi-ethnic approaches when the dominant culture has always enforced division and discrimination. The experience and consciousness of oppression does not exempt black men and women, including herself, from misrepresenting the Other or other minority women from being prejudiced against blacks. Smith does not idealize her Third World coalition, but she believes that her "umbrella" women have a central role in the expansion of contemporary historical and literary narratives.[29]

A radical opening to Otherness allied to literary and political concerns has characterized the work of Alice Walker, one of the best known black "womanist" (as she would rather call herself) writers in the United States. She also admits that her awareness of "the ignorance, arrogance, and racism" in what is traditionally taken as "Superior Knowledge" did not prevent her from expecting Cubans to have the same attitude about race as the people of her own country. A visit to the island nation showed her that categories are contextual and historical and that U.S. attitudes are not universal. Walker returned with the impression that in Cuba the dominant culture is "recognized as being the synthesis of the African heritage and the Spanish."[30]

Alice Walker echoes an evaluation of Cuban culture that harks back to Martí and lingers on in the rhetoric of Fidel Castro and the literature of Gabriel García Márquez. Whether she and they are overly optimistic about such syncretism is open to debate: the illusory quality of national myths of *mestizaje* has been a recurring topic in recent historiography and literature from Latin America. Today, García Márquez and the majority of Latin American intellectuals agree with leaders of liberation theology that history in "Our America" has also been written "with a white hand" and conciliation has always been imposed by the minority elite.[31]

In any case, one may connect Walker's perception of Cuba with the reaction of a Cuban man who was exposed to police violence in Minneapolis at the beginning of 1989. "In Cuba," he told reporters, "we all worked together, black and white. I learned I was black when I came to this country."[32] Evoking the experience of black psychoanalyst and political activist Frantz Fanon, the episode may indicate that the realities of racism and colonialism are not really faced while blacks remain among their own people. Fanon was not conscious of the power of racism while he remained in his native Antillean island of Martinique. Only in coming face to face with the European colonizer or a predominantly white society could oppression truly be unveiled and inner divisions be understood.[33]

The impressions of Latin American places reported by some black women writers from the United States do not prove the superiority of any culture over another. They do reveal, however, a wish to connect with and understand those cultures. Recounting a journey in the opposite direction from that taken by the Cuban man or by Fanon, black feminist writer Audre Lorde describes Mexico City as the site of a reverse kind of recognition, of the discovery of the friendly gaze of people similar to her own. By mirroring herself in their faces, she unburdens herself of a social alienation that had been the "normal" pattern for her until then: "Wherever I went, there were brown faces of every hue meeting mine, and seeing my own color reflected upon the streets in such great numbers was an affirmation for me that was brand new and very exciting. I had never felt visible before, nor even known I lacked it."[34] The affirmation of her own identity in the gaze of Mexicans erases the traditional contrast— always present in standard, representatively "American" narratives—between *I* here and *they* below the border.[35]

On a visit to Mexico earlier in this century, Harlem Renaissance poet Langston Hughes was pleased not to find there "any color line, or any Jim Crow." Yet his travels to Cuba and Haiti in 1931 showed him the sad realities of poverty and racism that still prevailed.[36] The feelings of self-assurance and recognition reported by Audre Lorde, along with the realization of the recurring economic and social inequality and racial oppression remarked by Langston Hughes, also inform the novels of Morrison, Marshall, and Jones and their linkage with the culture and history of the Americas.

Other black women writers in the United States have recently approached ideals of a Pan-African solidarity across the American continent or an interracial coalition of women within this country. Strongly supportive of liberation movements in the Caribbean and Central America, the work of poet and playwright Ntozake Shange emphasizes a common struggle uniting the *New World* and Africa against an obsolete and violent white West. It does not matter that languages are different and distances great; for Shange, union is possible, hope is strong, and a new, bright song echoes in the stories told by mothers to their children.

> but i have a daughter / la habana
> i have a son / guyana
> our twins
> santiago & brixton / cannot speak
> the same language
> yet we fight the same old man. . . .
> the same man who thought the earth waz flat
> go on over the edge / go on over the edge old man
> you'll see us in luanda, or the rest of us
> in chicago
> rounding out the morning /
> we are feeding our children the sun.[37]

Shange expresses her intense support for freedom and equality all over the Americas, her enthusiasm in being part of a movement for a *teatro libre* in all countries of the continent, and her faith in the union of peoples of whatever hue against oppression within the United States. In a combination of various languages and geographies, she joins "Nuestra America" and other "Third World American Writers [who] are rewriting American history from a subversive 'Calibanic' typology."[38]

> Lines and lines of raised hands blancas,
> morenas, indias, negras, aziaticas, our

hands together: tejanos / texans. We
reaching toward the sky / thru the fog
them sheets of fog. Maybe 'we' the sun.[39]

In the novel *The Salt Eaters*, by Toni Cade Bambara, the central
character, Velma, is a black woman whose search for meaning in her
African roots does not isolate her from peoples of other ethnicities
and races. On the contrary, her conflicts and dreams are associated
with those of other female friends whose stories also tell of disruption, oppression, and a common attachment to the land: the "Seven
Sisters"—Inez, Nilda, Chezia, Mai, Iris, Cecile, and Palma—all "colored" women "talking Spanish or West Indian or some other language." They are involved in different forms of contemporary protest
("No Nukes," "Stop the Esmeralda," "Get the U.S. Out of . . ."). 
They respect one another's cultures and practice mutual solidarity.
Sisters of the yam, of the rice, of the corn, of the plantain, their
memories reveal families, villages, rites of faith, spirits, and also dark
times of silence and pain.[40]

Women from other ethnic groups in the United States have tried
to escape the narrow confines of the black–white binary. The liminal
position in the border—*la frontera*, as Gloria Anzaldúa puts it—allows the possibility of reinvention and a larger degree of freedom, in
spite of the contradictions and the pressures from all sides. Anzaldúa
negotiates her own *mestizaje* within the borders of the United States.
"To live in the Borderlands means you are neither hispana india negra española," says Anzaldúa, and it demands much of you: that
"you live sin fronteras, be a crossroads."[41]

Also responding to a condition of liminality between her native
India and her home in the United States, Gayatri Spivak chooses to
avoid placing herself under exclusive "Indian" or "American" definitions. She would rather circumvent the pressure to produce "authentic" ethnic narratives by situating herself as a migrant or "manage-
able Other." Spivak argues for a truly cosmopolitan approach to
race, gender, and class that recognizes and respects differences
among women, people of a same race, and "Third World" groups,
avoiding ghettoization and the idealization of one's "authentic"
roots.[42] Anzaldúa and Spivak are only two examples of contemporary
reactions to the gap between ethnicities and the illusion of pure origins. As women placed by family and cultural backgrounds literally
between two distinct spaces, they have explored the creative possibilities of being "in between."

## Morrison, Jones, Marshall:
## Inter-American Connections

The novels of Toni Morrison, Gayl Jones, and Paule Marshall are undoubtedly black stories that problematize the history of the United States. They have undermined the conventional representation of the United States as a white nation or as a nation in black and white, resting isolated from the rest of the continent. They explore interracial contact and the very meaning of "blackness" in America. Herself a New Yorker born to Barbadian parents, Paule Marshall's novels focus on the relationship between Africa and a larger America that embraces the Caribbean, the United States, and Brazil, characterized by a diversity of colors and cultures. When Toni Morrison explores the complexity of mixed heritage in the United States and the Caribbean in her epic narratives of the African diaspora, or when she writes as a storyteller who brings the community together and keeps myths alive, she is connecting not only with the tradition of black women writers pioneered by Zora Neale Hurston but also with the literature of such Latin Americans as Gabriel García Márquez, as she openly acknowledges.[43] Gayl Jones's fiction is rooted in her desire to expose the lives of black women during and after slavery in Brazil as well as in the United States, but she also refers to García Márquez and Carlos Fuentes as major influences on her "notions of fiction."[44]

The conceptions of literature connecting Marshall, Morrison, and Jones to García Márquez and Fuentes have to do with the recuperation of memory through the tradition of storytelling inherited from mothers and grandmothers. Storytelling is a communal practice that frees history from the constraints of the dominant narrative, creating the possibility of a future outside the hegemonic social practice. Walter Benjamin connects storytelling with peasant societies and regrets its loss in the modern world, but it is clear that these contemporary novels recuperate it as a powerful emancipatory tool.[45] Many times, it is true, the stories leave the city to draw strength from the rituals and memories of village folk, as do Morrison's *Song of Solomon* and *Tar Baby* and Marshall's *The Chosen Place, the Timeless People* and *Praisesong for the Widow*. The village may be an isolated community that has preserved memories of the African past, as in the novels just mentioned, or an imaginary seventeenth-century Maroon settlement in the hilly forests of Brazil, as in Gayl Jones's *Song for Anninho*. The power of this literature lies in a kind of storytelling "that combines subjectivity and objectivity, that employs the insights and passions of myth and folklore in the service of revising history."[46]

The references to a multicolored, complex, and striving "America" in the works of Bambara, Shange, Walker, Jones, Marshall, and Morrison make an explicit connection between the black "nation" in the United States and the peoples and cultures living below the southern border. As for cultural linkages, Lorde, Walker, Marshall, Morrison, and Jones came to recognize them through family bonds, in their own travels to different countries, or by means of the growing number of historical and literary accounts that have accorded these linkages increased visibility. Family has tied Marshall to Barbados and the Caribbean culture, and a career in journalism allowed her long stays in Brazil and close observation of that nation's culture. Marriage to a Jamaican possibly helped Morrison to connect her birthplace in Ohio and her family roots in Alabama and Georgia to the realities of the Caribbean. Graduate school called Gayl Jones's attention to the colonial structure and race relations in Brazil. U.S.-bound migration from the Caribbean and Latin America together with the higher degree of physical mobility and the academic background of blacks and women from the United States have broken down the traditional cultural isolation of the two hemispheres and have opened the way for the inter-American literature of Marshall, Jones, and Morrison.

While these three U.S. women writers understood their cultural and historical connections with Latin America and the Caribbean through family stories, books, or visits to those areas, Colombian writer García Márquez discovered his own African roots on a trip to Angola. If Audre Lorde felt a sense of belonging in Mexico, so did García Márquez in Africa, even though his biological roots are elsewhere. He joins Marshall and Morrison in the affirmation of a great indebtedness to a Caribbean cultural center, and like Marshall, he believes that the Caribbean is "the natural geographical area of Brazil." The most phenomenal things happen in both places. The explanation lies "in the syncretism, in the Negro ingredient which distinguishes us," García Márquez says; "the human synthesis existing in the Caribbean reaches fantastic extremes."[47]

The novels discussed here resist formulaic categorizations, not only within the much disputed "modernist" and "postmodernist" classifications but also within the traditional spaces occupied by folklore, history, and literature. Does Paule Marshall write ethnographic novels, or fictionalized history? Where should we place Gayl Jones's version of slavery in Brazil? In terms of literary criticism, the novels created by Morrison, Jones, and Marshall also resist boundaries imposed by categories such as "black" or "feminist." In their cultural and literary complexity, they help rescue the genre from its announced "death" and also from the indictment of complicity with the social amnesia of modernity. The fiction of these black women writers in the United States attempts to recapture and reorganize the fragments of collective history into a new type of narrative. The originality of this narrative lies in the way it emphasizes the popular roots of contemporary culture, in the use of creative folk rituals, and in the interconnection between myth and imagination, all alongside the starkest representations of racial, sexual, economic, and cultural abuse. Rooted in culture and community, this narrative is an attempt to counter the versions of facts and truth presented by the colonizer of yesterday and today with the view from the dominated. The recognition of the exploitation and invisibility of the African Other throughout history may hurt, shock, and yet liberate, as happened with Fanon when he met the rejecting gaze of his model and oppressor.

In the varying perceptions of reality and the reactions to domination illustrated in their novels, Marshall, Jones, and Morrison use writing as testimony, as reconnection, and as a manifesto for change. For Jones, fiction is a way to elaborate the memories of rape that black women have suffered since slavery. Remembering the pain can be a subversive act against the oppressor, but how can it truly liberate and open up the future to change? Is pain synonymous with hate, or is it more complicated than that? Is there ambiguity in the relationship between the slave woman and the oppressor? For Marshall, stories are ways to express "the necessity of reversing the present order."[48] For Morrison, resisting the system goes beyond the realm of race, ethnicity, gender, or the need to rewrite the past history of peasants, women, and slaves. Resistance must also be an attitude of the present in the professional urban world of advanced capitalism and corporate management. As a well-known writer and editor, she assumes a political role when she urges all writers not to submit to censorship and marketing demands. Contemporary writing must resist capitalist pressures and be nonconformist: "We need a heroic writers' movement—assertive, militant, pugnacious."[49]

In a manner reminiscent of García Márquez, Toni Morrison uses her space and voice as journalist and novelist to speak out for a better social order and greater freedom. As authors of international acclaim, both Nobel Prize winners, the two writers use their public and critical prestige to promote the values of their peoples and their cultures. The issues that inform the literature of both writers and the communities they come from are closely related parts of their quest for identity and justice. W.E.B. DuBois, Aimé Césaire, Eric Williams, and Frantz Fanon, intellectual leaders of Pan-African resistance and solidarity in this century, have insisted on the need for economic and political empowerment of peoples of African descent, much as Martí advocated for Latin Americans as a whole. For U.S. blacks as for Caribbeans and Latinos, the reliance on inner cultural and political resources represents self-affirmation and resistance to alienating, exploitative pressures.[50]

Frantz Fanon specifically stressed the urgency of an "effort at disalienation" through self-consciousness and the use of "a positive voice" in political and cultural constructions. In ways that seem to have anticipated considerations about time and history made by French cultural historian Michel Foucault, Fanon elaborated on the complexity of the relationship between colonizer and colonized, the illusion of creating myths of a homogeneous (Pan-African) Third World and some privileged grasp of "truth," and the deceptive security of a frozen, immutable past. Decades before Gayatri Spivak and postmodernist visions of ethnicity and literature, Fanon warned against black–white simplifications and emphasized the continuous reinvention of culture. In Fanon's words, "Disalienation will come into being through their refusal to accept the present as definitive. . . . My black skin is not the wrapping of specific values. . . . I am not a prisoner of history. . . . I should constantly remind myself that the real *leap* consists in introducing invention into existence."[51]

Resistance to political, economic, and cultural control is a common feature in the discourse of a number of Latin American writers, who frequently are also political leaders and activists in the tradition of José Martí. Like Fanon, Martí believed that the tensions and contradictions of the past had to be reevaluated and rewritten if change was to occur in the present. Excited about the dawn of a truly new world, the nineteenth-century revolutionary affirmed the difference of an American perception of history against the fin-de-siècle pessimism in Europe. In response to the despondency of the French Romantic poet Alfred de Musset (1810–1857), who mourned the realization that he "had arrived too late to a world already too old," Martí hailed the possibilities of America: "The world is always young. My American world is always young."[52] As we reach the end of the twentieth century, writers from both Latin America and minority groups in the United States realize that there is still much to do and change in this world and a whole history to be written. "An endless task, the cataloguing of reality," predicted the Caribbean Frantz Fanon.[53]

Both Fanon and Martí stressed the need to unveil and overcome the absolutism of colonial thinking still at work in the *New World*. A century ago, Martí considered problems that would remain vital in the political and cultural shifts of the final decades of the twentieth century. Like Fanon, he urged new nations to resist "the excessive influx of foreign ideas and formulas" and to reinvent themselves: "'Create' is the password of this generation. Absolute ideas must take relative forms if they are not to fail. If a republic refuses to open its arms to all, and move ahead with all, it dies. Nations should live in an atmosphere of self-criticism."[54] Martí's advice is ever more necessary today.

Concern with the lingering traits of colonialism in the economy, politics, and culture of twentieth-century societies has informed the criticism and the literature produced in the last decades by minority writers in the United States and by many Latin American writers. Analysis of connections between the fiction of Toni Morrison, Paule Marshall, and Gayl Jones, on the one hand, and Latin American and Caribbean literature and history, on the other hand, discloses a variety of perceptions of memory, community, and the past, as well as different approaches to counter-memory and possible mechanisms of change. Criticism produced by black scholars during the 1980s has especially praised the Pan-African quality of Morrison's and Marshall's works in terms of their "communal version of history," the allegorical and "visionary sense of renewal through the recovery of culture," as well as the socioeconomic critique of the development of capitalism from an agrarian to an urban society.[55] In fact, the rewriting of history from an alternative point of view and the dialectics of tradition and change undergird the stories created by Jones, Marshall, and Morrison and Latin American writers such as García Márquez as well. A question to be considered here is to what extent those black women writers have inscribed other "colored," exploited, and disinherited people in their narrative. How cosmopolitan and inter-American is their work? Has any of them gone beyond Pan-Africanism to embrace other diasporas and other colors?

Having originated in historically specific circumstances, the popularity and critical acclaim in the United States of novels by both black women and Latin American "boom" writers mark a very significant moment in literary and cultural history. The publishing industry and the academy opened doors to newcomers from two cultural spaces that had long been denied recognition. Together, the writings of both groups can help bridge North and South in remarkable ways, taking the concept of "good neighborhood" out of the realms of political and economic interests once sponsored by the government of Franklin Delano Roosevelt, and relocating it in the arena of counter-memory and resistance. The blending of folk history and the miraculous in the tradition of epic storytelling brings together these novels as representative of the post–World War II period for *Third World* peoples. Marking the birth of new nations or simply evoking the struggle of postcolonial societies, these contemporary novels also recall the importance of the initiators of the genre that marked the birth of nations in the eighteenth and nineteenth centuries. As the narratives of newly visible "others," the contemporary works also reenact the role of print for their earlier counterparts in creating mutual awareness and "reading coalitions" to promote bonding between the North and South America of color.[56]

As historical and cultural texts, the works of Morrison, Marshall, and Jones are in dialogue with the already-classic texts on the struggle of nationalism and resistance, the works of Frantz Fanon and José Martí, and the traditions of Pan-Africanism and Pan-Americanism that they represent. In subsequent chapters, I examine the way these women revise the cataloging of reality in narratives that engage in a major continental debate with a host of historians, sociologists, and anthropologists. "History gives topic and substance to black women's writing," says critic Susan Willis.[57] Morrison, Jones, and Marshall present their testimonies as witnesses of the historical process and as black women. They have contributed immensely to the rewriting of a more just and complete American history, which would rescue the memories of the forgotten, the women, the blacks, other nonwhites, and the poor. That process is not mere intellectual practice; it represents a crucial factor in the revolution toward concrete change.[58]

Marshall, Morrison, and Jones have attempted to reread and better comprehend their own past as women and blacks in the United States by setting that history within an inter-American framework. As black women writers whose careers bloomed in the aftermath of the civil rights movement, they have assumed the role of what Toni Cade Bambara calls "cultural workers." Their novels represent the confluence of interests and affirmations that so remarkably characterized the moment in history when the movement for women's freedom paralleled the black struggle and the civilian protest against the Vietnam War. A demographic revolution was also in progress at that time, as increasing numbers of displaced peoples, poor refugees as well as émigré writers from all over the Americas, helped bring the Caribbean and Latin America literally into the United States. Even as the old order shattered inside the country, the new awakening in culture and politics absorbed the excluded outsider.

In the diversity of their works, Morrison, Jones, and Marshall have helped retrieve the history of racial and economic exploitation of black people in the Americas. Joining together the United States, the Caribbean, Latin America, and Africa, their narratives voice the anger of the women and men who have for so long remained at the bottom of every social scale, the spirit of black and feminist rebellion, and the myths once told but since forgotten. The three authors are members of a "community of black women writing in the United States" that "can be regarded as a vivid new fact of national life."[59] They hail the development of a literature, a literary criticism, and a historiography by and about women that greatly expanded throughout the 1970s and 1980s. In that development process, they have introduced the history and the literature of "the other America" into North American fiction, blurring geographical boundaries and challenging old antagonisms.

After the 1959 revolution in Cuba, a sometimes unlikely combination of interests—intellectuals, graduate students, and the U.S. State Department—produced a massive increase in the number of Latin Americanists in the universities of the United States. The emergence of works by Gayl Jones, Paule Marshall, and Toni Morrison coincided with the resulting proliferation of works on the Caribbean and Latin America in the social sciences and humanities. In addition to the distinctiveness of their creative imagination, Morrison, Jones, and Marshall have introduced to literature a Pan-Americanism that focuses on the empowerment of the voiceless and those subaltern all over the Americas.[60] Reflecting major explorations of their time, their works embrace the peoples and histories of the Caribbean and Latin America as vital parts in a common quest against exploitation (whether of a country, an area within a country, against a race, a class, or a sex). The three novelists joined the chorus of social scientists and researchers who have expanded their fields toward a comparative and cross-cultural approach, particularly on topics related to the history of slavery and race relations. As writers, however, they assume the position of the object of study rather than the stare of the outside observer. As women and as blacks from the United States, they enter the world of the Caribbean and Latin America with solidarity and recognition and help bind together two hemispheres constantly set apart by contrasting ideologies, cultures, and interests.

Complex questions emerge from the project of these writers. If the Latin-Caribbean world is perceived as largely "brown" and different in race and culture, how is it inscribed in the imagination of people in the United States who are also nonwhite? Considering that the construction of the Other is inevitably connected to the process of identity formation and the consolidation of national and group interests, how do historical and literary texts written by U.S. blacks negotiate such impulses when they look south of the border? The questions involve difficult and interrelated issues. For one thing, even though the black community in the United States may sometimes be described as "a nation within a nation," these two "nations" share mutual antagonisms and resemblances and are in themselves multiple and diverse.[61] Moreover, for U.S. "black America" as for "white America," the construction of that "other" America unfolds in a neocolonial space where power is strongly tilted toward the North in all respects, whether in world or hemispheric politics, economics, technology, or in the production and control of knowledge.

It is to be expected, therefore, that a multiplicity of views and a complexity of racial and national allegiances will inform the exchange between the Americas. Jones, Marshall, and Morrison are here grouped together but do not form a "school" of equal thought and style. They do not "represent" black Americans either, just as the authors that they refer to in their writings and interviews do not stand for a total Latin American culture and literature. In their geographical and historical crisscrossings and in the literary intertextuality of their narratives, Jones, Morrison, and Marshall create individual works even as they feed on the history and the memories of black Americans like themselves.

The history of the African diaspora and its reconstruction within a black framework necessarily embrace the whole area of "the extended Caribbean." The diaspora underwent related processes and left a similar heritage all along the Atlantic shores of the Americas. African descendants now try to make sense of fragments, of records, of erasures. Matters relating to the colonial world and neocolonial structures have been in a constant state of revision and redefinition within general historiography. Arguments and disagreements range from disputes over the site of Christopher Columbus's first landing to questions regarding the number of Africanisms and the extent of the rupture brought about by slavery in the *New World*. Easier access to information and greater geographical mobility have permitted and stimulated further comparative analyses. Throughout this century, immigrants to the United States from the West Indies and Latin America, travelers to the Caribbean and South America, and researchers and writers of different colors and perspectives all over the Americas have contributed to the intensification of the debate over the relations between races, the myths surrounding the Other and the past, and the best ways to evaluate that past and proceed toward the future. Within the black community in the United States, responses to history and literature from parts of the extended Caribbean lying below national borders have been closely connected with the general intellectual and political moment, as well as with specific agendas of black and feminist groups.

The visibility of literature by black women is a very recent phenomenon in the literary history of the United States, not to mention the American continent. In fact, the visibility of black women (and women of other colors) is a recent development in the social sciences as well. Contemporary research in social history has "discovered" the slave woman and her children, figures long considered marginal and unimportant in the social structure and traditionally disregarded in historiography.[62] Marshall, Jones, and Morrison are pioneer voices in the movement to rescue the past of black women from oblivion and invisibility and to open up spaces in fiction for issues of comparative history that have long been controlled by male scholars. Their novels bring together some of the focal points in comparative American historiography: the master–slave relationship, the slave family, slave resistance and rebellion, the plantation economy, segregation in the postbellum South, and the complex construction of identity by generations of descendants of former African slaves who nevertheless feel deeply "American," whether in Brazil, the United States, Barbados, or Jamaica.

The issues that have fed the often-heated debates among academics and civil rights activists over recent decades are also basic to the novels of Morrison, Marshall, and Jones. These issues involve the nature of slave systems and their differences from and similarities to one another; the interaction between the dominant class and subordinate classes (as well as between slaves and free Negroes) and the nature of these relationships after slavery was abolished; the degree of resiliency, agency, and power among blacks, under slavery and afterward; the degree of disruption reflected in the personalities of men and women, in the culture, and in family and social organization; and finally, the never-ending dispute between North and South over race relations and economic exploitation in our contemporary world. Escape, maroonage, and the rebellion of slaves and free blacks during colonial times are recurring themes in the novels by Jones, Marshall, and Morrison and have also received increasing attention in historical research throughout the continent since the early 1970s. The presence of women in history has finally been recuperated in recent historiographical developments. Enriching such studies with memories, myth, and imagination, the writings of Marshall, Morrison, and Jones inscribe the minds and emotions of black women in the new text of the continent.

Like these writers' novels, recent historiography has registered the concerted efforts to erase the rights and the memories of slaves and their descendants throughout centuries of American history. In Brazil and the Caribbean, most slaves could not read and write and could not record their stories; and in spite of the large number of narratives and recorded interviews by slaves, the slave past in the United States has also suffered deletions and distortions. In their novels, Jones, Morrison, and Marshall attempt to rewrite history as they record the oral accounts, passed from generation to generation, of their own ancestors. Their role is ever more important in view of the persisting discrimination and silencing of black women, even among activists of the civil rights movement in recent past.[63]

Besides relating to shifts in contemporary historiography, the novels of Jones, Marshall, and Morrison recall recent debates in the ethnographic field and often resemble narratives of cultural rituals and social dramas.[64] In their individual voices and sometimes contrasting tales, the three writers elicit a polyphonic and open-ended interpretation of "the black experience" that suggests discursive strategies in contemporary ethnography. Finally, they bring to mind the factor that has most contributed to revolutionizing contemporary anthropology: a postcolonial world that has blurred the boundaries between the privileged position of the observer and the isolation of the (usually *Third World* and uneducated) subject. Like the "primitive cultures" normally silenced in "classic" texts, which have recently returned the gaze of the ethnographer and started talking back, black women now read the various historical and anthropological narratives about themselves, respond in their own voices, and create narratives for themselves and the people they perceive as equals.

The formerly illiterate and silent woman is now educated and sophisticated and produces her own tale of a culture in flux, a contested and ambiguous terrain where identity and culture are in a continual process of recreation. The plural and complex views of sexual, ethnic, and national identity presented by Morrison, Marshall, and Jones also respond to the dynamic state of flux in personal relationships, community organization, and national allegiances in today's society. Although they are citizens of the United States, the social and cultural representations of these women unfold in a larger continental and international context where the *Third World* is no longer a separate and invisible entity. As in contemporary ethnography, these writers represent and record a postcolonial reality where cultural borders are relatively open and migration is the norm.[65]

Along with their blend of psychological, economic, and political aspects of life in parts of the Americas, the narratives of Toni Morrison, Gayl Jones, and Paule Marshall explore cultural meaning through ritual performance. Music becomes the crossroads where America meets Africa and Europe, memory blends with the present, and identity is recreated. The frantic drums and the excited dancing of contemporary Caribbean Carnival connect with traditional "ring shouts" and shuffle dancing in Marshall's cultural text. Spirituals and the blues are the points where longing and sorrow intersect with hope and endurance in Morrison's and Jones's *New World* narratives. In the work of all three writers, prose resonates with the magic and beauty of music and dance that is deeply African and American.

For Morrison, Marshall, and Jones, the identity and well-being of black people today depend on a reconciliation with the past. A meaningful self and culture must therefore be sought and reconstructed in the fragments of history and in the reinvention of culture. Marshall and Morrison place a strong emphasis on the need for a "spiritual return" to Africa for "the reintegration of that which was lost in our collective historical past."[66] Jones emphasizes a necessary reconciliation with and reevaluation of painful memories of the slave past in order to allow for personal stability and some possibility of loving relationships to develop in the present. All three authors rewrite important chapters of the history of blacks and whites in the Americas, helped by their own experiences and memories and the stories heard from their ancestors and communities.

For black writers and scholars in the United States, the historical and cultural developments in the Caribbean and Latin America are often felt as part of their own life and history. Major reasons for such interest and identification have been the Haitian Revolution, the Cuban War of Independence and subsequent occupation by the United States, and the history of slavery and race relations all over the Americas. In more recent decades, writings by U.S. poets, playwrights, and novelists have responded to and enriched a comparative field usually characterized by academic discussions or journalistic explorations.

Black women writers have contributed to the debate with their personal response, adding subtlety and contradiction to a picture often simplified and limited. When they go beyond the southern borders for themes or settings, they also recapture a tradition inaugurated in one of the first novelistic accounts written by a black person in the United States: *Blake, or the Huts of America*, published by Martin Delany in 1859, tells the story of a slave who tries to spread insurrection in Cuba.[67] The interconnection of the oppression and resistance of black people in the extended Caribbean and the confluence of individual and collective identities are similarly evoked in the works of Toni Morrison, Gayl Jones, and Paule Marshall.

The interest in the larger America that is shown by the three women novelists goes beyond liberal intellectual hopes of finding a peaceful solution for the "American dilemma" somewhere and moves away from a hemispheric contest for best performance in race relations. By combining their experiences and memories with those coming from Brazil, Jamaica, Cuba, Barbados, and other parts of America, these writers try to connect and make sense of a common fragmented history, retelling it with a sense of mission and love. Their novels must be read in the context of contemporary notions of ethnicity and of developments in women's studies and comparative histories of slavery and race relations during the 1970s and 1980s. They must also be understood against the competitive and often tense atmosphere that affects those fields and can be particularly strong in the inter-American dialogue.

To that dialogue, Morrison, Marshall, and Jones have made a powerful and beautiful contribution. By creating characters who are neither simply heroic nor victimized but who struggle with pressures and paradoxes to negotiate a meaningful identity, the three writers share the open spirit of new social history and interpretive ethnography. They wish to avoid simplifications and stereotypes of any kind, even as they search for their "mothers' gardens," their African roots, their myths, and the significance of their own womanhood within a space and a culture that stretches beyond their home country to embrace the continent.[68]

# 2
## From the Natives' Point of View: The Ethnographic Novels of Paule Marshall

> Nay, let them only see us,
> while
> We wear the mask.
> —Paul Laurence Dunbar*

A place of intersection for many cultures and languages, the Caribbean was the first geographical space in the recorded history of the countless encounters and clashes that have made up America. As a one-generation-removed daughter of the Caribbean island of Barbados, Paule Marshall reads that history with mixed anger and love. Like the Caribbean, her work contains a busy plurality of peoples, races, and colors in a continuous recreation of culture. The many voices and stories in her novels reveal the contradictions and the complexity of the legacy of colonialism at the heart of America.

As they interrelate times and continents in a revision of the past, the people in Marshall's ethnographic narratives not only retell America but also create their own possibilities of transforming the

---

*Paul Laurence Dunbar, "We Wear the Mask" (1895), in *Black Identity: A Thematic Reader*, ed. Francis E. Kearns (New York: Holt, Rinehart and Winston, 1970), 69. Dunbar was the first black writer Paule Marshall read; his poetry "instilled in [her] the secret desire to some day write" and pushed her on to explore other black authors (Paule Marshall, interview with Sylvia Baer, "Holding onto the Vision," *Women's Review of Books* 8, 10–11 [July 1991]: 24).

present and constructing a new future.[1] Against the official history of authorities and the organized hierarchy of races and classes, the stories and the memories of the common folk rewrite facts and dispute accepted "truth." She hears their stories and observes lives in their daily routines of home and work, in their memories of the past, in the hope or despair about the future, and in the songs and dances that they enjoy in the towns of her "extended Caribbean" map. Her ethnography is marked by the paradoxes of Merle Kinbona, major character and "informant" in the novel *The Chosen Place, the Timeless People,* and by the cultural pluralism and multivocality of the continent that is part of Marshall's own life story.[2]

The small island of Barbados in the Caribbean always looms large in Marshall's imaginative world. It was the homeland for her family before her parents immigrated to the United States, where she was born in 1929 in Brooklyn, New York, the family's new place and the main setting of her first novel. Marshall's version of the extended Caribbean, with roots spreading far into eastern United States and across the Atlantic—crisscrossing the routes of colonizers and colonized—is actually present in all of her novels and shorter works, from *Brown Girl, Brownstones* (1959) to *Daughters* (1991).[3]

## The Americas in *Soul Clap Hands and Sing*

The four novellas in *Soul Clap Hands and Sing* (1961) are individually dedicated to specific parts of Marshall's version of an extended Caribbean. Titled "Barbados," "Brooklyn," "British Guiana," and "Brazil," these early pieces dramatize several of the themes of her first novel and later works. The postcolonial reality of sharp class separation and a wide range of color contrasts prevails in all four pieces. The main character in each novella is invariably a man in middle or old age who is undergoing a period of personal contradiction and decay, longing for consolation and rejuvenation in a young black woman.[4] Colors, cultures, and generations contrast and combine in Marshall's version of a hybrid America, a dynamic terrain marked by continuous migration and interethnic contact.

Reflecting the political tensions and changes of the 1950s, the novellas approach the movement for political self-determination in the Caribbean islands, as well as the persecution of suspected Communists in the United States of the McCarthy era. As in her other works, Marshall uses her personal experience and observation to in-

form her stories. She had the opportunity to travel to Caribbean islands and Brazil on assignments for the small black magazine *Our
World* (she left the magazine in 1956).[5] Her observations of the interplay between races and classes in those areas surface in the four stories: the old structure, like the protagonists, is patriarchal and decadent, but young people and new ideals may announce change.

In the first story, an emigrant who has migrated back is the central character. Mr. Watford returns to his native Barbados rich but
despondent with the fortune he has accumulated over fifty years of
hard work in the United States. Born black and poor on the island,
he had worked for a white family at the age of eight, repressing
much hate and rebellion. An orphan at twenty, he left for the United
States, a country that "meant nothing to him" except as the place
where it was possible to find wealth (7). But after returning to Barbados, he reads only Boston newspapers, even if in late editions; he
dresses in starched white and walks with a stiff, self-conscious pace,
like a U.S. southern planter. The high gates and imposing columns of
his "American Colonial" house, his money, and his philosophy of
life set him apart from the "crude wooden houses" and the common
people of the village (3).

Times have changed since he left the island so many decades before. Influenced by the "do-it-yourself" mentality of the United
States, Mr. Watford believed in personal improvement through hard
work and in "learning a trade" as the remedy for social ills. Now the
young poeple wear buttons urging "Vote for Barbados People's
Party" and warning that "The Old Order Shall Pass," and Watford
feels that they implicitly accuse him of belonging to the socioeconomic order that they reject. The solemn whiteness of his clothing
and house contrasts with the "easy ways" of the islanders and a local
"nastiness" that he does not want near him. The spirit of the island
enters his home nonetheless, embodied in a quiet new maid whose
name he ignores but whose young body he desires. Dressing and
behaving like a dominating planter, Mr. Watford repeats the pattern
of class and sexual exploitation set up by the colonists, even though
his skin is black.

In the novella "Brooklyn," the Jewish professor of French literature, Max Berman, also wears a "starched collar," but his life story
differs substantially from that of the "Barbados" protagonist. Memories of guilt and humiliation torment him: the wife he never loved,
who was killed in a car accident; a second wife, also unloved; his

loss of "the faith of his father"; his experience with the Communist party and his frustration after the purges in Russia; the oppression suffered for being a Jew; his expulsion from "a small community college in upstate New York" and the inquisition ensuing because he had once belonged to the party (31–36). The past nightmares refuse to let him go: once again, his former political activities cause his dismissal from the small college where he now holds a summer job.

Much like Mr. Watford, Berman is victim and also victimizer. In the anger and loneliness of this stage of his life, he develops a crazy and intense attachment to a young southern girl, the only black student in his class, "a very pale mulatto with skin the color of clear, polished amber." (In this pairing of a Jew and "a Negro," Marshall connects their plights and anticipates *Chosen Place.*) They have in common skin of about the same color and a similar burden of isolation and loneliness. When Miss Williams first comes to see Professor Berman before class, he is disturbed that "he shared in the sin against her," even though he had also been sinned against as a Jew (38).

The Jewish professor attempts to seduce her, but she resists and assumes a voice of her own, breaking away from the circle of her seclusion (61–62). Still, the power held by the teacher makes this an early tale of sexual harassment, based on the author's experience. Like other middle-class blacks created by Paule Marshall and Toni Morrison, this young woman has well-off parents who insist that she keep away from both whites and "niggers." Her color and class confine her to a limited space. The story does not pass judgment on either race or either gender: bringing together a man and a woman whose colors and histories mirror each other to some extent, it probes into human frailty and alienation, reflecting on personal and social dramas.

In "British Guiana," the character Gerald Motley defends an imperialistic project: Great Britain and the United States would help Guiana build an army, buy guns, invade Surinam, declare war on Venezuela, and provoke Brazil.[6] In addition to merely showing power, such daring interventionist politics constitute "the only way the world will ever know there's a place called British Guiana" (98). Like his country, Motley also needs to assert his own worth and overcome his feelings of inferiority and insecurity as a person of mixed background. Representative of the island's ethnic formation, his family history includes a British army officer, a black slave woman, and later, some Hindu blood. From the color of his skin, one can tell that he is not black, white, or East Indian; he seems to have become an insignificant "neuter" in color and in character (125–26).

Motley's education in England and marriage to a fair-skinned woman should have secured him a place among the chosen few in the Guianan capital, Georgetown. His personal contradictions, however, draw him away from progress and respectability. When he betrays his wife with a young black-Chinese woman, his wife and daughter leave for the United States, "where they passed for white and forgot him" (71). A decadent and solitary rum lover, Motley befriends a young, poor black man named Sidney, who then hates his own condition and abuses the old man in return. A car accident concludes but does not resolve Motley's turbulent life. Small Guiana, like other abused places in the continent, also remains contradictory and unresolved, seemingly static and immutable, where "you could leave for a century and come back to find nothing's changed" (116). Much like Bournehills in *The Chosen Place, the Timeless People*, Gabriel García Márquez's Macondo, or Toni Morrison's Shalimar, it is the distorted legacy of a common colonial history.

In the final novella, "Brazil," the landscape of Rio de Janeiro supplies the background for the story of the retiring comic actor, Caliban. Some staple ingredients of "Rio" stories and movies are there: the Sugarloaf Mountain, the Corcovado with its open-armed Christ topping the mountain, the skyscrapers along Copacabana Beach, the black-and-white stone mosaic of the sidewalks, the Copacabana Palace Hotel, the poor *favelas* on the hills, the Carnival, the samba, and the *cafezinho* served in small cups around the city.[7] Marshall once again plays with the concept of identity and integrity within a postcolonial environment marked by class divisions, regional differences, and hybrid colors.

Rio itself is a city of paradox and contrast. Its most visible side has a welcoming beauty. The Sugarloaf is a solid and benevolent presence, "rising protectively over the sleeping city"; the sea is "vast and benign"; the bay has "sure, graceful curves, forming an arabesque design with the hills between." The city of dreams exudes a colonial sensuality, "white, opulent, languorous under the sun's caress," attractive to tourists and to Brazilian migrants in search of work and a happier life (148–58).

Glorious daylight gives way to hot nights of dancing and excitement in Rio's many clubs and bars. Black Caliban has long been the star of one such night spot, the Casa Samba, performing old jokes and caricature imitations. He is supported in the act by Miranda, a blond, younger dancer who is "one of those Brazilians from Rio Grande do Sul who are mixed German, Portuguese, native Indian and sometimes African" (132). Although he has made a name for himself, Caliban is now old, tired, and no longer funny. Paule Marshall uses the audience's reactions to illustrate the distinction she perceived between Brazilian and U.S. citizens regarding interracial and inter-American contact. In the show, Brazilians laugh "out of affection and loyalty," while tourists, "mostly Americans from a Moore-McCormack ship in the harbor," laugh loudly and self-consciously to protect themselves against the dangerous and lascivious Other. The closeness of Caliban and Miranda on stage threatens the tourists' principles of propriety regarding racial separation. They relieve their tension and alarm at seeing "Caliban's dark face around Miranda's white thigh" by reassuring one another that "this was Brazil after all" and not their familiar surroundings.[8] Surely, Miranda cannot be really white! Here "white was never wholly white, no matter how pure it looked." Their nervous laughter is not provoked by any joke, for they are unfamiliar with the language of the place: "I don't know why I'm laughing. I don't understand a word of Spanish. Or is this the place where they speak Portuguese?" (136).

The fact is that the Great Caliban, whose real name is Heitor Baptista Guimarães, is no longer great after thirty-five years in show business. A migrant like Miranda, he came to Rio a poor, young man from a small town in the state of Minas Gerais. At first he mopped floors and served food in a restaurant, but he achieved success and money after winning a stage contest at the important Teatro Municipal. His glories are registered on his walls in many mementos, awards, and photographs from the 1940s and 1950s where he appears in the company of the president of Brazil and the famous Carmen Miranda (153). Dressed in "flashy rings" and "stylish clothes," he now lives with a young and pregnant wife in a "modern house of glass walls and stone" in an affluent "suburb near Corcovado, the mountain of Christ" (152, 164). His wife, beautiful like "a Madonna painted black," is the granddaughter of a distant cousin of his, also from Minas Gerais (152).

After all those years of Carnival-like glory, Caliban hopes to recover a pure, lost Heitor and a life of peace away from the glitz and falsity of show business. It is not in Rio but in the provincial and Catholic Minas Gerais that Caliban/Heitor wants his child to be born.

He dreams of a stable family and a calmer love life now, leaving Miranda, his lover of many years, behind in the past. He refuses to concern himself with her future as he retires from a show where she always had the supporting role. He prefers to think that "she is like Rio. There will always be somebody to admire her," even if her youth and her charm are gone (146–48).

By forgetting Miranda and the show, Caliban hopes to recover Heitor, the past, and the person he was before coming to Rio. Caliban expects his young wife from Minas to support him toward that goal, even if "Heitor Baptista Guimarães" sounds like "the name of a stranger who lived at another time" (152). Trying to resurrect the dead, Caliban distances himself from touristic Rio and returns to places that postcards do not show and his memory had long "ceased to see." His search for himself takes him through the Rio that he once knew and that his fortune and career had erased from his consciousness. He passes dirty little children carrying tins of water on their heads, their empty eyes foretelling "the defeated lives they had yet to live" (164). The squalid slum makes his own life and the beauty of the city look like a sham and threatens their existence: "That squalor above Rio implied that Rio herself was only a pretense" (163). Marshall contrasts the stage and the street, the laughter and the despair, bringing out the paradoxes of the city. All dimensions of Rio, however, recognize Heitor only as Caliban.

Caliban/Heitor finds out that his "true" self does not exist anymore. Unable to find a mirror for his original identity anywhere in Rio, he takes revenge on Miranda, for in his mind she and her glittery apartment building symbolize the city. But destroying her place brings no solution. Dressed in a Carnival costume for too long, Heitor has become his disguise. Ironically, Caliban will now be someone only during Carnival; for the rest of the year, he has no role to play.

In "Brazil," Marshall explores a theme that recurs in her later novels: the quest for identity amid the paradoxical realities of class, race, and gender in the "extended Caribbean." Marshall's Caliban is a tropicalized play on William Shakespeare's character in *The Tempest*, his name an anagram of Christopher Columbus's reference to the "canibal" inhabitants of the Caribbean islands. The Shakespearean version of the relations between the European Prospero, his daughter Miranda, and the black islander Caliban has inspired a number of Caribbean and Latin American writers.[9] Marshall joins those who have made Caliban prototypical of Latin America and the

Caribbean. Rather than subscribing to an idealized dichotomy between the white and evil colonizer and the heroic and natural black man, however, Marshall subtly explores the interplay of domination in gender and race and the contradictory identity of a hybrid *New World*.

Cuban cultural leader Roberto Fernández Retamar asserts Caliban as the best possible metaphor for "Our America." The figure signifies both America's exploitation by white colonists and the possibility of radical reversal in the empowerment of the underclass and the affirmation of ethnic pluralism. "I know no other metaphor more expressive of our cultural situations, of our reality," proclaims Retamar.[10] Paule Marshall and other writers of the extended Caribbean take Caliban as inspiration for their own writing. Having learned the language of the master, they can use that tool in storytelling, for the revision of history, and as an effective form of action against conditions created and stimulated by colonialism.

## The Chosen Place, the Timeless People

The plot of *The Chosen Place, the Timeless People* unfolds in a symbolic Bourne Island that is modeled after Barbados, the homeland of Marshall's parents, a place she early associated with her cultural roots and Africa. Situated between the "Anglo" world and the "Latin" countries, the Caribbean islands mix many different cultures and symbolically connect the two hemispheres, like "steppingstones that might have been placed there long ago by some giant race to span the distance between the Americas, North and South" (13). The location of Barbados at the easternmost point in the Caribbean gives it a distinctive character in relation to the other islands and places it closer to Africa. It also links it in a special relation with the city of Recife in Brazil, one of the easternmost points of the whole American continent, a relation mentioned by Marshall in *Chosen Place* (471).

Smaller and more vulnerable than the other islands, Bourne Island/Barbados has an important symbolic role as it reaches out farther into the Atlantic:[11]

> Unlike the others . . . which followed each other in an orderly procession down the watery track of the Caribbean, the island . . . had broken rank and stood off by itself to the right, almost out in

the Atlantic. It might have been put there by the giants to mark the eastern boundary of the entire continent, to serve as its bourn. And ever mindful of the responsibility placed upon it in the beginning, it remained—alone amid an immensity of sea and sky, becalmed now that its turbulent history was past, facing east, the open sea, and across the sea, hidden beyond the horizon, the colossus of Africa. (13)

Most of the characters in *The Chosen Place, the Timeless People* are native islanders representing the different gradations of color and class in their specific locations: from the darker and poorer sugarcane workers of Bournehills, to the "red cross-bred" people of Canterbury (still poor but "superior") and the urban slums of Harlem Heights, to the lighter and more affluent professionals of New Bristol, and finally, to the few whites. The English colonizers imprinted the people, the language, the culture, the religion, and the economic and political organization of the island. New Bristol is the fictitious city modeled after the Barbadian capital, Bridgetown, in whose different neighborhoods, separated by color and class, the story takes place.[12]

The major conflict in the novel springs out of the interaction of Bourne Island natives with white American visitors, who are involved in anthropological research supporting a far-reaching development project for the stagnant area of Bournehills. Writing like an invisible ethnographer, Paule Marshall follows the encounter step by step and explores the conflicts and contradictions that gradually surface. Even though the visiting anthropologists represent an enormous U.S. corporation that obviously means to use ethnography for its own profit and advantage, Marshall's emphasis on the stories, rituals, and struggles of Bourne Island affirms the continuing possibility of people's empowerment and resistance.

After a late independence, the colonial structure lingers on the island, in the sugarcane fields and mills still controlled by English landlords and in the powerlessness of the "slave" class. The English and their descendants still retain major positions of power in urban society. In Marshall's novel, a large newspaper chain controls the local news in Bourne Island (the editor is the reckless and "openly supercilious" Englishman George Clough), and the economy still depends on the goodwill of sugar barons such as Kingsley and Sons despite the island's newly acquired "quasi-independent status" (52).[13]

The United States has rivaled Great Britain for effective interference in the island and control of other equally underdeveloped areas, both in colonial times and in the modern cycle of neocolonialism. In *Chosen Place*, the big investments promised by the American corporation are offered as a dramatic solution to bring progress to a stubbornly backward place. The company has the revealing name of United Corporation of America, UNICOR or "one heart," a "giant commercial complex which, like some elaborate rail or root system, endlessly crisscrosses the world, binding it up" (37). The huge result of a successful merger of "most of the old [Shippen] family businesses in Pennsylvania," UNICOR had originated in the commercialization of staple products like "cornmeal and flour, salted meat and fish, lumber, candles and cloth," which at first were shipped principally to the West Indies. In colonial times, the Shippens profited from the triangular trade that exploited the west coast of Africa for slaves; brought the slaves to the Caribbean islands; took sugar, rum, and molasses from the islands to Philadelphia; and returned to the islands other staple products that they did not produce.

Postcolonial control only expanded and modernized that power structure. The later UNICOR, a symbol of big business in general, expanded from huge sugar mills to "iron, steel, oil, the large-scale manufacture of munitions, uranium mining, banking." It associated with other foreign commercial empires such as Kingsley and Sons, "with its vast holdings in Africa, Asia, and smaller places like Bourne Island" (37). Disguised behind the respectable work of anthropology, the corporation supports the Center of Applied Social Research (CASR) that employs Saul Amron and Allen Fuso. Harriet Shippen, Saul's wife as well as the heiress of the Shippen fortune and history, is the agent responsible for bringing Amron out of Stanford University and into the development project.[14]

Anthropologist Saul Amron's role in the novel reflects Marshall's concern with colonialism and its influence on every "innocent" area of knowledge. It also vividly indicates the intense reevaluation of the anthropological profession that has been taking place in the United States since the 1960s. Ethnographers have traditionally belonged to a higher-educated class and a developed nation whose relation to the place and people under study is extremely asymmetrical. Even when they are not directly employed by an interested multinational corporation, their work may serve the interests and policies of neocolonialism. Marshall has created Saul Amron exactly at a time when "the potent historical conjuncture of decolonization and the intensification of American capitalism," in addition to stimulating resentment against the United States and a growing nationalism in new nations, has provoked a general self-questioning within U.S. anthropology.[15]

Saul Amron's personal life, like that of many ethnographers, is radically changed by fieldwork, just as he is supposedly discovering the reality of people quite different from himself. The Caribbean is, for him, the culminating center of the places and peoples that have intersected across the American continent. Saul, the "wandering Jew," finally belongs nowhere and sees everywhere. He talks and works with the poor of Bournehills, but it is mainly through the "native" eyes of Merle Kinbona that he comes to interrogate himself and his plans.

An articulate, British-educated woman who owns the local guest house, Merle shows the constant struggle of conflicting forces in her brown, lined face and in her outrageous outfits. Age has hit her hard and early: she has to disguise an "aging forty-year-old body" beneath "flared, one piece dresses she made herself" (64). She talks incessantly and nervously and laughs loudly. The struggle in her life is cultural and personal: she is the daughter of the upper-class Englishman Ashton Vaughan and "a real African" named Clara. Merle knows that her mother "was only sixteen but fat and pretty in her skin and black like a real African when Ashton Vaughan took a liking to her and bred her" (33). Clara happened to be the favorite among the many women he kept, a preference that cost her life: she was probably murdered in cold blood by Vaughan's wife. Nothing was done about the killing, and Merle disowned Vaughan as a father (357).

Not only the pains of family history disturb Merle Kinbona. Her struggle for personal coherence and cultural definition parallels the reaffirmation of a rebellious history in which slaves played the central role in Barbados. It is, for Merle Kinbona, "the only bit of history we have worth mentioning on Bourne Island," but once she tries to teach it, she is dismissed for altering the truth and trying to incite her high school students to rebellion (102, 229). Marshall now privileges Merle's long-suppressed version of history, and it is Merle who becomes the main informant for the American anthropologists. In her dualism and her complexity, she seems quite representative of the island and "a damn research project in herself" (119). Her Bantu face is symbolic of Bournehills and the country: "It had been despoiled, that face, in much the same way as the worn hills to be seen piled around her on all sides had been despoiled—stripped of their trees centuries ago, their substance taken. . . . It looked utterly bereft at times" (5).

The sunny island retains its beauty, however, in spite of the wreck. Merle's eyes, too, reflect an "inner sunlight," a beautiful "sense of life" beyond the chaos. With kindness, she offers comforting, healing words to the anthropologists, attentive to Allen Fuso's personal conflicts and to Saul Amron's opening of his "numb" heart and eyes, which until then had been "almost blind" (92, 119). Because Merle is so identified with the poor of the island, Amron becomes increasingly fascinated by her. At the same time, he enters the "true spirit" of the place, drawing away from the respectable middle class that seems to him "the same the world over" (74). There is an exciting mutuality in the discoveries and exchanges between Merle and Saul. Amron's discovery of the Other in fieldwork parallels the process of understanding and expressing his own deeper self. Merle also sees more clearly into herself and is transformed by their contact.

In the novel, the problematic Bournehills is constantly associated with the dark "shadows" of the unconscious and the forbidding realm of memory, like "some mysterious and obscure region of the mind which ordinary consciousness did not dare admit to light" (21). In the shadows lie personal conflicts and social ills that the upper classes would rather ignore. For Merle and the hills people, however, their history is heroic and beautiful. The Ashanti Cuffy led the first slave revolt in Barbados in 1675, and the cane fire still seems to be burning in the awesome and blackened Pyre Hill.[16] Named "Cuffee Ned" in the novel, the enslaved rebel is honored by Marshall as the greatest among her "timeless people," even if the Pyre Hill Revolt is banned from schoolbooks and classes and may never be mentioned to children. When Merle tries to break the ban in her school class, the headmaster tells her "to teach the history that was down in the books, that told all about the English" (32). Merle and the Bournehills people refuse to submit to an official narrative that denies black struggle and resistance; they preserve their history as a tale passed from generation to generation of "oral historians" and magical storytellers:

> "Cuffee Ned did it. He sent the whole thing up in flames during a little fracas we had down here . . . in the days when the English were around here selling us for thirty pounds sterling. . . . Cuffee

put a match to it one night. The entire hill up in flames now! Castle and all. The very sky that night was on fire, they say. . . . And that hill burned for five years. . . . Long after Cuffee Ned was dead and the revolt put down, the old hill continued to burn." (101–2)

The revolt was "the largest and most successful of the many rebellions to take place in the island" (102). Led by Cuffee Ned, the slaves "fired the hill and surrounding cane fields and captured Percy Bryam, who died shortly afterward yoked to the mill wheel at Cane Vale, where he had been tied and tortured." The slaves were armed with weapons they had raided from an arsenal and resisted for over two years as a free nation under the leadership of Cuffee Ned; for Merle, he is "the only real hero we've ever had around here" (102). It is true that, in the end, the English soldiers "took his head off and left it for all to see on a tall pike along Westminster Low Road," but "we don't ever forget anything, and yesterday comes like today to us" (102). The dream of freedom, the brave resistance, and the final restoration of the dominant rulers—publicizing a death and a victory that will always be denied in the memory of the people—recall the stories of Zumbi of Palmares, as retold by Gayl Jones in *Song for Anninho*, and of the couple Will Cudjoe and Congo Jane, celebrated in Marshall's *Daughters*. Cuffee's story is a symbol of African resistance and endurance in Barbados, in the Caribbean, and throughout the American continent. It is reenacted every year in the Carnival festivities of Marshall's Bourne Island.

An appropriate symbol of the Caribbean crisscrossing of cultures is the pre-Lenten Carnival festival that overtakes the islands with colorful costumes, steel-drum beats, and calypso rhythms. The utopian quality of Carnival still finds renewed expression year after year in different parts of the American continent, combining basically European and African traditions but gradually incorporating the influences of incoming cultures. From the two largest countries, the United States and Brazil, to the small Caribbean islands of Barbados and Trinidad, multiethnic Carnivals dramatize dilemmas and tensions at once particular and universal. Rituals of music and dance allow Marshall to explore the complexity of racial, class, and gender relations in specific locations of the Americas but also to relate such locations to one another and delve into issues of colonialism, old and new.

Though the Carnival season itself is brief, the tropical island's abiding carnivalesque spirit of sensual abandon invites transgression. (This spirit has also been associated with Brazil, especially Rio; Port of Spain in Trinidad; and New Orleans.) Carnival simply brings that mood to a climax, allowing some people to push the boundaries of personal and social freedom; for others, however, even a temporary lapse from traditional morality and rules associated with race, class, and gender is an unbearable fall into chaos. To such an outsider, the laughter and release are threatening and frightening.

The comic and the tragic combine as euphoria builds in the transgressive rituals of Carnival, inspiring "both phobia and fascination."[17] It is not coincidental that those rituals originated but have been repressed in Catholic European centers; they have long been marginalized to "extended Caribbean" areas, sites of fantasy and hysteria in the imagination of colonial powers.[18] In Paule Marshall's Bourne Island, Carnival helps unmask the hypocrisy hidden in the big development project, as well as the contradictions within each individual. By contrast, the harsh reality and the repressed anger of the poor Bournehills people are dramatically evoked and somewhat exorcised during the Carnival festivities. Marshall's novel performs a similar role of denunciation on the one hand and evocation on the other, through the play of a variety of people coming together to tell their stories and possibly transforming themselves and their lives through the storytelling.

The parades and masquerades of Carnival stimulate play between paradoxical elements: dream and reality, fantasy and truth, laughter and death, the private and the social, the religious and the profane, the past and the present. This play raises complex and fascinating questions about the possibilities of psychological rebirth and "truly human relations," which have been associated by Russian cultural theorist Mikhail Bakhtin with the Carnival spirit. Paule Marshall's *Chosen Place* seriously and creatively addresses whether, with its masks and theater, Carnival comes closer to "truth" than the bland "reality" of daily life. The novel weighs the force and effect of transgressive action, considering the relation between "authorized transgressions" such as Carnival and the truly revolutionary acts defined by Umberto Eco as "unexpected and nonauthorized carnivalization."[19]

Mikhail Bakhtin has described medieval European Carnival as a truly popular celebration in which oppression is forgotten in the congregation of happy revelers. During Carnival, free gestures and profane words are not meant to offend; they express open fraternization and camaraderie and mock the traditional restraints and hierarchy in behavior and language. Customary "barriers of caste, property, profession, and age" give way for the experience of "new, purely human relations," and utopia becomes reality. In spite of the binding restrictions imposed by modern government regulations and bourgeois social control, Carnival can still reveal ancient human longings and deeply hidden voices; it can still create magic and invoke freedom amid the efficient modernity and mechanical alienation of our age. "The principle of laughter and the carnival spirit," says Bakhtin, "frees human consciousness, thought, and imagination for new potentialities."[20]

For a few days, the world seems to have changed into a place of equality and love, where barriers of ethnicity, race, and class are naturally overcome. "We all is one," sings a famous calypso composed by the Mighty Sparrow in Trinidad in 1958 and remembered by Paule Marshall in her work. The song celebrates the ideal of unity and solidarity among all West Indians at a time of independence from the old colonial rule, its refrain echoing in Jamaica's national motto. "Let us join together and love one another, we all is one," dream the Carnival revelers as they dance to the powerful drumbeat of the Carnival song.[21]

In the West Indies and in all the places where Carnival occurs, power and hierarchy are normally restored to the same individuals and groups—the male, the rich, the white—as soon as the feast is over; for Carnival is theater, not actual revolution. It only sings and plays games of a new order, rekindling hopes and illusions of beauty, happiness, and equality for all sexes, classes, and races. It nevertheless seems that by participating in that brief game, people can express and renew themselves as they are invited to overcome boundaries, joining voices and hands together. Talking and singing are themselves personally and socially affirmative acts, and the content of Carnival parades and songs, as in Paule Marshall's novel, may take an additional counterhegemonic stand and assert the power of people against an oppressive history.

Under the ideological emphasis on "one country, one people," Carnival has gained official and popular support as the great expression of a "national theater," particularly in the cases of Trinidad and Brazil. Throughout this century it has passed through similar phases in different countries. Evolving from street bands and masquerades in restricted, usually poor and black groups, it has steadily gained wider acceptability and assimilation by the larger society. As Carnival becomes big business and a source of ever greater media attraction, negotiations between popular free play and the interests of the dominant power become more complex. Though the powerful remain strong, popular organization and cultural conscience have grown in recent decades. The forms of liberation and power reversal in Carnival are similarly experienced from New Orleans to Rio, in spite of the varying degrees of social and racial participation, fraternization, government and business sponsorship, and the varying size of the "theaters" in which Carnival occurs.[22]

Marshall's *The Chosen Place, the Timeless People* presents Carnival in several layers. First, it is part of the spirit of the island and so, in a way, a constant presence there. It is explained to the American ethnographers (and to Harriet, who is actively helping in the research) before the celebration takes place, and readers can watch different people prepare clothes and moods for the event. It is then described in the full euphoria of Monday and Tuesday nights' ball dances and in the street parade all day on Tuesday, which swells to a crescendo of emotion and heat at the reenactment of Cuffee Ned's heroism by the Bournehills band and the joining-in of a wild guerrilla band that has come down from the poor Harlem Heights. Finally, it lingers in memories of the transgressive time and, more dramatically, in the actual changes it brings about for individuals and groups and in the possibility of further change.

The memory of Cuffee Ned's emblematic slave rebellion persists in its symbolic reenactment by the poor people of Bournehills, year after year at Carnival time. Despite the control exerted by institutions and European politics and culture, African pride and history emerge disguised as a Carnival play put on by the Bournehills people.[23] Every year, the cane cutter Stinger revives Cuffee Ned's heroic role, embarrassing the respectable middle-class mulattoes who abhor such "ignorance" and violence, which threatens their complacent accommodation. In their opinion, the Bournehills act disturbs the peaceful and playful character of a properly civilized Carnival; only the happiness of the country should be played out. Paule Marshall shows the bourgeoisie, both black and white, rejecting but often joining in the festivities in Bourne Island; the parade is a blend of masquerade and consciousness raising.[24]

The medical officer for Bournehills, Miles Wooding, a black man whose "subtle reddish cast to his dark-brown skin" and professional status place him in the middle class, voices the opinion of those on Bourne Island who would rather forget slavery and its violence. Carnival should be a pleasure for tourists, not the "foolishness" of "those brutes" putting on that "same masque about some blasted slave revolt." Although "a bit of history" was interesting for a while, the repeated reminder "of that old-time business" has become unbearable and should be banned from sight (59–60). City leaders actually would like to eliminate Bournehills itself from hearing and sight, not just the masquerade: ban the actual hills and their history altogether, for they disturb the landscape of the island.

By contrast, Carnival gives the upper classes a rare opportunity to mix with the people in the crowded streets. They praise the remarkable experience of emotion, release, and the feeling of oneness with the crowd, thrilled with the democratic dismissal of race and class barriers that Carnival produces. Both the white Englishwoman Dorothy Clough, married to the local newspaper editor, and the lawyer and government official Lyle Hutson, an Oxford-educated mulatto with whom Dorothy seems to be having an affair, are enthusiastic about the event. "All o' we is one," the Carnival motto, proves "true more or less for the two days carnival lasts," says Dorothy. "You see all sorts of people, rich and poor, black, white, and in-between, dancing together in the streets, laughing and talking to each other." It can be an idyllic scene of solidarity and equality, "a marvelous sight, and a much needed one," Dorothy recognizes, "in a world where all of us manage to be so ugly to each other, especially over this whole stupid question of race and color" (200).

But Carnival can be a disturbing sight for white middle-class Europeans and Americans who are not used to such transgressions. Dorothy Clough's "solidly middle-class English soul" suffered initial shock at the pagan holiday and panicked at the crowd, but she enjoyed it all after her cultural barriers broke down. She has become aware that the togetherness of Carnival is only a passing illusion. Back in England, she will return to the usual hierarchies and boundaries, but on the island, Carnival has given her a good taste of social unity and personal freedom (199–200). Would the dominant classes still enjoy Carnival if its transgressions became permanent? Marshall implies that they would not.

Paule Marshall chooses Carnival as the central event and decisive turning point in her novel. She paints it in all the colors and sounds of a great celebration, modeling it after the great Carnival parades and dances of Trinidad and Montserrat.[25] Traditions brought over from the balls of France and from Venetian masques and African dance, music, and clothing join together in the street parade. People dress up in all types of costumes, depending on their own fantasies, priorities, and dreams, from the revealingly mild "sailors" of the English and middle-class ladies to the grotesque "white mime" of Vere's ex-girlfriend, disguising her darkness in stark white makeup, tulle, sequins, jewels, and a blond wig (271). In contrast, poor slum children come down from the hills barefoot and in their usual rags; the young guerrilla band members emulate Fidel Castro in the threat of an armed revolution, exhibiting beards and cigars in the manner of the Cuban leader, "dressed in olive fatigues, heavy combat boots and helmets camouflaged with leaves," and all of them, "even the women, brandishing cardboard machetes and grenades" (289).

Marshall's novel and its Carnival parade reflect the revolutionary mood of 1960s and 1970s politics in the Caribbean and especially emphasize the historical roots of contemporary popular culture in the plantations of the seventeenth century. According to Caribbean social critic Patrick Taylor, "popular culture was political" from the start, as it brought together "African-based, European-influenced religious and aesthetic symbolism" against "slavery and oppression." Oral tales of "survival and struggle" passed from generation to generation and were "later picked up in literary works."[26]

In Marshall's novel, memories of peoples and events from different times and places join together in the paradigmatic celebration. The Bournehills people come into town in slave costumes copied from library books that described Cuffee Ned's clothes: a "standard Osnaburg tunic over a pair of homespun pantaloons," to which women have added heavy silver bracelets that look like handcuffs (284, 269). The African slaves are preceded in the parade by a procession of "brilliantly costumed marchers, huge bedecked floats . . . rivalrous steelbands which would, many of them, clash as the day wore on"—revelers carrying all kinds of messages (279). The powerful and the tragic in history are now burlesqued in Marshall's Carnival scenes:

> This year, along with the usual large and noisy contingent of sailors and whooping American Indians, there were bands depicting Cleopatra's Egypt, Hiroshima—with a mass of twisted wreckage and corpses—The Garden of Eden, Wars to Come, The

Fall of the Roman Empire—with a stout black Nero, a chaplet of leaves around his forehead, fiddling in the midst of a fake fire— Life on the Moon, The Twenty-sixth of July Guerrilla Band, The Parade of the Dolls. (279)

Bournehills, once the winner of the "Best Local Historical" award, finally enters the street looking "across a great vista of time." It differs from the other bands in the slow, dragging movement of the dancers and in the awesome sound produced by the stomping feet and echoes of chains in the loud clashing of countless bracelets. It is "a somber counterpoint to the gay Carnival celebration," bringing memories of the selves and the culture set in exile (282).

The band members ask with their eyes for the acknowledgment and love of the watching crowd who have gathered for the "mammoth parade." Observers at first complain and resent the insistence of the Bournehills people in repeating the same theme after so many years, but they soon are touched by its powerful message. There is deep silence when Delbert announces in his conch shell that the pageant will start. Carefully dressed like Cuffee, Stinger reenacts his power and courage; wearing "a long nightshirt" and "an old fashioned nightcap," flour-whitened Ferguson exaggerates the shock and the pleading howls of landlord Percy Bryam (284). Fake flames rise up and a mock battle between soldiers and slaves ensues, but victory is soon announced. The arms of the Bournehills people fling to the skies, free of their bracelets and chains, and in "a triumphal dance" with "joyous leaps and bursts," voices soar in a "triumphal song." It is a long hymn of jubilation, telling the details of the uprising and the almost three years of resistance, a struggle compared to those of Jamaican Maroons and Guianan Bush Negroes: "free, at peace, dependent only on themselves, a nation apart" (285–87).[27]

The Carnival celebration reaches a cathartic climax. Screams come from all sides; in the frightening and dense moment, it seems as if the hills really are burning. The paraders hail the force of people working and fighting together: they had once been great, had been a people, and they can be as strong and united again. But the rhythm of the moment slows into mourning, as the low, sad tones sing of Cuffee's defeat by massive government action. But he was prepared and ready to die, and death is also victory in a way: a hunter and warrior once again, his spirit could return to his African homeland (288). The story told by the Bournehills band seems the dramatic representation of a general plight of dispossession and exploitation, ending in a cry for change:

> They were singing, it is true, of Bryam, Cuffee and Pyre Hill, of a particular event, place and people. . . . Yet, as those voices continued to mount the air, shaking the old town at its moorings on the bay, it didn't seem they were singing only of themselves and Bournehills, but of people like them everywhere . . . the experience through which any people who find themselves ill-used, dispossessed, at the mercy of the powerful, must pass. (286–87).

The watching crowd understands and joins in, singing and swaying with the Bournehills band. Saul Amron relates the story to the suffering of the Jewish people for thousands of years and sees its enormous importance in spelling out methods for change, with "history as a guide" (315). The Bournehills people will soon apply Cuffee's lesson of union to their struggle against Kingsley and Sons, whose economic domination and absentee power repeat the colonialist pattern. People learn to organize and carry out their own "development programs," as Cuffee's message had so long proclaimed (354, 404).

Merle Kinbona guides the anthropologist Saul Amron in the Carnival pageant and the late-night ball at Sugar's. The place had been a sugar warehouse and a slave "barracoon" in earlier times and still smells of the dark flesh whose essence had been "distilled over the centuries and locked into the stone" (316). Brought together by a sense of mutual understanding in their shared Jewish and African heritages of sorrow and endurance and helped by the overall Carnival mood, Saul and Merle reverse ethnographic roles. Returning his gaze, she plays the "objective impersonal interviewer" and probes into his darkest secrets and contradictions in a way that he had never allowed to happen before.

Saul tells Merle about his first marriage, the tragic miscarriage of their child, and the death of his wife Sosha, a Jewish survivor of a Nazi concentration camp; his despair with "Western man's alienation and disaffection"; his refusal to accommodate in the United States after the radical dreams of his youth had proved unreachable; and his wish to get out of that closed, racist world and live among "people of different colors and cultures" (321–22). In return, Merle tells of her personal tragedies and paradoxes: her love–hate relationship with capitalism; her past love life, divided between a rich, exploitative Englishwoman and a proud and committed African male economist; and the consequent separation from her only daughter. The two share heavy burdens of guilt and grief, feeling stricken and exhausted after removing their social masks.[28]

Their mutual confessions happen in the midst of the noise and craziness of the last Carnival ball, and dancers around them seem to participate in and respond to the unfolding of their stories, the crowd stopping in a moment of silence for Saul's infinite sorrow and in a look of concern at Merle's rage (325–27). As the end of Carnival approaches, Saul and Merle dare a bigger transgression, staying together for the rest of the night. She agrees to do it only if he does not "make much of it, meaning it goes no further than tonight" (389). After Carnival, all rules, boundaries, and traditions should be restored. Yet even if it is a passing phenomenon, Carnival may help a person and a society come to terms with dilemmas and discover solidarity. It does go further, and never again will Merle or Saul be the same.

In or out of Carnival time, the Caribbean island described by Paule Marshall adheres less to certain Western inhibitions and taboos than would be tolerated in parts of the United States and Europe. The Yankee Harriet is horrified by a sensuality and a relaxation of racial barriers that her family tradition taught her to avoid (100, 420). At the mere touch of Lyle Hutson's hand on her arm, some "dark unknown part of herself surfaced" (425). Repeating the experience of her English acquaintance Dorothy Clough, she gets caught in the apparent chaos of street Carnival, but unlike the other woman, she is unable to overcome her panic, fear of impending death, and disgust at those thousands of sweaty black bodies pressing against hers. The reversal of roles becomes suddenly unbearable: she, the white heiress so used to admiration and command, is now dressed like a slave in a costume given to her by the Bournehills people. The dark warriors in the guerrilla band do not seem to see her or hear her voice and are not "shocked" at having a white woman in their midst. Harriet is physically and mentally overcome by the hysterical fear of being pushed into the sea and dying, and she passes out in that moment of terror and disgust. For her, Carnival is not a ritual of release and catharsis but a nauseating crisis of grotesque proportions.

The incident was not "a minor thing," as she later reports to her husband and friends. She is deeply disturbed within herself, a fact perceived by Lyle Hutson, who tries to shake her "American" barriers to his advances by telling her of Saul's "liaison" with Merle. Such one-day affairs are a common occurrence during Carnival, he says, when "practically everyone takes advantage of the opportunity" (426). Merle and Bournehills become one and the same obsession for Harriet from then on. The place now seems a solid black block, responsible for all her tragedies.

While his wife rejects the island, Saul Amron faces a crisis with the United States. From the island, the anthropologist looks back to his homeland. He sees that the United States "never honestly faced up to its past, never told the story straight," and he wonders if it ever will (359). Saul's and Merle's criticism of the United States likely voices Marshall's own anger at the racial violence going on in the country during the years when the novel was being written (1963–1968). They also reflect disbelief in the existence of racial paradises in the *New World*. Perhaps only a "God's forgotten" place like Bournehills can allow different races to meet and become true friends (469).

The United States is also under the critical scrutiny of Allen Fuso, the white anthropologist who accompanies Saul Amron in the development project, and Lyle Hutson, the mulatto lawyer from the island's upper class. After having interacted with other races and classes in the Caribbean, Fuso resents the ethnic bigotry and the regimented lifestyle of his family and town in the United States. Back home, he had been a "red-blooded" patriot like the others, marched in "Columbus day parade" with his father, and even made plans to join the marines. Now he hates the memory of it (377). Lyle Hutson contrasts the West Indies with the United States, "a most unfortunate country," although he admits that Bourne Island is not the happy "multiracial society" that people talk about (422).[29]

In her critique of neocolonialism, Marshall is careful not to indict "America" and not to identify "Americans" as generally exploitative and cynical, even if their business deals recall and perpetuate the old colonial rule. The anthropologists Allen Fuso and Saul Amron have "decent faces" and sincere intentions. Allen, who had been on the island before, is well liked by Merle and by the common people of the hills. Marshall shows deep sympathy for Allen's "strong Mediterranean coloring," the result of a mixed ethnic background combining "various strains" (including an Italian father who is despised by a bigoted Irish mother); his sincere smile and self-criticism; and his confused and repressed homosexuality (17, 310–12, 377). Saul Amron is another example of possible solidarity coming from a North American, again not the Anglo-Saxon type. He is a Jewish man with family and personal ties to Latin America. His mother, a Sephardic Jew from New York, had filled his imagination with stories of her ancestors who had made it to Latin America and the Caribbean after the Inquisition. In practical life, his fieldwork has taken him to many different places in the continent. Being by family, taste, and profession a person of the world, Saul welcomes difference. Even his looks are hybrid: along with a pale face and curved nose, Saul's hair is "coarse and rust-colored," resembling "nigger hair" (17).

By contrast, Saul Amron's "pure bred Anglo-Saxon" wife, Harriet, is a descendant of the powerful Shippen family from Delaware and heiress to an enormous wealth, accumulated since (and because of) the slave trade. The family name is a play on the continuing impact of U.S. shipping and trading on the West Indies and other parts of the world. Harriet Shippen is constantly associated with the colonial powers: in her family history; in her civilized, contained manners; in her inability to accept the touch of a black hand; and in her naive and hypocritical moral rectitude, which refuses to face her family's and her own guilt and complicity in the evils of the world. Even so, she is portrayed as an ambiguous and divided woman who constantly depends on men, lonely and human in spite of her immense power.

*The Chosen Place, the Timeless People* illustrates the complex relationship between the Caribbean of today and the traditional colonial order. European privileges continue to exist only at the expense of the continuing poverty and exploitation of black people. Among the island's middle classes, the lure of social prestige has led people such as Lyle Hutson to collaborate with the dominant order. He had been a radical socialist while studying in prestigious English schools such as Oxford and the London School of Economics. Merle was then in England, and they were lovers for a short time. Back on the island, however, and parted from Merle's radical influence, Lyle gave up all his plans for fighting Kingsley and Sons and nationalizing the sugar industry. He married quite comfortably into "the famous Vaughan family" (his wife is therefore a relative of Merle's father) and joined the power circle and the status quo (61). And there are others like him, black men who "for the most part had passed through the white prism of their history and been endlessly refracted there, altered, alloyed" (53). The Parliament that governs the island is made up of such men, and the colonial reality of the past remains barely touched in the present—a reality that Marshall also explores in her latest novel, *Daughters*.

The *Chosen Place* also connects paradoxes in issues of race and class with the complexities surrounding gender and sexuality. The radical Merle once yielded to the favors and money of an English protectress-lover in London; for a while, she had agreed to prolong an economic and emotional dependence on a richer white person of her same sex. Homosexuality is twice presented as an option in the novel, in Merle's story and in Allen Fuso's attraction for Vere (both cases are international, interracial, and interclass). After Merle is well established back in the Caribbean, her house depends completely on another woman, the black Carrington, "the last keep-miss" who came to Merle as an inheritance from her father, along with the Vaughan colonial house (110).[30] In both instances, with the English protectress and the native servant, Merle reproduces aspects of a colonial order that she fiercely criticizes. She realizes that she lacks energy to change as much as do the other people in Bournehills, all in need of "a miracle" to cure their paralysis (230).

If the upper middle class goes to school in England, many of the poor look for jobs there and in the United States. The exhaustion of the island's soil and the scarcity of resources push young men such as Vere Walkes to search for a way out in the United States. He returns after three years to find his mother, Leesy, in the same half-acre she has always owned with pride, in spite of all her destitution and solitude. On the wall of their tiny home, she keeps photographs of the queen side by side with a "pale suffering Christ" and a number of relatives already dead or "emigrated to England or America" (28). In the hope of making money and returning a successful man, the young Vere, actually too young to be allowed to emigrate through the Labor Program, picked fruit in New Jersey and cut cane in Florida, where many ran away from the horrible working conditions. He was refused help by an uncle who lived in comfort in Brooklyn but was more concerned about breaking the law and his own security than about Vere's welfare (30).[31] Frustrated, Vere returns to the island with nothing more than a new taste for cars and races, only to find more disillusionment in the destitution of his home, the ever-permanent threat of the closing of the sugar mill, and the cold indifference of his former girlfriend.

Vere had been only seventeen when they had a son, and his mother, Leesy, had believed the relationship to be a complete mistake, her first objection being the "red" in the young woman's color, an indication that she was "cross-bred and worthless" (31). Marshall again illustrates the hierarchy of color and class in the Caribbean and the antagonisms and injustices that it perpetuates.[32] Leesy blames Vere's former girlfriend, a young prostitute, for killing the couple's son, neglecting and abusing him only because he was "too black" (32). Despised by both blacks and whites, the young Canterbury woman is one of the *backras* of that area, "meaning more white than black and poor as the devil" (85).[33] Vere ultimately dies in one of the car races he learned to love so much in the United States. As his father had died in a 1950 accident after slipping "into the roller pit at Cane Vale" (28), old Leesy is left the sole, faithful survivor of the family, a symbol of the immutable hills where machines and progress have brought no good. She is symbolic of the enduring African woman, nurturing the family, anointing the sick, and holding onto a sacred—however small—piece of land to pass on to the children. The tragic irony is that in this modern America black children die young.

Marshall, however, in no sense idealizes the suffering black Bournehills or the mixed population of other parts of town. Full of their own contradictions and flaws, "the people" must often share the guilt and the wrongs of history with those in power. Group rivalry and individual selfishness delay or eliminate unified, effective action. Leesy herself remains static in the past, faithful to the British rule represented by the queen, and holds onto old class and color divisions between the poor, as does her son Vere's former girlfriend. Vere buys into values of consumption, puts all his money in an old German-made General Motors car, and races it to his death. Cane workers such as Stinger and Gwen have turned into automatons in their daily lives, seeing nothing besides the cane, stultified by the endless work (162).

For one reason or another, the working men and women cannot bring about change. The island's labor union leaders go to Washington, D.C., for "a conference of Caribbean trade unionists being held under the joint sponsorship of the American labor unions and the State Department," but the leading unionists are not interested in a backward place like Bournehills (393). Bournehills workers, for their part, have lost the power to react. Ferguson, one of the oldest men in the Cane Vale mill, is proud of his ability and critically aware of the injustices around him, but his wish to imitate Cuffee Ned and revolutionize the mill conditions is kept from fulfillment by his heavy rum drinking. He feels choked and numb, and his protest dies in his throat (222). In the Bournehills bar, there is "a never tiring talk of Cuffee Ned," and all wait for a new Cuffee to come; but day-by-day life is paralyzing and dull.

The people of Bournehills at least keep African memory alive by talking and singing about Cuffee Ned's resistance. Those who rise in the social scale to a better life would rather erase all traces of the slave past. The school headmaster defends a history told by the conqueror, the winner and the model for all. Others with less education, such as the black Parliament member Deanes whose dark color and heavy island accent hold him down among politicians of lighter color and higher prestige, are too afraid and insecure to rise and take a stand on anything. The Cane Vale sugar mill manager, Erskine Vaughan, a relative of Merle, takes anxious care of the English property, he more than anybody controlled by the business and afraid to lose his job. He knows of the dangers from the deteriorating equipment and machines, but like Deanes, he is afraid to do anything: "He wouldn't ask the Kingsley people to put in new ones not for Thy Kingdom come! He's frighten they'll get vex with him if he asks for anything" (155). Vaughan instead blames the workers for the bad condition of the machines. For the poor, life is simply too hard to leave room for improvement. For those in power, change cannot occur because, as they understand it—or prefer to believe—the poor hold back progress and refuse to change. Hence the old order remains, riddled with intricacies and paradoxes.[34] Can a development project sponsored by U.S. interests improve conditions at all in a place like Bourne Island?

The project itself is at risk: to avenge the pain and humiliation of losing her husband to a black woman, Harriet uses her power with the foundation backing the project to change Saul's position, taking him away from the island. Saul is outraged; he is tired of being manipulated by big interests and now sees his dependence on the personal moods and social insensitivity of his wife. Saul accuses her of being like all of "her" people, unable to share power and to respect the feelings and needs of others. In addition to his own life and his career, the fate of Bournehills is being manipulated by Harriet, just as it has always been controlled by the commercial and political interests of England and the United States. "What is it with you and your kind, anyway?" Saul cries out in anger. "If you can't have things your way, if you can't run the show, there's to be no show, is that it?" (454).

In the end, Harriet lets the shadows of the place enter her home and the memories of the past invade her soul. Bournehills becomes the arena where deep psychological troubles as well as fierce social and cultural dilemmas come to battle. For Harriet, as for Saul and others, "Bournehills could have been a troubled region within [themselves] to which [they] had unwittingly returned" (100). She finally faces her complicity in the impoverishment and destruction of the world and confronts the guilt and the paradoxes she has been trying to shut out of sight for so long. She sees her father and his world as dedicated to "money and mergers and manipulating the market." She thinks of the "unreconstructed Southern belle who had been her mother," with her way of speaking to the maid Alberta as if she were "a lesser person" (457–58). Harriet also stops evading the terrifying image of her first husband, Andrew Westerman, "a physicist who worked at" the atomic Proving Ground at Aberdeen directing a "huge secret laboratory" (38–40). In the recurring nightmare that has haunted Harriet's nights, a massive explosion erupts the center of the earth into a huge cloud, leading to final and empty silence. To her dismay and horror, she realizes that her hand rests on Andrew's—the Western man—and directs the lever, triggering the holocaust (39). Symbolic of the ultimate power of her class and race to build empires and destroy them with equal recklessness, Harriet in her dream guides the hand of science but realizes with terror that final supremacy will also signify the destruction of the victors.

Unable to go on living under such a "horror at herself," Harriet seeks death by drowning in the sea. It is ironic that she willingly kills herself in the same Atlantic that had taken so many African bodies in the diaspora, a sea that sounds as if it mourns them all, the great boulders taking on the fantastic shapes of gravestones. The sea was often noisy and violent, echoing cries from centuries past, "a loud unceasing lament—all those, the nine million and more it is said," who lost their lives in the Middle Passage (106). From her first moments on the island, the thunder of the ocean had reminded Harriet of the detonation of atomic bombs and her recurring nightmare (107). During her marriage to the atomics expert, that vision of the apocalyptical end had made it impossible for her to go on living with him, and it prevented her from talking about such feelings even years afterward. But on Bourne Island, Harriet finally faces her inner darkness, "her complicity in the destruction," and purges her guilt in the roaring Atlantic. She walks numbly on and on, feeling the gaze of the hills people on her, and meets "the massive detonation set off by the breakers on the reefs. And then the spray rising in the dazzling white toadstool of a cloud" (459). In her self-sacrifice, she finally rejects the history of violent domination and oppression in which she and her family participated. She also escapes her own contradictions, unable to solve them otherwise, disappearing in a natural explosion whose noise and form recall her fearful dreams.

After Harriet disappears into the waves, their outrage seems somewhat appeased. The water regains color and clarity, "as though it had been endlessly filtered to remove every impurity." With the seaweed gone and the sand finer and soft, it seems "a new sea" after the storm, more reconciled with its history and more appeased in "its usual hysteria" (461).

The daily repetition of the tides, like the Carnival parade reenactment year after year, suggests a cyclical pattern of return. Harriet's tragic end repeats the fate of other women of her color and race who were defeated by patriarchal domination, even if they held power over other races and classes. Harriet is a complicit member in a deeply oppressive structure, but she is like other abandoned women who face rejection and betrayal by the men they love. In her composed figure and in her fate, she mirrors her mother, a Virginia belle who committed "a protracted form of suicide." Harriet's isolation and despair also recall Daphne Pollard, the British wife of a sugarcane field manager in the early history of the island, whose tragic form of death Harriet reenacts (173). Ultimately dependent on the wishes of their fathers and husbands, the three white women share deep internal conflicts stemming from the racial, patriarchal, and religious rules that control and destroy their lives (437).

In *The Chosen Place, the Timeless People,* Marshall also dramatizes the economic and racial tensions of former European colonies where blacks and whites are taught the superiority of Western civilization and must live accordingly. Her characters represent the variety of hues and levels of prestige within such societies. The person who is lighter and more closely imitates the European is the most respected and, of course, the richest. Lyle Hutson effectively represents this dilemma. His house is constructed according to a grotesque but popular hybrid architecture that aspires to Greek nobility and American efficiency and modernity (54). Hutson himself, a lawyer who does not dare question the real crimes being committed against the people, "is in league with Kingsley & Sons, even if he didn't know it" (67).

The hope for truth and creativity lies in the poor people, whose allegiance to African roots and the memory of black resistance can help them resist corruption and assimilation by the distorted values of the dominant order. The physical features of some island people are still distinctly African, such as Ferguson's "beautifully sculpted Benin head" (396) and Merle's face, one "that might have been sculpted by some bold and liberal Bantu hand" (5).[35] Africa is also present in the rhythms that poor blacks have imposed on the language of the conqueror, infusing it "with a raw poetry, transforming it, making it their own" (122). Because Europeans regard their language and their Africanness as inferior, the history of the Bourne Island blacks is ignored and despised. Only by recovering their history and rejecting English or American notions of "progress" can they achieve the union of the people and action as heroic as Cuffee's to bring about change in the social structure (135).

Marshall dramatically emphasizes the repetition of historical cycles and the connection between peoples and individuals of different places and times. In Bournehills, present and past share a similar colonial order, with the English and the American alternating roles of domination. The other Third World countries in the hemisphere endure similar processes in their cycles of "discovery," exploration, and decay in the hands of European colonizers. The barren hills of Bourne Island remind the ethnographer Saul Amron of other impoverished lands of the continent: "Bournehills . . . was suddenly the wind-scoured Peruvian Andes. The highlands of Guatemala. Chile. Bolivia, where he had once worked briefly among the tin miners. Honduras. . . . Southern Mexico. And the spent cotton lands of the Southern United States. . . . It was every place that had been wantonly used, its substance stripped away, and then abandoned" (100).

The fate of the working class and the black race is the same in Bournehills and the United States. Migrant workers in the United States live through an odyssey of exploitation and escape quite similar to slave life, while the English monopoly of sugar in Bourne Island and other Caribbean islands retains the tradition of absentee landlords and depleted lands. The women in the *Chosen Place* also share similar burdens related to ethnicity and gender. Merle's lined face recalls the suffering of Saul's first wife, Sosha, linking the plights of Africans and Jews.[36] In spite of the radical contrast between their lives, Saul's second wife, Harriet, is like Sosha in the sense that both women have followed a husband in his professional career. Harriet is also like other white women of her family and class, apparently powerful and privileged but still controlled by patriarchal rule. Both the women and the men in the novel share in different degrees and for various reasons their measure of oppression and guilt.

The repetition and crisscrossing of patterns of domination across the Americas and the world is the major emphasis in the novel, where the Shippens, Kingsley and Sons, and other commercial empires; members of Parliament; lawyers; overseers; and the middle classes in general cooperate and support one another in the exploitation of the bodies of the poor and the resources of the earth, in the name of civilization. Centuries have passed since the five-year burning of Pyre Hill and the death of Bourne Island's owner, Percy Bryam, under torture on a mill wheel at Cane Vale, yet "yesterday comes like today" in a place where the sugar enterprise remains in English hands and overseers and managers keep the island and its people under control, "like [ghosts] from times past" (161). The opportunity arrives for the workers to control their own labor when the Kingsley roller machine breaks down and they must take over the cane processing. Erskine Vaughan is ordered by "the people in London" to close the mill down (392). The workers have to organize and haul their cane to grind somewhere else, excited by the possibility of cooperative work directed and done by themselves. The novel here suggests the hope for a beginning in the concrete practice of life, without romantic heroism, and again recalls contemporary efforts toward cooperative action in the Caribbean islands.[37]

Repetition and circularity also mark Merle's final return to Africa, where she will try to recover her daughter. However, Merle is now a new woman, stripped of such European ornaments as the weird earrings depicting Westminster saints and of all other signs of a divided self. She is able to assume a happier and more beautiful identity (468). Saul will pursue an independent career, firmly convinced that it is the people themselves, not any corporation, government, or power from above, who can produce real change. That is also the message of Bournehills' Carnival dramatization and of the book as a whole. It took the anthropologist just a little longer than it took the illiterate Leesy Walkes to question the sincerity and efficacy of foreign aid and to realize that much more radical action is necessary for real change. The only way to change is to "start fresh" and not try to build on the same old, corrupt order (142–43).

Paule Marshall raises profound questions about the process of decolonization and the establishment of an independent cultural identity in modernizing societies that were originally rooted in African slave labor under European rule. Published in 1969, *The Chosen Place, the Timeless People* reflects intellectual and cultural issues brought to the forefront in the 1960s and 1970s, especially questions of gender, class, and racial differences in the United States and the British Caribbean; the interrelatedness of the two socioeconomic areas; the need for change; and finally, the forms of political, economic, and cultural action that the dominant system can accommodate. In the novel, people are empowered through the spontaneity of Carnival costumes and rituals, education, the renovation of ties with the past, pride in the history of the poor and the black, cultural memory, and cohesive political organization and action.

Carnival allows for the expression of the sensuality, the pride, and the power hidden under the social masks worn in everyday life. Before people openly claim their space and alter the social structure, Carnival masquerades can be their only moment of affirmation and visibility. They evoke ancient myths and miracles: revelers can feel a special power and beauty by wearing costumes and escaping the uniform mechanization of their daily routines. Costumes and dramatizations allow people to express the selves that they feel within, empowering images of beauty and strength, rebels and warriors who could perhaps transform the world. Grief, pain, hope, rebellion, and a history not told by the official records can come out in that transgressive moment.

In Marshall's novel, costumes and parades are strategically used to address central issues of our time: the relations among races, ethnicities, genders, and classes; between the colonizer and the colonized; and between the hegemonic and the popular cultures. In the words of poet and historian Edward Brathwaite, the novel is concerned with "the orbit of American cultural and material imperialism" that characterizes the West Indies, associated with the "Euro-colonial past" that may distort, contrast, or negotiate with people's "active memories of Africa and slavery."[38] In her concern with the recuperation of popular myths and histories of Africans in the Caribbean and with the reformulation of the concept of national identity, and in her critique of (neo)colonialism, Marshall shares a common ground with several writers from Latin America and the Caribbean. Her focus on popular rituals and her discussion of different forms of resistance are also of major interest to contemporary U.S. ethnographers, colleagues of Marshall's Saul Amron.

*The Chosen Place* explores the need to address personal, social, national, and regional identities in a constant process of creation and transformation. Time and space are interconnected in the shared history of struggle and resistance under persisting colonialism. All the continents of the world are linked with past, present, and future action taking place in England, in the United States, in a Caribbean "Bourne Island," in Brazil, and in Africa. Marshall's character Merle judges the United States on the basis of her own experience in England and on news of increasingly violent U.S. racial and foreign relations. Merle would rather avoid the country, especially in the company of a white man like Saul (469). Through Merle's vision, Marshall urges radical change in the traditional colonial mindset that justifies the lack of civil rights at home and the exploitation of poorer nations abroad. Written amid the turmoil and rebellion taking place between 1963 and 1968, the novel joins in the widespread protest of the time against racism, militarism, and economic oppression on national and international fronts.

As the novel closes, Merle looks forward to a brighter future, while Saul feels too despondent to go on doing fieldwork. He does not want to return to the United States, where he would feel an outsider, one "who's simply awaiting either the return to sanity in the country or the end" (468). But Merle needs to reconnect with Africa before she can be a mature and productive woman in her own Caribbean space: "Just being there and seeing the place will be a big help for me . . . in some way it will give me the strength I need to get moving again" (468). After her trip, she will return home to Bournehills, for it is on the island that she can influence social and political change. She feels like a new person who will never be "bought or bribed" as she had been in England, accepting checks in exchange for protection and favors at the cost of her marriage and daughter. As she plans her journey of reconnection, she is already different: within herself, she has already reached freedom, maturity, and wisdom (441). Merle is Paule Marshall's favorite character or the woman that she "would love to have been." Representing the struggles of black people in the Caribbean, according to her creator, "she embodies an entire history. She is the child of the hemisphere."[39]

En route to Africa, Merle reconnects with Africans who had been brought in their diaspora to neighboring Trinidad or who cultivated and processed sugarcane in Brazil, farther south in the "extended Caribbean." She refuses to go through New York and London on her journey, symbolically moving within the Third World in the Southern Hemisphere and drawing a circle uniting the Caribbean, Brazil, and Africa in her quest for a more complete identity as a Caribbean person in a broader frame of reference. Marshall describes Merle's Third World journey:

> She was not taking the usual route to Africa, first flying north to London via New York and then down. Instead, she was going south to Trinidad, then on to Recife in Brazil, and from Recife, that city where the great arm of the hemisphere reaches out toward the massive shoulder of Africa as though yearning to be joined to it as it surely had been in the beginning, she would fly across to Dakar and, from there, begin the long cross-continent journey to Kampala. (471)

In writing about Cuffee Ned's struggle and Merle's journey to Africa as symbolic of a necessary reconnection for the Caribbean, Marshall approaches Barbadian and Caribbean identity as "an act of imaginative rediscovery," which also entails becoming and transforming oneself and the culture.[40] Although Marshall echoes the *Aeneid* in different points in the story and Saul Amron compares Bournehills to "the crude seat of some half-ruined coliseum, where an ancient tragedy was still performed" (99), that ancient tragedy may evolve into a less-despairing, more-promising future. For that reason, Marshall refuses to dwell on the violence of the past; it happened and must be remembered, but people and history move on.[41]

The combination of an emphasis on cultural empowerment and a broad inter-American scope characterizes Paule Marshall's work. *The Chosen Place, the Timeless People* and the more recent *Daughters* are her most multicultural and polyvocal works: parts of the continent crisscross, races mingle, and American cultures connect with Europe and Africa. In *Chosen Place*, Carnival festivities provide an occasion for the intensification of the tension, the violence, and also the beauty of the continuous making and remaking of the *New World* as we know it. Marshall's other stories and novels, set in different parts of the Americas, add more color and people to the new inscription of the continent.

## Completing a Trilogy:
### *Brown Girl, Brownstones* and *Praisesong for the Widow*

Marshall's three novels *Brown Girl, Brownstones; The Chosen Place, the Timeless People;* and *Praisesong for the Widow* form a trilogy in their shared theme of return to Africa or to African origins in the Caribbean.[42] Her first novel, *Brown Girl, Brownstones* (1959), explores the conflicts and negotiations in the lives of an immigrant Barbadian family who have settled in a brownstone apartment building of Brooklyn, New York, where a young Bajan (Barbadian) community flourishes.[43] More than a study of immigrant life, the novel is, according to the writer, "a kind of commentary on American society."[44] There is strong pressure on the newcomers to conform and "make it in America," but the central character, Selina Boyce, resisting the group and particularly her mother, finally makes the journey back to the Caribbean as the novel reaches its conclusion.[45]

By contrast, Selina's mother, Silla, is obsessed with forgetting about the Caribbean past and saving to buy a house in her new land. She has assimilated what makes Marshall "so unhappy about American society: this kind of almost blind absorption in the material" that results in "a kind of diminishing of life, of feeling." But the existence of people like Silla in Marshall's experience has not been strong enough to dim the cultural and political brilliance of other women, a fact Marshall highlights in the book through Selina's escape from the alienating influence. The first history lessons in Marshall's own life came from the memories and ideas of some remarkable women. Her inter-American and diasporic perspective grew in large part from the influence of women of the Barbadian community in Brooklyn where she was born and grew up. These simple domestics, day workers, and sleep-in maids held strong political beliefs, a diasporic conscience, and supported Marcus Garvey and his UNIA (the Universal Negro Improvement Association). Marshall writes of them, "They also saw themselves in terms of the larger world of darker people. . . . They saw themselves not only as Black Afro-Americans or Afro-Caribbeans living in this hemisphere, but they saw themselves as part of that larger world. And this has become, of course, one of the themes of my work."[46]

In *Praisesong for the Widow* (1983), the main character, Avey Johnson, is a middle-aged, middle-class woman who finally rediscovers her connections with Africa and the black Caribbean and also a self repressed since childhood. Like Silla, she had chosen to trade the history and culture of her African ancestors for the prosperity and comfort of modern-day urban life in the United States. Her friends are people like the near-white Thomasina Moore, who tries to keep away from "niggers" because they "mess up ever' time" (*PW*, 27). Avey and her husband, Jay Johnson, tried to forget the hardships of their Brooklyn childhood and the segregated buses in Washington, D.C., by distancing themselves from the poor and the oppressed. Avey lived through the harshest moments of the 1960s and 1970s "as if Watts and Selma and the tanks and Stoner guns in the streets of Detroit somehow did not pertain to her" (140).

Avey's assimilation of the values of Western culture and modern capitalism coincide with her distancing from her African roots. For the sake of social acceptance in a white world, young Avey and husband, Jay, hid away their Africanness and stifled their spontaneity and love. Her "Bantu behind" and her "gulla-gold skin" lost any reason for joy or pride; the small rituals that had been so important, such as their sensuous dancing and playfulness or his love of poetry and music, were forgotten in the endless marathon to prove themselves successful and respectable (137). Even more than political and historical awareness, Marshall here seems concerned with reconnecting her lost characters with the cultural and spiritual influence of Africa. In *The Chosen Place, the Timeless People*, the anthropologist Saul Amron realizes that academic and practical knowledge are not enough to understand a place like Bournehills; only "soothsayers and diviners" might be able to comprehend its deeper, elusive meanings, although the Cuffee Ned masque seems to clarify some of them (*CPTP*, 316). In *Praisesong for the Widow*, Marshall brings the African power of divination and healing to the forefront along with African-Caribbean folk dance and song. She privileges the cultural realms of folklore and myth in the process of disalienation and reconnection.

Avey's cultural awakening occurs during a cruise to the Caribbean, when the European music, food, and ambiance of the white ship are abandoned for the drumbeating and the dancing of black people on the island of Carriacou. Before Avey's departure from the United States, her daughter Marion spoke against a vacation on the *Bianca Pride*, a ship that glorifies whiteness even in its name: it would be a "meaningless cruise with a bunch of white folks" (*PW*, 13). As a graduate student, Marion belongs to a generation weary of the manipulation of history and the traps of assimilation. Echoing Merle Kinbona's choices on her final trip in *Chosen Place*, Marion previously had urged Avey to take trips to Brazil and Ghana (*PW*, 13). But at this point, Avey cannot resist the dazzling attraction of the luxury cruise and the opportunity to feel rich and elegant, sporting the contents of her six suitcases, shoe caddy, and hatbox (16). She travels with Thomasina Moore and Clarice, women who, like her, are in their fifties and sixties and who are most interested in the pleasures made possible by the continuous economic struggle of past years.

Like a white explorer interested only in buying the pleasures available in that part of the world, the imperial liner sails through the waters of Mexico; to the Carnival in Cartagena, Colombia; and amid the striking colors of the Caribbean. Always proper and civilized, Avey is disgusted when her black friend Clarice gets off the ship to swing "her bony hips to the drums" of the Cartagena Carnival parade (25). The ship allows its passengers a safe distance from the land; the economic, historical, and cultural dilemmas of the region bear no relevance for the happy cruisers. They are occupied with their vanity and their own little theater, staged in highly decorated rooms reminiscent of the grandeur of Versailles.

Marion's warnings prove both true and false. The liner is indeed a gaudy white prison, but the trip is by no means meaningless. The waters and the spirit of the Caribbean win over Avey despite her careful resistance, carrying her on a journey within herself, through her Africanness and her past. Thoughts of Jim Crow segregation and lingering police brutality against blacks make the polite normality on the ship strike her as false and hollow. Feeling isolated from other passengers on the boat, Avey escapes into the company of female mentors from different generations. The presence in her mind of her daughter Marion and her father's aunt Cuney seems more real than her artificial surroundings on the *Bianca Pride*. Marion's critical whisper points to the symbolic meaning of the ship's Versailles Room: "Versailles. . . . Do you know how many treaties were signed there, in that infamous Hall of Mirrors, divvying up India, the West Indies, the world?" (46).[47] Marion's broad historical references remind the reader of Saul Amron, and these ideas and the overall framework indicate Paule Marshall's priorities and her expanded awareness of world domination.

As Avey retreats into herself, dreams and visions bring back her childhood vacations in the company of Great-Aunt Cuney on Tatem Island, a black enclave in South Carolina. Stories told by Cuney recalled the robbery of land owned by blacks but also the vision and endurance of the African slaves who arrived at the island's Ibo Landing. Back home, Avey retold the stories to her brothers, word for word, having absorbed the emotion and power of the narrative: how the Ibos, reaching America in chains, envisioned everything that would happen to them from slavery through emancipation up to "the hard times of today" and simply walked back to Africa, wading into the water without any need for boats (38–39).

Guided by her daughter and her great-aunt, Avey is finally taken over by this new–old person being born within her. She undergoes inner turbulence and physical pain in a ritual of initiation and rebirth that clears her mind and opens her eyes to the beauty of her heritage. This process is symbolically completed at the center of the Americas, when Avey discovers the Grenada hidden away from chic hotels and the "tropical" package tour. She must rewrite her life story, beginning with the recovery of her name—Avatara, given to her by Great-Aunt Cuney after Cuney's own grandmother, a name long forsaken by the pressure to Americanize and to sound pleasant to English-speakers. The Sanskrit word *avatara,* origin of the English "avatar," signifies descent and reincarnation of a deity or "an incarnation or embodiment of another person."[48] The name suggests a reconnection with Great-Aunt Cuney and a reincarnation of her spirit and her culture. Receding step by step into the past, allowing older memories to return, Avey undergoes a "descent" that takes her through usual stages of spirit possession until she can rise to a higher state of consciousness of herself and her heritage.[49]

In turmoil, Avey's mind spins and aches, obeying the command of her visions. As if the "old" Avey were sleepwalking, she leaves the fancy hotel in Grenada where the *Bianca Pride* passengers are staying. She wanders along the beach to the rum shop of Lebert Joseph, an old black man who resembles an African griot in his storytelling and his wisdom. He has been waiting for her; he listens to the tale of her recent hallucinations and dizziness with no surprise and invites her to a popular festival on neighboring Carriacou Island.[50] In that annual festival, local people gather to dance and sing to the memory of their "old parents" and "give them their remembrance." Lebert Joseph is concerned when, questioned about her nationality, Avey can say only that she is from New York, the United States (168). He knows that his own descendants now living in the United States and Canada are probably like Avey, knowing nothing about the "Big Drum" and "the nation dance," having lost their ties with Africa (166). But in Carriacou, at least once every year, all the people join together in songs and dances that retell the past. Lebert Joseph is a storyteller who seems to have known all ages and to have followed his people along changing geographies and continents. He is Avey's guide to the African world submerged within herself and within the culture of the Americas.

In a language that mixes and transforms English and French with African sounds and words, the old man names and describes the Creole dances. He sings the "Bonzo Song," telling the story of the disruption and sorrow of a family on their way to America: the husband was taken in chains to Trinidad, the wife sold to Haiti, and the children left in Carriacou. The song is also the collective history of African families in the *New World*. Joseph sings it not as "something he had heard, but an event he had been witness to." He also tells Avey of glorious imperial Juba, a city at the foot of the Nile River whose memories "had come down to him in the blood." Filling up the present with history and memory, Joseph incorporates the pain and the grace of the events and people involved in the tales (177–78).

On her journey of reconnection, Avey follows the old man to Carriacou, leaving behind the weight of disturbing thoughts and elegant clothes. She feels so different that even the name Avey sounds strange and alien to her now. The women on the boat bring back to her mind the old women in the church she used to attend, the powerful sermons, and the call-and-response rhythms of the congregation. The boat and the memories rock her wildly; it seems that "her entire insides erupt" as vomit, acids, bile, tears, mucus, and the food in her bowels are all expelled by her aching body in spasms of purification. The "church mothers" on the boat and in her mind hold fast to her; they know that the present ordeal is a necessary and good phase for Avey. The boat is compelled to rock violently because, just like Avey/Avatara, it is crossing a rough channel where two opposing currents clash. It recalls other boats that crossed those hard currents in the Caribbean Sea, carrying stricken African people who suffered a much greater agony than Avey ever will (204–9).

The novel comes to a climax of joy and reconciliation in the "Beg Pardon" ceremony in Carriacou. Lebert Joseph's daughter Rosalie shares with her father the power of "seeing and knowing," and she bathes Avey in lime-scented water with the care of a mother. The silent ritual takes Avey even deeper into herself and further into the past. If on the boat she felt like a child, vomiting and dirtying herself all over, now she feels like a clean baby. At the same time, the hands massaging her with baby oil after the bath awaken her body to a sensual pleasure that she had believed to be lost (218–24). Avey is now physically and spiritually ready to join the celebration of life and memory with the people of the island.

Carriacou seems to join other areas of the *New World* through the intense beating of its drums and the joy of its revelers. A clanging iron sends out loud calls that can be heard "from one end of the archipelago to the other" (246). The sound of drums evokes the Carnival celebrations in Cartagena, the beat of all Carnivals in the "extended Caribbean," and the drums in the dance halls of Harlem. The landscape of the tiny island—the hills, the darkness—the food, the look of the people, the dancing shuffle, the movement of hips from side to side, all remind her of Tatem Island. Those apparent strangers around her "had become one and the same with people in Tatem" (250). The steps and rhythms of the "Carriacou Tramp" are the same as those of the ring shout of Tatem Island, the dance of Africans in the *New World* that interconnected the continent and helped to "stay the course of history," bringing the memory of the past to join the present (250). Now it is even possible to imagine Avey's "nation": from her height and the way she dances, she must be an Arada (252).[51]

Avey's great-aunt had passed on to her the responsibility of remembering and retelling the story of her people even as a child, "a mission she couldn't even name yet had felt duty-bound to fulfill" (42). For a long time she had forsaken the task, running away from her great-aunt and from her heritage, but now she is determined to revive Cuney's house in Tatem and educate her grandchildren there, resuming her mission. She is also ready to go back to New York and awaken all those who live as she had been living, rushing "in and out of glacier buildings, unaware, unprotested, lacking memory and a necessary distance of mind" (255).

Paule Marshall passes on the tale of faith and resistance to her readers, deeply concerned to present a collective history put together by her African ancestors. She heard many such stories from her family and neighbors in Brooklyn and from people in Barbados. Like Avey, Marshall is determined to fulfill the mission passed on to her by her own family and community. "It was my mother and West Indian friends who really taught me how to write," she recognizes in humility. As a writer, she emphasizes "the presence of Africa in our lives" and a reconciliation with the past and the culture.[52] In *Praisesong for the Widow*, history is enlarged beyond its sociopolitical and economic aspects to include not only joys and anxieties, dances, celebrations, and people's daily lives (which already enter Marshall's earlier works); but also the spiritual and mythical legacies of African ancestors.

## Bridging the United States and
## the Caribbean: *Daughters*

Marshall's latest novel, *Daughters* (1991), alternates scenes and people from the United States and from Triunion, a paradigmatic Caribbean island once occupied by the "big three" colonial powers of France, Spain, and principally England. Like ancient Gaul, it had been "one little island under three flags. The French up this way, the Spanish to the South, and the English everywhere else," until England reached total control (138). The mixture of languages is evident in the Creole speech of the "poor-behind villages of Morlands" (132), the combination of Creole and English, the official "standard" English, and the Spanish presence in the southern bay.[53] Symbolically combining the histories, cultures, languages, topographies, and peoples of different parts of the West Indies, the island of Triunion recalls the major European powers but also Marshall's persisting dream of national and regional unity. Her fiction reflects her hope in "the day when the islands of the Caribbean—English, French, Spanish, Dutch—will come together in some kind of federation." In her books as in real life, she sustains the belief that only union will bring power, enabling the small West Indian nations "to come out from under the shadow of Big Brother to the north" and to win respect "in the councils of the world."[54]

As Marshall emphasizes in *The Chosen Place, the Timeless People*, the lessons of independence are spelled out in colonial history. While European rivals fought one another for the complete domination of Triunion, making the small island the battlefield of twenty-three wars, slaves from its several regions united in a historic rebellion. Their leaders now stand in the form of four giant stone figures in the Monument of Heroes, placed away in the North District and constantly evoked in *Daughters* (129). They represent the three big divisions of the island and the many slave rebellions that happened everywhere in the "extended Caribbean." Père Boussou, the old man from the northern Gran' Morne, had the mission to spread the news of the uprising "from one estate to the next" with his conch shell. The statue of young Alejandro from the southern Spanish Bay depicts him carrying the sword "he had taken off a conquistador." Will Cudjoe and Congo Jane were "coleaders, co-conspirators, consorts, lovers, friends" (14). They are both depicted as armed with cutlass and musket, but she is also adorned with the lace shawl taken from "the woman who owned her" when "the great house" fell apart (138–39). The pretty shawl had not only embraced her shoulders but also provided bandages for their wounds. Will Cudjoe was injured in his forehead. The slave woman's body, as often happened in history, was cruelly deformed: similar to Almeyda's ordeal in Gayl Jones's *Song for Anninho*, Jane's breast "had been left in shreds" (376).

According to Paule Marshall, the four Triunion heroes are "inventions based on a number of black heroic figures" from the history of the United States and the Caribbean islands. Congo Jane, for instance, was inspired by the early eighteenth-century figure of Nanny, who founded the Maroon community of Nanny Town in the Blue Mountains of Jamaica.[55] Historians also refer to a Jamaican Maroon leader named Cudjoe. Marshall rescues their names and their feats to correct unjust or biased accounts in traditional historiography and to inspire courage and pride today. Through Congo Jane, Marshall specifically underlines the importance of women in revolutionary struggles. Fighting side by side, Jane and Will Cudjoe remind readers that goals can be accomplished if men and women support each other and unite for a common cause on equal footing, as they did in slave times.

Those three men and a woman in the Monument of Heroes symbolize a utopian union in the same struggle of all African descendants on Triunion and the harmonious combination of colors, languages, and cultures in one same society. Although their people have since populated the island, they have not been able to overcome the legacy of rivalries and hierarchies inherited from the colonial powers. Like Cuffee Ned in *Chosen Place*, the four heroes inspire a present still disturbed by the values and prejudices of the past. The two novels actually resemble each other in their intertexts of history and anthropology, in their urging for unity, and in their inter-American character.

*Daughters* focuses on personal, cultural, political, and economic relations between the West Indies and the United States. Ursa Beatrice Mackenzie, the protagonist, resembles Paule Marshall in "the two worlds she inhabits."[56] Although she was born and educated in the United States, Ursa's childhood memories kept her rooted in Triunion. With a father from the island and a mother from the United States, Ursa inherited traits and interests from both sides, as well as the conflicts between them. Her father is "the P.M.," Primus Mackenzie, member of the House and a prime-minister hopeful who bears the looks and the charm of a real one; thus the initials of his name, P.M., match his drive for national power and his control over Morlands, the poor North District of Triunion, and over the women who dote on him. They form the constellation of which he is the sun, the first, *primus*. His only daughter, Ursa, actually has several mothers, all in love with her father.

First in that constellation of women is Ursa's biological mother, Estelle—*stella*, "star," the small, light-skinned wife that he met in the United States. She has a fragile body but an acute mind. In spite of her modern upbringing and liberal principles, she must learn to share her West Indian husband with his "keep-miss" Astral, a beautiful woman with the dark, straight hair and warm color of the island's Spanish Bay. She must also bear the jealous gaze of the dark and faithful maid, Celestine, brought into his house by his authoritarian mother when they were both children. With Celestine the P.M. had his sexual initiation; although he treats her as a master, she remains at his beck and call, always ready to serve him. In their varying degrees of skin tone, health, education, and independence, these women constitute the P.M.'s heaven and gravitate around him.

Ursa needs to spend years away from his world before she is able to understand him and her "mothers" and to construct an identity beyond his orbit. She displays pieces and memories of her extended family inside and outside herself. She has her father's "plum black" skin and high forehead (55) but is small, thin, and critical like Estelle. She braids her hair in a circle around her head like her beloved Celestine and shares with her long-time friend Viney the same sisterly bond that Astral has with her lifetime friend Malvern. Motherhood is a prevailing motif in the novel, woven into the web connecting Ursa and the three women who loved the P.M.—Estelle, Astral, and Celestine. She is the only child that those three ever "had."

Abortion and thoughts of an unborn child also haunt the memories of Estelle, Astral, and especially Ursa. Celestine has given up on having a family of her own: she dotes on the Mackenzie family that she serves, sublimating her own desires. In fact, she considers herself more Ursa's mother than Estelle and would probably take care of Ursa's child if she had one (18). Although Estelle is in the supposedly comfortable position of wife, she nevertheless has suffered a series of miscarriages before she was able to keep a pregnancy and give birth to a child. Because of the violent racial episodes in her country during the 1960s, Estelle doubts for a while whether she really should "bring another child this color into the world" (171).[57] Astral's beauty and health in her youth attracted many lovers but did not entitle her to a happy family life. Blinded by pain after an early abortion, she felt as if she carried "the wire thing inside" her (126). Always speechless in public, Astral carries the frustration of the mistress who never gives birth to a child and remains secondary in her lover's life. The social and cultural circumstances, much like those in colonial times, continue to devastate the bodies and the spirits of women for the pleasure and convenience of their masters.

The novel begins and ends with Ursa struggling with pain, having gone through the abortion of (possibly) a daughter. Her pains have to do with both the loss of a child and the loss of herself as child, finally reaching maturity and independence. She must reconcile herself with her own role as the daughter of a special and disturbing man. In her memories of childhood, the P.M. blocks the sunlight: with his body and big head in front of her, Ursa wasn't "able to see the trees or even a patch of the sky" (355). She must literally and symbolically get away from his shadow if she wants to see the light and feel free. Before she can give birth to a child of her own, she needs to assert her existence and first "abort" the imposing figure of the father as her controlling center.

Ursa's ordeal reflects Marshall's complex relationship with her own father, Samuel Burke, to whom the novel is dedicated. Primus Mackenzie is "handsome," "charismatic," and makes women suffer, much like Marshall's father. Ursa spends years struggling to make peace with her father, just as Paule Marshall did.[58] But *Daughters* goes beyond mere autobiography, and its subtle exploration of conflicts related to motherhood and feminine identity transcends its "Caribbean" and "American" territories. In this respect, the novel tells the stories of specific women in a particular place and time, but the stories reverberate with the stuff of ancient myths and worldwide feminine dilemmas.

At the insistence of her mother, Estelle, Ursa was early sent to school in the United States, where she would remain for graduate study and work. At present Ursa Mackenzie is a contemporary black woman struggling between ideals and reality in her academic, professional, and personal lives, realms in which the United States and the Caribbean both mix and clash. As a student, she experiences the rejection of a long-dreamed research project on the positive relationship between men and women under slavery, a theme inspired by her childhood memories of the statue of Will Cudjoe and Congo Jane. Raising Ursa up to touch their toes, Estelle had early called Ursa's attention to the greatness of their deed, even if the important people of the island did not recognize it (167). In the United States, they receive similar treatment: the verdict of Ursa's professor is that the theme is "not historically consistent." As with Merle's teaching experience in *Chosen Place,* Ursa pursues but is barred from a version of history that emphasizes the strength and determination of slaves under oppression and assigns central roles to black people.

Marshall here returns to a favorite theme: the rewriting and reinvention of history. Lies and stereotypes fill literature, history, and popular culture. Of her own experience Marshall remembers that the little history about black people that she was taught in school "was far from the truth." For that reason, there is an urgent need "to set the record straight," writing a new history that will be "an antidote to the lies." Like Merle Kinbona and Ursa Mackenzie, Paule Marshall is interested "in discovering and in unearthing what was positive and inspiring about our [black] experience in the hemisphere."[59] She personally contributes to that task in *Daughters* as in all her earlier works, and in *Daughters,* she rewards the efforts of all idealistic educators by having the schoolteacher Justin Beaufils, with the help of Estelle and Ursa, be recognized by the people and elected to the Triunion House.

In professional life, Ursa Mackenzie hopes to feel worthy as a black person and to help improve the lives of black people. She leaves a profitable position with the National Consumer Research Corporation (NCRC) in New York because she is afraid that she is turning into a typical black New York YRUM (the Young and Restless Upwardly Mobile, a term of Ursa's creation). Well dressed, with a nice car and a modern apartment, she has felt cut off from her real self, her black roots, and her aspirations. After a twelve-year interval, she decides to go back to graduate school and resume her long-desired research project. At the same time, she wants a job that will not repress her blackness in exchange for money and status. "Afros, dreads, and braids had not been allowed at NCRC," and she longs to throw away hair relaxers and put on a braid, "the way Celestine always wore her hair" (48). She also hopes to work not for the wealth of big companies like American Leaf and Tobacco and other NCRC clients but for the empowering of black people.

The opportunity seems to arrive when she is hired by the Meade Rogers Foundation to participate in a team study supporting the mayoral campaign of a black candidate in Midland City, across the Hudson River from New York. Her early enthusiasm proves misguided. She later returns there to realize that the social and economic prestige of commuting suburban professionals ranks way above the well-being of the poor and decadent black community of Midland's South Ward. After the black candidate is elected, bulldozers cut through that neighborhood to prepare for the construction of a highway passing over the place. Burned-out houses, litter, and hopeless young people coexist in the Beirut-like chaos; drugs and sex make up for the loss of community, the impossibility of pride, and the scarcity of jobs and schools. The bulldozers also bury the political promises of a black politician, who becomes like all others when he reaches a position of power.

Frustration is also the norm in Ursa's love life, now limited to a dragging story of noncommunication with longtime boyfriend Lowell Carruthers. She prefers to keep him ignorant of her pregnancy and abortion. His dissatisfaction with his work dominates his thoughts and stiffens his behavior. Like so many black men who struggle for "a place in the world," Lowell has submitted to the rules of a competitive and sterile job and announces his frustration in his permanent frown. Ursa blames it for the lack of enthusiasm between them, while he blames her unreasonable attachment to her father. Ursa resents Lowell's interference in family matters, but she knows that, in spite of the eighteen-hundred-mile distance and her four-year absence from Triunion, she must still clarify that relationship before she can really love a man and give birth to her own daughters.

Characters and sites from the Caribbean island of Triunion and from the United States meet and crisscross on personal, social, economic, and political levels. Parallels with *The Chosen Place, the Timeless People* often arise. As in the case of lawyer Lyle Hutson in the earlier novel, the P.M.'s socialist ideals give place to accommodation and admiration of "things American" as he grows older and more ambitious. The United States directly influences that transformation. In *Chosen Place*, the State Department and a large U.S. labor union sponsor a conference for Caribbean trade unionists in Washington, D.C. In *Daughters*, Primus participates in a tour designed to show democracy at work to young potential leaders of the Third World, organized by the Carnegie Endowment on International Relations (27, 204). He is impressed with the progress and the greatness of North America, "where everything's the size of the Grand Canyon and the possibilities are limitless" (144).

It was in that visit to the United States that young Primus met Estelle, then a petite student from Hartford, Connecticut, one of the Delta sorority girls invited to greet and lunch with the touring visitors. She later visits Triunion and falls in love with the man and the place, overcome by Primus's royal treatment of her and the beauty of the island. She also admires his political drive, at the crucial moment when the island people have just achieved "home rule and they are pretty much governing themselves" (30). The P.M. is still an idealist, critical of the island's internal divisions, planning big changes, aware that power comes from union. "We might all finally come together—French, Dutch, English, Spanish—all o' we one!" he tells Estelle, "so that even Big Brother would have to respect us" (144–45). Sounding like Paule Marshall herself, he represents the Caribbean hope of the 1960s, when the newly independent or semi-independent islands of the Caribbean dreamed of socialist resistance to outside control through self-determination and the joint efforts of all islands.

As a young politician, Primus Mackenzie repeatedly accused Triunion's government party—"the Democratic National Party, or the Do-Nothings as Primus calls them"—of inefficiency and corruption (128). He was immediately accused of being a Communist "in the pay of Moscow" (220). Years later, he cannot be distinguished from his opposition, just like the Midland City mayor in the United States. His promises for the poor are replaced by projects for the rich and the foreign. The P.M. gets politically and personally involved in a "multi-million-dollar" project designed to turn "the empty tract of Government Lands" of the North District into an expensive tourist resort. He puts his own money down alongside investments by U.S. and Canadian developers and Triunion's Planning and Development Board, of which he is a member (43, 129, 310). The episode recalls Paule Marshall's earlier incursion into Caribbean politics and development projects in *Chosen Place*.

But here, too, Marshall stresses hope in spite of the contagious corruption and the persistent inequality. At the end of *Daughters*, the P.M. loses his seat to the young schoolteacher Justin Beaufils, whose name signals his role as a good and just son of the island as well as his membership in the "minority" group of French creoles, traditionally poor and alienated from power decisions. Justin had been one of Ursa's childhood playmates, though he came from a lower class. His father worked "day and night at the sugar mill in Morlands," and he was one of the "'ti garçons" who helped Celestine in errands and small chores. Now an aspiring politician, he frightens Celestine with his courage to challenge the old order. His wife is from another minority group and is a strong ally in his campaign; from Spanish Bay, she attended "some big school in Cuba" and speaks, writes, and prints as efficiently as he does (304). Justin and wife are lovers, co-leaders, and co-workers, repeating the roles and renovating the dream of Will Cudjoe and Congo Jane. Members of a social class that is usually exploited and dominated, they voice the ideal of equality between races and genders on the island.

Estelle, Ursa, and even Astral approve of the political change and abhor the P.M.'s pact with the forces that he had long opposed. Celestine remains uncritical; like the people who traditionally voted for him, she cannot forget that Primus was "Mis-Mack's boychild" (303) and son of the most important man from Morlands, entitled to their eternal respect and gratitude. She is also afraid of disorder and violence. As with every election since the island became independent, the United States is keeping close watch from the battleship *Woodrow Wilson*, stationed at the bay. Now it displays even more threatening force: besides the usual weapons, it carries deadly Tomahawk cruise missiles, ready to be used on the island. Celestine is horrified at the prospects: "O ciel eternel, it could be finish with Triunion!" (304–5).

Celestine in *Daughters* and Leesy in *Chosen Place* seem to play similar roles in their endurance, their basic goodness, and their love for the children. They are both strong survivors of a time already gone. In many ways, they are voices from that past, symbols of stability and tradition. They are reluctant to change and have accommodated to the existing order. Celestine hates gas stoves ("Food don't taste right"), is suspicious of political radicalism, antagonizes Estelle's "American" modernity and her light skin ("the blanche neg'"), and accepts traditional "extended Caribbean" mores. "And what if the woman [Astral] is his keep-miss?" argues Celestine in defense of Primus Mackenzie. "Show me the man in this place that don't have one and sometimes more than one" (198).[60]

In spite of their reactionary politics, Celestine, Leesy, and other similar women of Marshall's novels are ancestral figures, heroic in their nurturing ways. They are modeled after Marshall's maternal grandmother, nicknamed Da-duh, who "remains an important presence" in her life and work and has inspired women of "special force" and "resiliency." Like Great-Aunt Cuney in *Praisesong for the Widow,* Celestine represents ancestry and reconnection for Paule Marshall, embodying "that long line of unknown black men and women who are [her] forebears."[61] In a more contemporary and political way, Viney's grandfather from Virginia also has the voice of wisdom, and his words to his granddaughter underline Marshall's central message in this novel. "The woods are on fire out here," he says of the situation of black people in the United States, but he does not despair or give up. "We need everybody that can tote a bucket of water to come running," he pleads (102).

The memory of roots and the support of such enduring figures are necessary for black people to counterbalance the disrupting pressures of history and the disturbing social conditions of yesterday and today. The Caribbean island and the United States share a heritage of racial divisions paralleling economic inequality. Dark-skinned people like Primus have to prove themselves to be the best before they can hope to be accepted among lighter-skinned people. Poor boys with holes in the seats of their pants walk along the roads of Triunion; there are many poor blacks in the country and in the city, both on the island and in the United States. The Caribbean island, like other dependent places in a neocolonial world, exports its best students to universities in England or the United States, as happened with Primus and his daughter, Ursa (and Merle Kinbona and Lyle Hutson go to an English university in *Chosen Place*). The poor and the young also leave in search of better salaries and working conditions and in response to the attractive promises of the First World. On the island, power and money remain under the control of people with "names like Allenby and Shepard, Forsythe and DaSilva," and with complexions that are almost completely white, who inhabit the "big pretty houses" on Garrison Row and Raleigh Hill (159). Decades later, black Primus, like other blacks, would rise in the social scale and occupy one of those "white elephant" houses in the elegant "highbrow part of town" (169). Like Lyle Hutson in *Chosen Place,* Primus displays that house as a badge of honor, a sign that he is equal. Ironically, he has become too equal, having absorbed the values of those people he had once antagonized. "More British than the British," this class of islanders puts a premium on whiteness and cultivates the culture of the European "motherland" (167).

Progress and development often mislead blacks in search of "the American Dream." Harlem is a traumatizing place that, seen from above, looks like Dresden after the massive bombing of World War II (256). But "there is no escaping Harlem" for a black person, as Lowell Carruthers recognizes, "not even for the white folks" (96). Black youth are threatened by poverty and despondency in Midland City, often resorting to alcohol and drugs for consolation or money. Debris, garbage, and decay fill the burned-out, Beirut-like streets of such neighborhoods, in the United States as on Triunion (296). In the slums of Armory Hill, near the city of Fort Lord Nelson in Triunion, and in the Spanish Bay, the young also have no jobs. They will get away "in leaky boats" as soon as they can (144). Astral's friend Malvern has seen almost all of her children emigrate to the United States. Although they try to save and buy her a few signs of comfort, she remains sick and poor, like so many others on the island. Crime is the easiest way for idle slum dwellers to show some prosperity. Malvern wonders, "Where they getting all this money I ask myself and they ain't working no place" (213). The Caribbean sky is bluer and the stars are brighter than in New York City, but Fort Lord Nelson is plagued with the same social ills: contraband, beggars, male and female prostitution, poverty (106–8). The persisting heritage of colonialism shatters black communities: it is a war of centuries still raging against the black and the poor.

Outsiders to the dominant culture, contemporary black youngsters are perceived only as suspects by the police, even in a renovated, middle-class neighborhood in Brooklyn (323). Present and past coincide in many ways: "the more things change the more they remain the same." Viney's thoughts on the bitterness of the Civil War (always recalled by the battlefield across the road from her family home in Petersburg, Virginia) combine with her suffering for her son Robeson, who was arrested by the police when he was playing a game around parked cars.[62] In violent and racist New York City, all blacks are considered possible thieves and murderers, even small children.

Memories also weave scenes of recent black history into the present. The absence of restroom facilities along the poor northern roads in Triunion reminds Estelle of earlier trips into the U.S. South, when her family drove from Connecticut to Tennessee to visit her mother's family. Going by car saved them the trouble of using segregated transportation, but it presented other difficulties. It took a long time for any "toilet with a Colored sign to appear," so they had to squat "behind a bush, a rock, a tree or between their old Hudson and the shoulder of some road below the Mason-Dixon line" (146). Segregation had all sorts of absurd consequences. Estelle's old parents died on that same road to Tennessee when her father "suffered a massive stroke at the wheel." Jim Crow was officially gone, but he "refused to take the bus or train down," holding onto the driving that symbolized both his stigma and his rebellion (381). In spite of the new laws, white southerners would not let the old system go. Amid the generalized violence of the 1960s, Estelle's brother Grady had his hip broken in an Alabama jail; that was his punishment for "working on the voter registration drive" (223). Worse than that, children were killed in Georgia "for *supposedly* talking back to some white shopkeeper." The news makes Estelle terribly upset, and she writes from Triunion, "What kind of barbarians do they have in Georgia? What kind of country is it? When is it ever going to change?" (170).

People in Triunion follow such news with disbelief. They soon become aware of the anger of the U.S. black population, manifested in loud protests and cries of Black Power. Malvern fears reprisals and even more poverty if such ideas spread in Triunion; she tells her man, a bus driver who works for the government, to stop talking about Black Power before he loses his job. She discusses the news with Astral: "There's too much of this Black Power talk from the United States flying about the place. Do you read about all the demonstration and rioting and burning and thing going on up there? The American black people—them! are saying they want their rights" (212). By contrast, Estelle rejoices at the expanding activities of the civil rights movement in her country. Disturbed by the unchanging political and social conditions in Triunion, she dreams of the new possibilities represented by the impressive March on Washington of 1963 and by all the demonstrations against segregated facilities in the South. She already combs her little daughter's hair in the Afro style and hopes that she will grow up to represent her in the barricades. She writes in excitement, "No more back of the bus, no more bushes, no more you can't eat or sleep here even if you do have the money. All of that finally at an end. I can't get over it. Black folks—no more Negroes or "cullud"—finally moving, a-moverin', the Movement, I love it!" (223).

Through Estelle and other characters, Paule Marshall highlights and connects major struggles in the history of black America: the slave rebellions, the civil rights movement, and the possibility of true political empowerment for blacks and equality for women. The 1960s and 1970s are insistently recalled in memories of violent racial warfare in the United States and the absurd Vietnam War in Southeast Asia (it killed Lowell Carruthers's brother-in-law, and Lowell barely escaped the draft). Those years are also recalled in the protest songs and marijuana joints popular among students and young people in general. Ursa and Lowell enjoyed both the music ("What's going on across this land?" sings Marvin Gaye) and the "high-quality Mexican weed" when their love was young and they could feel happy in their togetherness (95).

In spite of all the tensions and divisions, *Daughters* emphasizes the possibility of peaceful coexistence among people of different racial and ethnic backgrounds. Contrasts do exist but should not represent barriers. Triunion and the United States are combinations of peoples of several colors and ethnicities; the message of union and solidarity holds for both places. Reflecting the true situation of the 1980s, New York City is a place open to the migrants of the world, many of them Caribbeans. Ursa relates to them with sympathy. There is the Dominican Carlos, the doorman in Lowell's building, who is anxious to retire, put on his Guayabera shirt, and return to the Dominican Republic; in Triunion, one could buy those shirts made in Spanish Bay. There is the Latina receptionist at the abortion clinic; in spite of the tense moment, Ursa is comforted by a smile that is "patient, solicitous, saying, Hey, *mina*, it's all right. . . . I know how it is." With her pretty looks and her bright colors, "she could be from Spanish Bay back home." The feeling of recognition from someone similar to her in gender and origin "makes Ursa like her all the more" (5). Along or near busy Columbus Avenue where the more affluent walk (Lowell Carruthers and Ursa, for instance, on their outings), there are Korean fruit stands, Japanese restaurants, and cafés full of "black, white, Latina, Asian but mostly white" faces (52).

Because of ingrained racism and unequal living conditions, New York may often turn into "the Big Rotten Apple," with interethnic relationships easily going sour. Viney Daniels has to threaten an Eastern European taxidriver with deportation when he refuses to take her to Brooklyn. He was not the first foreigner to show fear at the reputation of the place and a quick absorption of the prejudices of the city; a Slavic driver had once "shouted nigger bitch after her." Even before learning to speak the language, these immigrants understood sexism, racism, and segregation (319). Brooklyn did look like

Harlem and other run-down black ghettos before many of its old houses and brownstones were renovated. Ursa's friend Viney Daniels left an elegant apartment in Manhattan for an old house in Brooklyn that would become her haven and her badge of pride. Like Ursa in her job change, Viney moved to an area more like herself. As another feature of the 1980s presented in the book, decadent neighborhoods are gradually transformed and "gentrified," losing the stigma of a ghetto. In Viney's multiethnic block, "almost as many white as black and Latina faces were to be seen" (70).

Viney's elongated beauty connects different worlds. She has the elegance of a dancer or fashion model and the sharp assertiveness of a Triunion market woman (61). She and her son show different aspects of their ethnic mixture: while she has the color of caramel, he is darker, like coffee. But both mother and son have an Indian nose: "Some Chickahominy in Virginia long ago left his or her signature on the Daniels family tree before being force-marched on the Trail of Tears" (64). Robeson's birthday party reveals the multiethnicity of their new lifestyle and the possibility of peaceful coexistence for new American generations; the children who come to celebrate are "black, white, Latina, Asian—a mini U.N.—tearing around the yard in some free-for-all game" (253). Interclass and intergender relations are also emphasized in the close friendship of Robeson and little Dee Dee. Robeson can enjoy expensive toys, ample spaces, and loving attention in a comfortable house proudly announced in the entryway to belong to "V. Daniels and Son." Dee Dee, in contrast, lives in the "unsightly group of walk-ups and old-law tenements" still standing at the end of the same block, and spends most of the time in Robeson's home (60). In religion, Viney is able to sway "like some elderly mother" of the Triumphant Baptist Church in Petersburg, Virginia, but also to sit like Buddha and share Ursa's practice of Eastern-style meditation and prayer (83).

Yet if traditional Caribbean islanders like Celestine reject whatever they consider "American," New Yorkers often treat those islanders with derision. Even Ursa's best friend, Viney, attributes anything disagreeable in Ursa to her West Indian heritage. Like Paule Marshall, Ursa Mackenzie is sometimes viewed with suspicion in the United States, not recognized as equal to U.S. blacks because of her slight accent. A black skin does not exempt people from being prejudiced.[63] Even though Ursa was born in Hartford, Connecticut; had a mother from Hartford and a grandmother from Tennessee; and lived most of her life in the States, some "Black Folks" (as Viney refers to U.S.

blacks) would easily cross her out as "immigrant, alien, islander without a green card . . . monkey chaser" (86). Viney is "a kind of foreigner herself," a Virginian who had to face the prejudice of her countrypeople from Connecticut and New York. If she let her southern ways show in an occasional "y'all" in class, she was stared at by both whites and blacks as if she "just crawled out of a bale of cotton and still had lint all in [her] nappy head" (65). Viney herself has to learn a kind of bilingualism and adopt strategies to cope with discrimination. Ursa voices Paule Marshall's reaction at the discrimination she feels as a woman who carries more than one nation in herself, and she knows the difficulty of accepting difference. Like Ursa, Marshall had to master several variations on English—standard, West Indian, and U.S. black English—to move among the different groups in her own adolescent life in Brooklyn.[64]

Because of the multiplicity within her, Ursa has an eye and a sympathy for the ethnic variety surrounding her in New York City and for the segmented population of Triunion. Like Paule Marshall, she welcomes the beautiful colors and exciting plurality that make up New York, Triunion, and the Americas. *Daughters* also hails the wide range of experiences of black women in both the old and the contemporary "extended Caribbean," from Congo Jane to Ursa Mackenzie. Sometimes victimized by sociopolitical and economic circumstances, sometimes frustrated in their hopes, they may either have professional respectability and affluence or be exploited and worn-out slum dwellers. They may be lovers and wives or feel the loneliness of no companionship. They may enjoy an independent life or mold themselves to fit the structure of a family or the whims of a man. They may be quiet domestics or heroic warriors. They may be married or single mothers, may never have had children, may have needed to abort the child that they would have had, or may have lost their children to more prosperous nations in the usual processes of neocolonialism. In their differences and contrasts, these women are America: Paule Marshall's novel is a sensitive tribute to their greatness.

## Conclusion

If once it was possible for the Caribbean and Latin America to be ignored and forgotten in the United States and in Europe, that reality has now dramatically changed. Calibans of all sorts are invading the land of the rich in search of work and a way out of poverty or seeking larger audiences for their music and their stories. Furthermore, if once it was possible to overlook Paule Marshall and keep her out of print for many years, that reality has also dramatically changed. The new editions of her early works signify the increasing attention paid to her inter-American and intercontinental voice in literary criticism, anthologies, and the classrooms of the United States.

The influence of Caribbean culture is evident in Marshall's writing: as she herself has remarked, the Barbadian women in Brooklyn taught her as a little girl to think in terms of continents and larger worlds. Her concern with the culture and history of Africans in the *New World* is intertwined with her observations of the political and socioeconomic complexities inherited from the colonial structure. Paule Marshall's stories are forceful reminders of the colors and shades of the peoples of America from North to South, their contradictions, and their struggles. In the midst of Carnival in Barbados or shuffle dancing in Carriacou, in show houses in Brazil or in the jazzy streets of New York, Paule Marshall is the native and the ethnographer, both living and recording the changing spirit of the Americas.

# 3

# The Redefinition of American Geography and History: Toni Morrison's *Song of Solomon* and *Tar Baby*

> Definitions belonged to the definers—not the defined.
> —Toni Morrison, *Beloved*

The yarn used by Toni Morrison to weave her beautiful novels represents several shades of America. Most obvious are the lyrical and at the same time harsh colors depicting black life throughout the history of the United States. The different migrations and dislocations in that life are the focus of all her novels, whether she is recalling the traumatic Middle Passage from Africa and the southern plantation world or examining later life in the northern states. In *Tar Baby*, Morrison introduces the Caribbean with its migrations and similar dilemmas, a geographical space, an economy, and a people carrying on the heritage of colonialism and slavery. The Caribbean joins the colors of Colombia to intensify the magic of *Song of Solomon* in its intertextual dialogue with Gabriel García Márquez's novel *One Hundred Years of Solitude*.[1] Brazil never becomes a visible presence for the reader in Morrison's work, but its records of slavery contributed to the background of her novel *Beloved*.[2] Intent on recovering the memory of her people and on challenging the traditional European whiteness of the U.S. literary canon, Toni Morrison finds alliance and support in the history and the literature of the "extended Caribbean." This chapter focuses on the inter-American bridges that she creates in the novels *Song of Solomon* and *Tar Baby*.

## Deciphering the Codes of History:
### *Song of Solomon* and
### *One Hundred Years of Solitude*

*Song of Solomon,* the widely acclaimed novel published by Toni Morrison in 1977, has attracted the attention of a legion of critics from the United States and different parts of the world. It shows an effective interplay of black culture and history and follows a tradition of magical storytelling deeply rooted in Africa. For a reader familiar with Latin American literature, *Song of Solomon* also brings to mind *One Hundred Years of Solitude,* the landmark novel by Colombian writer Gabriel García Márquez, published in 1967. Some connections between the two novels have been pointed out by literary critics in the United States, but a more extensive exploration deserves to be undertaken.[3] Separated from the Latin American writer by race, gender, and nationality, Morrison has nevertheless expressed enthusiastic admiration for García Márquez and praise of "South American novelists" in general as her "favorite writers." In Morrison's view, they "have the best" literature in the world over the last quarter of the twentieth century.[4] She has officially joined García Márquez and other prominent writers as the Nobel Prize committee selected her for the literature award of 1993. In the eyes of the world, Toni Morrison "has the best" literature in the last decade of the twentieth century.

With the work of Mikhail Bakhtin, Julia Kristeva, and Umberto Eco, contemporary criticism has abandoned traditional notions of hierarchical "influence" in textual production to assume that every text derives from a multiplicity of other texts, absorbing and transforming them in the process of that dialogue. The author writes as a reader and will, in turn, be "rewritten" by future readers.[5] My discussion of *Song of Solomon* focuses on intertextual bridges between Morrison and García Márquez. Far from diminishing Morrison's narrative, the echoes of *One Hundred Years of Solitude* double its strength and set it in an expanded inter-American context.

Morrison is one of the many writers and critics in the United States who have praised the power and beauty of Latin American literature in recent decades, when, in an unprecedented way, Latin American works have directly intersected the literature of North America. That breaks a Eurocentric tradition in U.S. literature and also challenges the hemispheric cultural order, that is, the predominance and prestige of U.S. culture that has accompanied the country's economic and political hegemony in the continent. García Márquez is proudly aware of his own popularity and that of other "boom" novelists in the traditionally dominant "North," along with the enormous effect that Latin American immigrants have had on food, music, language, and cultural habits in the United States. He revels in the new possibilities of such a Calibanic turn in the inter-American power balance—a reversal in the direction of cultural penetration, with Latin America now thrusting into the United States.[6]

Like many of the novels by black women in the United States, the works of many writers from Latin America are fueled by the magic and wonder of their land and their people. That awe and respect for the geography and culture of Latin America have earned García Márquez's *One Hundred Years of Solitude* hyperbolic praise throughout the world, describing the novels as "a masterpiece," "seismic," or "an earthquake." An enthusiastic admirer from Spain called him "the most popular writer since Cervantes."[7] The worldwide success of the novel helped dismiss the notion that Latin American fiction "never sells" or that it presents mere "anthropological interest," as Lionel Trilling reportedly told his students at Columbia University in 1968.[8] Throughout the 1970s, works from Latin America came to be hailed as "probably the most energetic and inventive body of literature" in the world, "particularly where the novel is concerned." The "center of creative gravity" was "shifting away from French and English to Spanish," since only Latin American literature seemed able to deal with the universal theme of alienation with "force and imagination," setting the individual plight "in the extremely vast context of a clan and a world."[9] For Latin America, the fame of the boom writers was hailed as a sign of cultural emancipation, reinforced by the 1982 Nobel Prize awarded to García Márquez. In the United States, some writers have left French "models and mentors" for the "vital lessons from their South-American writing kin."[10] In 1983, even the highly conservative critic Joseph Epstein admitted that the most impressive writers were those connecting fiction and history; "even Gabriel García Márquez," said Epstein, "a writer in whose politics I find nothing to admire."[11]

The work of García Márquez is set at a crossroads of traditions that critics have tried to squeeze into the most diverse *-isms*. He has been called an heir to the Bible, to fable, to Latin and world mythology; to Cervantes, Tolstoy, Dostoyevski, Balzac; to realism, naturalism, modernism, and magical realism; to Kafka, Joyce, Faulkner; to Borges and postmodernism.[12] Like García Márquez, Toni Morrison is willing to go beyond literary enclaves and even national boundaries, interested in energy and creation, affirming the new empowerment of former "subgroups." According to Morrison, "Categories like black writer, woman writer, and Latin American writer aren't marginal anymore"; for her, "The thing we call 'literature' is pluralistic now, just as society ought to be."[13] Nevertheless, although early in her career she was irritated by the insistent label "black woman writer," Toni Morrison has more recently come to find it glorious.[14]

The persistence of racial boundaries in the United States and the need to negotiate an identity despised by the dominant groups has usually directed black writers and critics inward in their themes and criticism—into their own black community. Black cultural and historical roots are woven into the booming literature of contemporary authors. That community, however, may be expanded to embrace connected histories. Morrison has family roots in the United States, but marriage to a Caribbean man and a home in his native Jamaica gave her years of physical proximity to García Márquez's Colombia and a taste of the folklore of the area, so similar to her own. García Márquez has been called "a trans-Caribbean bard," and his literature is as hybrid as his country of origin.[15] "The Caribbean coast of Colombia where I was born," he says, "is together with Brazil the Latin American region where African influence is most deeply felt." During his 1978 trip to Angola, García Márquez realized that his country was not just "Spanish," as people are taught to believe, but also African; he discovered that it was mestizo, with a culture rich in its diverse elements.[16] In the Caribbean coast of Colombia, the Caribbean islands, and Brazil he sees a "somewhat magic way of looking at reality." Paule Marshall would certainly agree with García Márquez's view that "the human synthesis and contrasts that exist in the Caribbean are nowhere else in the world."[17]

Growing up in mixed neighborhoods helped Morrison develop a concern for interclass and interracial union against exploitation, even if her imagination is fueled by the black experience in the United States.[18] Still, it may seem surprising that a modern, independent woman of an advanced society so conscious of women's rights should enjoy reading a male writer from a world traditionally regarded as sexist and repressive. However, an examination of the backgrounds of Morrison and García Márquez and of some personal statements and public pronouncements, as well as a close reading of their two novels, may actually reveal a common bond uniting not only their works but also the concerns of contemporary writers from the Americas and Africa.[19] Their impulse toward a new art goes beyond mere aesthetic concerns to reveal a deep preoccupation with affirming and reinforcing popular culture against models inspired or imposed by the dominant culture, whether from inside or outside national boundaries. Traditionally dependent and underdeveloped, the culturally and economically threatened "nations" of the *New World*—whether they exist as separate political units or as peoples within a larger context, such as Indians and blacks in the United States—have discovered a common, fertile ground.[20] Analogies between *One Hundred Years of Solitude* and *Song of Solomon* may show how cultural roots can be deep and strong enough to cross borders, hemispheres, and oceans; can erase the usual East–West and North–South divisions; and finally, can meet in the far recesses of human myth. Both Gabriel García Márquez and Toni Morrison are interested in writing about history, their peoples' plight, their families' memories, and the stories of "their tribes," which have much in common after all.

The personal family histories of García Márquez and Morrison have been constantly invoked by critics to support interpretations of their fiction. Their strong family ties and attachment to their ancestors surface in their clan-centered plots and the oral quality of their narrative style. García Márquez was born in 1928 in the small town of Aracataca in the province of Magdalena on the northern Atlantic coast of Colombia. He came "with the umbilical cord tied around his neck," he reports, as if referring to one of his famous characters. He was the first of sixteen children born to telegraphist Gabriel Eligio García and his wife, Maria Márquez Iguarán. His father's job forced his parents to move and leave the boy in the company of his maternal grandparents, Colonel Nicolas Ricardo Márquez Iguarán and Tranquilina Iguarán Cotes, until García Márquez was eight, when the death of his grandfather sent him back to his parents.[21]

Those first years of his life in small Aracataca played a central role in the development of García Márquez's creative imagination. The magical stories that his grandmother and an old aunt used to tell him, together with the natural, unsurprised style of their narration, have found a permanent place in his writing. Peruvian writer Mario Vargas Llosa believes that García Márquez's grandparents were "his most solid literary influences."[22] García Márquez himself has categorically emphasized the importance of those early years for his writing. "Everything I have written I knew or had heard before I was eight years old," he affirms. In the process of searching for a satisfactory personal narrative style, he discovered that the secret was to imitate the magical, entertaining, flowing stories that he had heard as a boy: "to tell the story simply . . . in an imperturbable tone," as his grandparents had told it, with serenity and certainty.[23] He went so far as to say that the style of his books "is almost entirely that of [his] grandmother." The easy way she invented tales and fantasies that would keep the boy from being "saddened by the truth of things" helped him lose the fear "of doing some things in literature, because anything is possible—just as it had been in [his] childhood."[24]

Besides style and mode, García Márquez's family provided him with themes and characters: the strong, supportive, nourishing mothers; the patriarchal adventurers and soldiers; a grandfather's loving authority. His grandparents settled in Aracataca when it was just a village, immediately following the Colombian civil war known as the War of a Thousand Days (1899–1903). His colonel grandfather filled his imagination with fantastic accounts of the disputes and heroic deeds of Aracataca while it had been a liberal outpost in the war against the conservatives (a war in which the Dutch banana companies played an important role). The boy was proud that his grandfather was one of the most respected and esteemed men in the village and the house they inhabited the most prominent. That house would become his most vivid childhood memory.[25]

The economic growth induced by the "banana fever" and the United Fruit Company in Macondo, a banana plantation near Aracataca, made the town "the most prosperous in Colombia." It brought with it the illusion of modernization and the impression that the old feudalism had been defeated and replaced by a more sophisticated and democratic order. But that was a fever only, a happy mirage. The town followed the boom-and-bust cycle typical of every area in the Americas that has been exhausted by intensive monoculture under the control of a foreign economy, whether the place is called Bournehills, Pernambuco, Shalimar, Aracataca, or Macondo. Some seven years after his grandfather died and García Márquez left the town, he went back there with his mother, who meant to sell the old house. He was shocked to find that the mythical, great house and town of his childhood were "shrunken, empty, altered." The contrasting visions of growth and decline were crucial to the writer's decision to "find and preserve the Aracataca of his grandparents, the wholeness of his first world," in his imaginative writing and to explore the sociopolitical and economic implications of such cycles in the town and the country of his birth.[26]

For Toni Morrison as for García Márquez, family and childhood provided a personal and cultural nourishment that would stimulate similar responses. Born Chloe Anthony Wofford in Lorain, Ohio, in 1931 to George and Ramah (Willis) Wofford, she has roots that go back to the South on both sides of the family. Her maternal grandparents, John Solomon and Ardelia Willis, worked as sharecroppers in Greenville, Alabama, after losing their land to whites; the same happened to "a lot of black people at the turn of the century," Morrison explains. Her grandfather tried to make better money by playing his violin in Birmingham, but around 1910, his wife felt that she had seen and feared enough of the Deep South. She decided to join the epic caravan of black people headed for a "promised land" in the north, taking with her seven children and little money. Like the strong matriarchs that Morrison would create in her novels, Ardelia Willis trusted that her own strength would suffice to protect her daughters from the sexual violence of white men and to provide them with a better life, preferably one away from poverty and racism. Her husband met her as she was on the road, and they went through Kentucky to head farther north. The stories Morrison heard about their flight and their quest would combine in her memory and imagination with the real–surreal accounts of the violence suffered by her own father in his home state of Georgia.

The American Civil War, the persisting racial war in the South during and after Reconstruction, the flight north in the first decades of the twentieth century, and the hardships of the Depression—in addition to the whole dark history of slavery that preceded all these events—can no doubt match or surpass the violent absurdities of Colombian history. But along with the tragedy, Morrison received from her family a sense of the magic and beauty of life, as did García Márquez. Her grandfather played the violin while her mother sang, decoded dreams, and told terrifying ghost stories in the intervals between the "humiliating jobs" that paid for Morrison's education.[27] Thanks to her immediate family, Toni Morrison's early years were full of "black lore, black music, language, and all the myths and rituals of black culture," even as she learned about the cruelty and the injustice of their life.[28] Like García Márquez's storytelling, her narratives must contain all the magic and suffering of her people and still appear simple and true, like her family's stories. Language must sound effortless; "it must not sweat."[29] Morrison justifies her attachment to grandparents and African roots as a way of keeping her own identity and at the same time contributing to the preservation of their culture: "It's DNA, it's where you get your cultural information. Also it's your protection, your education. They were so responsible for us, and we have to be responsible to them. If you ignore ancestors, you put yourself in a spiritually dangerous position of being self-sufficient, having no group that you're dependent on."[30]

Storytelling was "a shared activity between the men and women" in her family, and she attempts to write within that oral tradition. Morrison deliberately pursues an "oral quality" in order to "capture the vast imagination of black people."[31] Like the family and neighbors of García Márquez's Aracataca, Morrison's folks "were intimate with the supernatural"; the "real" for them went far beyond the limitations of the five senses.[32] "Birds talk and butterflies cry, and it is not surprising or upsetting to them" either.[33]

Morrison seems to have been successful in incorporating the magic qualities of ancient storytellers in the way she writes and speaks. "Her voice is so sure . . . she lures you in, locks doors and encloses you in a special, very particular universe—all in the first three pages," says Toni Cade Bambara of Morrison's narrative.[34] Like a true griot, Morrison "recalls the rich sound of our best preachers . . . she is sister, teacher, aunt . . . she speaks with wisdom," marvels Elsie B. Washington.[35] Morrison is aware that she has a role to play in transmitting a sense of magic, harmony, family, and community, as well as the pains of history, particularly to a younger generation that tends to ignore all of those elements. It disturbs her that "some young people" want to deny that past, focusing only on economic affluence and scientific progress.[36] Like her other novels, *Song of Solomon* attempts to recapture the missing power and the lost magic in an imaginative reaffirmation of black memory and resistance.

In this novel by Morrison, the protagonist, Milkman Dead, embodies the modern, rootless youth, enclosed in the selfish capitalist mentality of his father and the incestuous alienation of his mother.[37] In this suffocating environment the Dead family heads toward extinction, just like the Buendías in García Márquez's novel. Milkman is attracted only to the male prerogatives of gold and power. He is deaf and blind to his culture and therefore a perpetuator of the racial and sexual exploitation that characterizes the traditional system. After his "sterile childhood," he avoids facing truth and making any commitments, either political (as represented by the character Guitar) or cultural (Pilate): "He wanted to know as little as possible, to feel only enough to get through the day amiably" (181).

Not mere stories about a male protagonist, *One Hundred Years of Solitude* and *Song of Solomon* read like family and cultural epics. A diagram of the Buendía genealogy actually precedes the text of García Márquez's novel, which spins the long, marvelous yarn of the family led by the patriarch José Arcadio Buendía.[38] He was "the most enterprising man ever to be seen in the village" of Macondo, and his story and his legacy is carried on through the course of the novel by six generations that include three other José Arcadios, one Arcadio, the impressive Colonel Aureliano Buendía—father of seventeen Aurelianos and one Aureliano José—Aureliano Segundo, and two other Aurelianos. They are all mirrors or alter egos of the patriarch. The memories held by the Buendía family, whose hundred-year story starts in March sometime in the nineteenth century, stretch as far back as Sir Francis Drake's attack on Riohacha in the sixteenth century, an event that encircles the whole story.[39]

Incestuous relations or desires recur in all layers of the family history, beginning with the marriage of patriarch José Arcadio to his first cousin Úrsula Iguarán and ending with a baby-monster produced by the illicit love of the last Aureliano and his aunt Amaranta Úrsula. The family alienated and destroyed itself, and incest—regarded by all societies as a threat to social vitality and therefore as evil—is an outward sign of that closed circle. Yet incest is often present in mythical families. The theme links García Márquez not only to the Bible, the Greek classics, and older legends but also to the modern novels of William Faulkner and the contemporary work of Toni Morrison.

In *Song of Solomon*, Ruth Dead marries Macon Dead when she is sixteen, with no love on either part (70). Before marrying, she had been living alone with her father since the death of her mother, whom she strongly resembled. She dedicates a strong and strange love to her father, and he is glad that she marries early, for the ecstasy that "seemed to be shining on Ruth's face when [he] bent to kiss her" feels "inappropriate," to say the least (23). The attachment between the two remains, however, long after her marriage. When her doctor father finally dies, her husband finds her lying on the same bed with the corpse, "naked as a yard dog, kissing him" (73).

Ruth's suspicious son—also named Macon, like his father and grandfather—would years later discover that her nightly escapades were visits to her father's grave.

Incestuous bonds connect Ruth both to the man who fathered her and to the one whom she mothered. She attempted to transfer her lack and her love from her father to son Macon, nursing the boy with a pleasure that "made her daily life bearable" in "strange and wrong" afternoons, long beyond his reasonable nursing age (14). Part of the pleasure came from the shady room where she offered the boy her milk and her body: it had been the doctor's study, and she symbolically embraced both father and son in those solitary and dreamy afternoons. The town's discovery and censure would be forever stamped on the name they rebaptize the boy with: Milkman. Ignored by her husband and without a companion to love, Ruth loses then the son who had never been "a separate real person" to her but always "a passion" (131).[40] When it is his turn to explore sex, Milkman enters another incestuous and disastrous relationship with his cousin Hagar.

In terms of form and theme, *Song of Solomon* in many ways recalls *Hundred Years*, the most visible being the biblical-mythical isolated family world of the Macon Deads: "Macon Dead who begat a second Macon Dead who married Ruth Foster (Dead) and begat Magdalene called Lena Dead and First Corinthians Dead and . . . another Macon Dead, now known to the part of the world that mattered as Milkman Dead" (18). The sounds and letters of "Macon Dead" also echo "Macondo," "the part of the world that mattered" in García Márquez's novel. The recurrence of the father's name reflects the patriarchal order that has been a stable and basic feature not only of American society but of Western civilization as a whole. The woman's name disappears, along with her identity and her sanity. The cultural repression and suffocation of the female, as both a person and a feeling, and the vicious circle of pride, hatred, and isolation that ensues from that negation will lead to the inevitable decline of society. For Morrison, the family is Dead alive, without a history, a past, and a community to integrate in. As with many blacks living today in former plantation societies, the slave past is forgotten, with names changed in the records and denied in history, so much that "it's a wonder that anybody knows who anybody is" (328). The story narrates the tragicomic fiction of history, with its illogical reason and its ironic twists:

"They all had to register [in 1869]. Free and not free. Free and used-to-be-slaves. Papa was in his teens and went to sign up, but the man behind the desk was drunk. He asked Papa where he was born. Papa said Macon. Then he asked him who his father was. Papa said, 'He's dead.' Asked him who owned him, Papa said, 'I'm free.' Well, the Yankee wrote it all down, but in the wrong spaces. . . . In the space for his name the fool wrote, 'Dead' comma 'Macon.'" (53-54)[41]

Milkman Dead, therefore, must face the riddles of both his first and his last names, as well as the mystery of his whole African-American past. To discover his identity, he would have to overcome the sickness and the decadence of mother and father, as well as his own ignorance and narrowness. He would have to literally dig deep into the family, community, and culture, overcoming the ideal of individual success with which he had been inscribed since birth. He would have to shed the "milk" whiteness of his name and upbringing to allow black traditions a chance to manifest themselves and grow. He would also have to understand and accept the world as male and female, leaving the exploitative "macho" kingdom where men enjoyed "dominion won by fear" (178).

As in many legendary journeys, García Márquez's and Morrison's male protagonists undergo a mythical quest in search of the meaning and truth of their lives. Both the last Aureliano and the last Macon (Milkman) Dead combine fragments in their solitary pursuit of the clarification of the puzzle. In *Hundred Years,* Aureliano finally discovers the language code and deciphers the parchments containing the written saga of the Buendías. In *Song of Solomon,* the words of the "song" are pieced together and understood at the end, and Milkman is able to read himself in the history of his ancestors. In both cases, human history is invested with myth, and each individual life is connected to hundreds of years and generations of people who came before. The final unfolding of truth takes place in deep solitude and has the quality of a dramatic ritual.

To unravel the mystery of their identities, Aureliano and Milkman need to ponder over obscure texts—the unknown symbols of an old parchment or the puzzling words of a song. Their stories are as much about their quest as about the writing of language and history. The two novels explore the complex relationship between language and history in the American colonial past and the exploitative realities of today. García Márquez evokes the ambition to name and control the

unknown that has endured since the arrival of Christopher Columbus and other European explorers. When the Colombian shores
were reached and Macondo was founded, the new places and things
had to be given names or else they would lack "an identity." When,
much later, a plague attacked the town, causing insomnia and memory loss, the names and functions of objects were tagged onto the
objects themselves: "in all the houses keys to memorizing objects
and feelings had been written." A large sign on the road said MA-
CONDO and another even reminded the townspeople that GOD EXISTS.
"Thus they went on living in a reality that was slipping away, mo-
mentarily captured by words, but which would escape irremediably
when they forgot the values of the written letters" (*Hundred Years*,
53). People then invented a "more comforting" system to deal with
reality, creating one "invented by themselves," reading the past and
the future in cards, making up stories, until Macondo could celebrate
"the recovery of its memory" (53–55).

In a similar way, blacks in colonial America were tagged with
arbitrary names by those who mastered the language and the history.
Their past was forgotten and killed "dead" by regulations, prejudices, wars, and their own tragic loss of memory. The Macon Deads
also suffer amnesia and are parodies of people, bearing grotesque
labels that both distort and suggest historical "truth." Things and animals are also labeled with irony, and here the humor is less tragic:
the Not Doctor Street, the No Mercy Hospital, the horse President
Lincoln, and the pig General Lee (*SOS*, 3, 4, 52). But they all bear
the irony of truth; after all, though the Dead family name was not
"real" but one more legacy of slavery and its aftermath, the living
members of the family are culturally and socially dead. They represent the thousands of black Macons in Alabama, Georgia, Missis-
sippi, Tennessee, North Carolina, Missouri, and Illinois (states that
have towns and counties named Macon) and people in the whole
slave region and in all the Americas, reaching down to Macondo,
who have been cut off from their African roots and their meaningful
past.

The sense of urgency that has been attributed to Latin American
literature is also present in Morrison's, derived from the same concern with cultural identity and memory. Afraid of her people "being
devoured," Morrison uses her writing to "try to shake them, cause a
reaction." A powerful voice indicates solid cultural roots and a recognized social space. Morrison hopes "to restore the language that

black people spoke to its original power," countering the country's dominant idea of "the black" as usually "the pariah."[42]

*Song of Solomon* points to the problems that affect the black community from without and within: the plague of memory loss (Milkman, all youth, the middle class); the aimless, sterile violence (the Seven Days); ignorance and poverty; and the imitation of bourgeois values and attitudes by the black middle class and even by the poor (burlesqued in Hagar's fit of consumerism, for instance). Only empowerment through language—the original name—and the recovery of roots can still reverse the fate of a people threatened by sterility and violence.

From modern Michigan, where he lives as a young adult, Milkman must retrace the history of his ancestors back to the preindustrial village of Charlemagne, or Shalimar, or Solomon (the name is linguistically and symbolically mixed, biblical, Western, heroic, and magically Oriental and African at the same time), a nobody's land lost somewhere in the Blue Ridge Mountains of Virginia (246). In that imaginary locality and through that solitary odyssey, Toni Morrison leads her hero from his lost and devious ways to an awareness that is both very particular and localized, familial and racial, but at the same global and multicultural in its scope. She weaves together the diverse threads that make up the culture and heritage of the Americas, symbols and cosmologies from different continents, religions, and races that have come together in the *New World* and in this new American narrative.

Milkman actually makes no decision to undertake the journey in search of his own identity and history. On the contrary, he travels to Danville, Virginia, only to look for the gold that he and his father believe is still hidden in a cave that is ironically named "Lincoln's Heaven." The gold was supposedly left there by Milkman's grandfather, on the farm that once belonged to that "tall, magnificent" black man, but was taken by the whites who had killed him (222–37). It is for gold and power that Milkman leaves the home of his parents and sets out on his own journey.

From the men of his family, Milkman learned that money, property, and power should be the major goals of life. For a long time, he shared with them and the dominant culture that male-capitalist obsession: "To win. There was nothing like it in the world" (253). Both of his grandfathers had been men admired by their communities for their economic success. Like most former slaves, Macon Dead had craved and struggled for a piece of land he could call his own. Land symbolized the respectability and the economic freedom that he had for so long been denied. People who had known him remembered his determination and force: "[He] was the farmer they wanted to be. . . . [His death] was the beginning of their own dying" (237). For those men who survived him in the Dead family, however, his community ties were forgotten. To them, his story only reinforced the belief that it is through property and wealth that blacks can achieve power.

In urban, Midwestern Michigan, by contrast, Milkman's maternal grandfather, the famous Doctor Foster who had a street named (and "Not" named) after him, also enjoyed the admiration of other black people for the position he had reached. "He was the biggest Negro in this city. Not the richest, but the most respected. . . . Negroes . . . worshipped him." Milkman's father was, in turn, feared by all the tenants of his many properties; he had no patience and no pity for the lower classes. Although the two men were perceived differently by the community, Milkman's father and his doctor grandfather despised poorer blacks and were interested only in their own possessions and social prestige (71–72).

Milkman's early admiration for and wish to emulate these men are gradually shaken by two other major influences in his life, his radical friend Guitar and his aunt Pilate, "a natural healer" (150). Guitar calls his attention to the ills and wrongs of a white society that is deaf to its most sensitive voices, the "writers and artists," who "for years" have been exposing its distorted values and "unnatural" racial norms (157–58). Guitar is enraged not by the slave name he kept but by the "slave status" of his people, which men who act "white," like Milkman's father, the second Macon Dead, help maintain (161). Milkman is finally convinced that both his father and his grandfather had learned the lessons of Western capitalism: "owning, building, acquiring" was the lesson left to him (304).[43]

It is not only the rich men, however, who are self-centered in their use of people and things. Recalling conflicts within the civil rights movement in the United States during the 1960s and 1970s, Morrison suggests that political radicalism does not make men less sexist or selfish. Guitar is as obtuse as Milkman in relation to women, while the Seven Days group chose "never to have any children" and concentrate only in taking over the establishment (336). The characters were undoubtedly inspired by male radicals of the

1960s Black Power movement, who, in Morrison's opinion, were engaged in a male war against whites for the title of "King of the Hill."[44] Violent radicalism is not necessarily liberating either. In one case or the other, in the Deads' accumulation of wealth or in the Seven Days' indiscriminate violence, individual revenge against the colonial system impedes a real political activity and any community organization for change.[45]

Modeled after the strong black women of Morrison's personal experience, Milkman's aunt Pilate is the only sign of a vital black tradition surviving in the urban industrial environment. Like a tribal woman, she keeps her family name in a box hanging from her ear. She was "not born natural," a different person from the very beginning: she had "borned herself . . . popped out" of her dead mother's womb, without a navel, like Eve (144, 246). In her strong and wise ways, she is an African mother but also seems to combine traits of several strong female figures in *One Hundred Years of Solitude*. She has the memory of place and family embodied in Úrsula, the enduring and ageless mother of all; the priestess quality of Pilar Ternera (whose name actually resembles Pilate's), her ability to know past, present, and future and to teach the history that is not in the books; the musk odor and supernatural power of Remedios the Beauty; and the physical animality and naturalness of Petra (from the Latin for "rock") Cote. A primitive goddess herself, Pilate offers peaches and cherries for food, makes wine and whiskey, carries rocks around instead of jewelry or souvenirs, and has a "pebble" voice (151). Like most of García Márquez's mythical women, Pilate is more than natural, male–female, independent, and full of energy.

Pilate also recalls features of the gypsy Melquíades in her wandering style of life and in her wisdom. Even though she had been told that "colored people . . . ain't supposed to go nowhere," it was "as if her geography book had marked her to roam the country" (146, 148). She carried with her some quaint belongings, "six copper pennies, five rocks, the geography book, and two spools of black thread" (145). Above all, she had a mind that also "traveled crooked streets and aimless goat paths," reaching the rare wisdom of the young children and the sage, and the power of talking to the dead, which taught her that "there was nothing to fear" (149). Closer to nature's voices, Pilate followed none of society's rules and did not live by the clock (183).[46] In *Hundred Years*, Melquíades is the prophet who stands beyond human or geographical limitations. An extremely old, sick man, he was reported dead, only to reappear in Macondo "youthful . . . recovered, unwrinkled, with a new and flashing set of teeth" (*Hundred Years,* 17). His Eastern magic and mystery are evoked in the United States context by the magical brewing and cooking of Pilate. She steadily infuses the air with whispers of ancient memories in its "heavy spice-sweet smell" that "made you think of the East and striped tents and the sha-sha-sha of leg bracelets." But shut in their safe, air-conditioned homes, modern people sleep in oblivion and ignore her ginger-sugar magic (*SOS,* 185).

Another Marquezian female character in Morrison's novel is Circe, who keeps "Lincoln's Heaven" isolated from the white world after the death of its fraudulent owners (her former masters). Avenging the memory of her dead (Dead) friends and the history of her race, Circe has vowed that "everything in this world they lived for will crumble and rot" (250). It is her way to rebel against a system that enslaved, segregated, robbed, and killed her people and made her do the low jobs that it would "kill a white person to do" (249). Like Melquíades, Circe is extremely old but also young, taken as dead but unnaturally alive, so that "out of the toothless mouth came the strong, mellifluent voice of a twenty-year-old girl" (243). Literally a healer and a deliverer, she helped deliver Milkman's father and his sister Pilate and later "risked her job, her life," to hide the children from their father's assassins, some powerful people who "owned half the county" (248, 234). Circe later rescues Milkman from his ignorance, guiding him to the cave where he believes gold will be found and adding some pieces to the complicated puzzle of his past.[47]

After an awkward struggle through the brush, the creek, the rocky ground, the hills, and the woods of the abandoned land, a sweating and hallucinating Milkman reaches a dark hole filled with rocks and bats but no gold (252–55). He parodies classical heroic quests and recalls a similarly "reckless adventure" by García Márquez's patriarch José Arcadio Buendía. Firmly believing that he would "extract gold from the bowels of the earth," Buendía led an expedition to the swampy brush of Colombia. In the unbearable heat and amid a vegetation that grew "thicker and thicker," his men found no gold but "felt overwhelmed by their most ancient memories in that paradise of dampness and silence, going back to before original sin" (*Hundred Years,* 11, 19–20). In his own "descent to the underworld," Milkman also seems to return to the state of a primitive caveman, "clawing, pulling, fingering" his way in the total darkness, "hollering a long awwww sound into the pit" (*SOS*, 255).

Shedding his modern artificial self, Milkman is getting ready to absorb part of the wisdom of his ancient race. His journey continues toward Shalimar, where he finally finds the "gold" of his name and his cultural identity. He can now put together the pieces of the puzzle, able to "rewrite" and "read" the "Song of Solomon" and thus magically transform himself into a new man in the sacred ground of myth.

He is totally alone, with "nothing to help him" or weigh him down, such as "his father's money, his car, his suit, shoes"; he discovers then that a man is "what he was born with" (281). With his watch broken and time changed into a different realm, Milkman goes back into a far, deep past, into "what there was before language. Before things were written. . . . And he was hearing it." He also learns to speak the primal language and to communicate with the elements, whispering to the trees, trying to understand the earth's message like a blind man, using his fingertips (282). By listening to the earth, to the people, and to the children, Milkman finds his self, his "tribe of niggers" (332), and his community. They prove to be one and the same thing: Solomon is his ancestor's name and also another name of the village of Shalimar.[48] Only then does he become a whole man and capable of real love. Like a mythical goddess, the beautiful Sweet joins him to complete this magic paradise of natural freedom and true happiness.

Aureliano, the last Buendía in *One Hundred Years of Solitude,* also undergoes a long and difficult process to decipher the truth about himself and his family. Instead of having to learn the language of nature and folklore, as Milkman does, Aureliano dedicates himself to the study of Sanskrit so that he can read and understand the ancient wisdom written by Melquíades. As if he were in a primitive cave, Aureliano finds Melquíades' parchments "intact among the prehistoric plants and steaming puddles and luminous insects that had removed all trace of man's passage on earth from the room." To ensure his isolation in such a ponderous moment of discovery, he even "nailed up the doors and windows . . . so as not to be disturbed by any temptation of the world." He finally realizes that he can read very easily, as if the characters in those magical pages "had been written in Spanish and were being read under the dazzling splendor of high noon" (*Hundred Years,* 381).

The cavelike surroundings, the darkness, the solitude, and the timeworn manuscripts set the proper stage for the enactment of myth. As Aureliano "pursued the hidden paths of his descent," fascinated by the disclosure of his beginning and end, the wind outside was blowing strong and warm, "full of voices from the past, the murmurs of ancient geraniums, sighs of disenchantment" (382). The story he reads tells of the hurricane that destroys Macondo; the novel we read narrates how the "cyclonic strength" of the wind "tore the doors and windows off their hinges, pulled off the roof, uprooted the foundations" (382). Absorbed in his reading, Aureliano does not even notice the "whirlwind of dust and rubble being spun about by the wrath of the biblical hurricane" (383). While in the end of *Song of Solomon* Milkman "surrendered to the air," finally at peace (*SOS,* 341), Aureliano is to be "wiped out by the wind" along with "the city of mirrors (or mirages)" that had been Macondo (*Hundred Years,* 383). As far as the reader "knows," however, Milkman is suspended in the air, at a mythical moment when he is at last one with himself and his past history. Aureliano is still in that dark room, immortalized, "decipher[ing] the instant . . . prophesying himself" (383). García Márquez closes his novel with the destruction of a stagnant society; Morrison closes hers with the possibility of reinvention and salvation in black culture.

Walter Benjamin has contrasted the rapid, efficient, informative style of modern novelists with the art of marvelous repetition and layering of facts by ancient storytellers. A story is rich in myth and in wisdom, and the storyteller is akin to "teachers and sages."[49] Drawing on Benjamin, Italian writer Italo Calvino has similarly pointed out that the primitive narratives of ancient tribes and folktales handed down from generation to generation have fixed structures but at the same time "allow for an enormous number of combinations," with myth as their "hidden, underground part." The telling of a myth is never an ordinary event; springing "from the storyteller's combinatorial game" with the fable and reaching far beyond its codes and formulas, it is a rite that "feeds on silence" and "demands to be recited in secret and in a sacred place."[50] Gabriel García Márquez and Toni Morrison rescue the novel from the dry "objectivity" that Benjamin attributes to the genre and retell the myths and facts of their histories and their cultures with the creativeness and care of village storytellers. They keep company with Gayl Jones and Paule Marshall in their loyalty to the memory and art of their ancestors for a renewed transformed retelling of history, stories, and songs.

Similar motifs and images repeatedly link the novels *Song of Solomon* and *One Hundred Years of Solitude,* both written in a language carefully woven, both poetic and physical, complex but "apparently effortless," as García Márquez and Morrison would like.[51] Time is repeated by successive generations, and especially in García Márquez, tenses are constantly interacting, past, present, and future coexisting. The linguistic device is indicative of a social reality that combines different centuries in the same historical moment—the often inseparable yesterday and today of Latin America.[52] García Márquez's novel opens with a statement that has become a standard example of the technique:

> Many years later, as he faced the firing squad, Colonel Aureliano Buendía was to remember that distant afternoon when his father took him to discover ice. (*Hundred Years,* 11)

Morrison similarly plays with different times in the second sentence of her novel, though in this case the future does not look back but is brought closer to the present in the premonition of events:

> Two days before the event was to take place he tacked a note on the door of his little yellow house. (*SOS,* 3)

The choice of imagery often connects Morrison and García Márquez in these two novels. Bird images, for instance, provide a central motif in *Song of Solomon,* which contrasts the "white peacocks" in modern society—too heavy to fly, symbols of white male artificiality, arrogance, and doom—with the flying powers of the archetypal Negro, Solomon, and the culture of his wife, the Indian Singing Bird (179). In *Hundred Years,* birds are symbols of memory (223) and make deafening noises (18). Solemn peacocks also strut on the "extensive blue lawns" of the fancy houses of the gringos who control the banana company in Macondo (214). While in both novels peacocks are related to male sexual and economic power, Morrison more directly links "peacock" to male urinating, an analogy suggested by the very spelling and sound of the English word. Milkman is a thoughtless, insensitive "cock" that repeatedly urinates or "pees" (an activity also constantly performed by García Márquez's Aureliano). By "peeing on people" at home, Milkman plays out an ironic scene of patriarchal power (*SOS,* 216–18).

The idea of flying, which Morrison borrows from black folklore, is also part of universal myth and countless folktales.[53] It inspired García Márquez for an earlier short story called "A Very Old Man with

Enormous Wings"[54] and for the flying carpets and balloons of the gypsies in Macondo (*Hundred Years,* 213). The old man's aborted flying project in García Márquez's story echoes at the beginning of *Song of Solomon,* where the insurance agent Robert Smith meets his death attempting a heroic flight (or suicide?) on blue silk wings. A plain, civilized man with no magic, his deed serves to remind the town and the boy Milkman that "only birds and airplanes could fly" (*SOS,* 5–9). Despite its frustrating aftermath, the event does have a touch of magic. Mr. Smith is going to leap from Mercy Hospital when Milkman's mother enters the hospital in labor. At that moment, the powerful contralto singing of the "Sugarman" spiritual resonates outside, while red velvet rose petals blow around in the air and fall on the snow. They announce the birth of a new Solomon/Sugarman, a birth that will be realized only at the end of the novel. Similar magic surrounds the death of García Márquez's patriarch José Arcadio Buendía: it is greeted with "a silent storm" of tiny yellow flowers that cover streets and roofs like soft snow (*Hundred Years,* 137).

The logic accepted by Morrison's town, acknowledging the impossibility of human flight, is true only to a certain extent in both novels, in which flying, resurrection, and assumption to heaven are miraculous events that do occur to superior beings. In *Hundred Years,* Remedios the Beauty waves goodbye to her townspeople as she rises through the air "in the midst of the flapping sheets" that she had been folding (223). Black people hold similar supernatural powers in Morrison's novel, for she knows that flying is "one of [their] gifts." Morrison learned that "from her family and her community, from the stories, the spirituals, and the songs they constantly repeat."[55] In the novel, the old spiritual affirms that "Sugarman done fly" (*SOS,* 9). The children of Shalimar add to the myth and the tradition by repeating and preserving the story, even as they transform the lyrics in the cyclical rounds of their play (306).[56] Their song, emphasizing the refrain "Solomon done fly, Solomon done gone / Solomon cut across the sky, Solomon gone home" contains not only Milkman's family history but also the myth that supported many Africans through slavery. According to tradition, black slaves like Solomon/Sugarman were able to fly back to Africa, taken by their longing for home and their refusal to submit to servitude. Milkman will physically and mythically repeat Solomon's feat, leaping into the air at the very end of the novel, "as fleet and bright as a lodestar" (341). He is light and sure enough to leap into the air and challenge the laws of logic. In space, he will embrace his ancestry, his history, the myth of his culture, the recreation of himself.[57]

Milkman realizes that the wise Pilate shared in the same myth and power as their earlier ancestor, for "without ever leaving the ground, she could fly." Magically, two birds come down to honor her when she dies and take away her earring—her self, her identity—to the skies (340). The dream of resurrection and of the power of life over death resonates in Pilate's end but also echoes throughout *Song of Solomon*, a longing both religious and secular, natural and biblical, a symbol of the favorite human utopia: "the Risen Son and the heart's lone desire. Complete power, total freedom, and perfect justice" (186).

Biblical images of exodus and salvation recur in *Song of Solomon* and *One Hundred Years of Solitude*, along with the opposing metaphors of genesis and apocalypse. Primitive rocks, mythical Jordan Rivers, and ancient towns make up the scenery in the two novels. Although the wrath of the gods will blow it away in the end, Macondo seems at first a fantastic Eden, "built on the bank of a river of clear water that ran along a bed of polished stones, which were white and enormous like prehistoric eggs" (*Hundred Years*, 11). Creation is also invoked in the naming of things unknown, in the "seven metals that corresponded to the seven planets," which Melquíades owns (16), and in the "rock" names of Petra Cotes and Pietro Crespi.

In *Song of Solomon*, the biblical-mythical black family has its American origins in a primitive village located by a river and surrounded by rocks. The two "flat-headed . . . outcroppings of rock . . . looking over a deep valley" at the place called Solomon's Leap will be the final scene for the fictional and cultural synthesis that the novel seems to propose (*SOS*, 339). By contrast, creation is ironically parodied in the name and purpose of the radical group Seven Days, made up of seven men who want to recreate the world in their own image but are enslaved by their hate and by obsession with a tragic past.

Some biblical female names in *Song of Solomon* recall characters from *Hundred Years*. Rebecca (also called Reba in *SOS*), is the name given in both novels to characters who share an uncontrolled sexual life, going "from one orgasm to another" (*SOS*, 151). The opposite type of woman is also present in the novels: the frustrated sexual life of Ruth Dead can be compared to the frigid, repressed lives of the wives of the Buendía clan. The spinsterhood of Morrison's First Corinthians and Lena can be related to the solitude of García Márquez's Amaranta. First Corinthians shares a "good" education with Amaranta Úrsula, but their academic background does not push them out of the cycle of female submission and inferiority. Corinthians, for instance, learns in college "how to be an enlightened mother and wife" and how to contribute "to the civilizing of her community" (189). Besides decrying the traditional liberal arts education, Morrison indicts a black bourgeoisie alienated in a safe haven of comfort and forgetfulness. Rich Corinthians finally discovers love and loyalty in working-class radical Henry Porter, although her conventional middle-class status leads her at first to be ashamed of him.[58]

The character Hagar in *Song of Solomon* strongly reminds the reader of other desperate women who hunt their men and die for them in *Hundred Years*. Both Morrison and García Márquez suggest that our social conventions have made female life sterile and claustrophobic. Real love is rarely found within the institution of marriage; it can bloom only in a freer world, without repression and hypocrisy. This is the case with the love relationship of Aureliano and Petra in *Hundred Years* and with the final meeting of Milkman (now Sugarman) and tender Sweet in his ancestral hometown.

Morrison and García Márquez both pay homage to their families and cultures by means of names and references in their novels. Although Toni Morrison vows "not to write autobiography," *Song of Solomon* recalls hardships and journeys in her own family history.[59] The glorious patriarch Solomon, hailed in song by the children, immortalized as a rock (Solomon's Leap), and mirrored in the townspeople—the key to all history—bears the middle name of Morrison's maternal grandfather. García Márquez recalls his grandfather in the character Colonel Gerineldo Márquez, who refuses to back up Aureliano Buendía in "a senile war" (*Hundred Years,* 246). His grandfather is again remembered in the social prominence of the Buendías, in Aureliano's many illegitimate children, and in José Arcadio's killing a man and moving away to found Macondo.[60] The family name Iguarán is given to Úrsula, the first matriarch, who, like García Márquez's own grandmother, was her husband's cousin. Úrsula Iguarán embodies the strength of García Márquez's mother and grandmother and is the ideal, paradigmatic woman of his imagination.[61]

Petra Cotes, the lover of Aureliano Segundo, bears the last name of the Colombian writer's maternal grandmother. She is a strong and joyful character who "makes a man out of" Aureliano, perhaps indicating the role of the Cotes women—or of all women—in the world (*Hundred Years*, 193). Although the name does not directly indicate the connection, the magical powers of Pilar Ternera also remind us of the "pillar-like" quality of García Márquez's grandmother and the magic of her life and her tales.[62]

In addition to honoring their biological families, both García Márquez and Morrison pay homage to brothers and sisters in their cultures, not only by writing epic narratives based on their peoples' history and myths but also by directly invoking the traditions into which they insert themselves as writers. Always conscious of his *Latinidad*, García Márquez includes in *Hundred Years* names of characters from novels of such Latinos as Carlos Fuentes, Julio Cortázar, and Alejo Carpentier. "A passage recalls Juan Rulfo and there are scenes consciously in the manner of Carpentier, Astúrias and Vargas Llosa, in a kind of affectionate homage," says critic Alastair Reid.[63] The novel sends "messages to Borges . . . and to Carpentier," in what can be considered a kind of "interpretive meditation" on Latin American writing.[64] In Melquíades, García Márquez seems to honor all writers, all imagination, and all creation.

Morrison's work pays similar "homages," but instead of referring to other writers, she chooses to honor the music makers of her black world. They are her colleagues in the sense that she would like her novels to sound like the blues and play the same role as music for the black community. When Milkman tries to think of men who "bore witness" in his race, he lists blues singers such as Muddy Waters, Lead-belly, Bo Diddley, and Fats (*SOS*, 334). At the end of the novel, Guitar (a name that invokes the major instrument for the blues) and Pilate (herself a singer of spirituals and blues) are contrasted, juxtaposed, as if to indicate that the worlds which they symbolize—cultural roots and political action, female and male—must join together to create beautiful, meaningful music.

Spirituals and other folk music reverberate from beginning to end in the novel. It is, after all, titled *Song*, and Morrison has constantly emphasized that black music is the best way to convey the culture. She would like her work to be "like something that has probably only been fully expressed . . . in music, or in some other culture," she says revealingly.[65] She wants to write in a mode that would "do what the music did for blacks . . . in that civilization that existed underneath the white civilization." As a kind of blues singer, she wishes to express and eternalize the traditions, the sorrows, and the joys of black life. At the same time that the blues and jazz represent a return to origins and roots, they imply improvisation, creativity, and openness—both repetition and constant recreation. Here Morrison is unequivocally connected to *Corregidora* and the creative work of Gayl Jones, another major blues novelist. Like the childhood stories and African traditions made alive by memory, music celebrates a people and a culture, a place, a nation, the beautiful world that Africans and their descendants have been able to create but that was suppressed in historical and cultural records.

Both in her life and in her literature, Toni Morrison has testified as a black person and as a woman against racial and gender discrimination. "Racism will destroy love," says Morrison, and "the conflict of genders is a cultural illness."[66] She shares with Gabriel García Márquez and other Latin American writers the hope in a more unified and just society, in which the identity and value of the people can be recognized and stimulated. The past must be correctly reread if one wishes to influence the present, and the whole notion of history must be changed from a static narrative that is told and controlled by the dominant power to a dynamic story of many actors and creators.

In his own rewriting of history, García Márquez retells the discovery and exploration of Colombia from the days of Sir Francis Drake and the Spanish galleons to the arrival of modernity and prosperity. Drake the Englishman is replaced in the twentieth century by "slippery" gringos of a banana company, who talk "only in a strange tongue," are accompanied by "languid wives in muslin dresses and veiled hats," and isolate their style and ethnicity in "a separate town" for themselves (*Hundred Years*, 238). The Colombian people gain in sweat and hardship from their presence. García Márquez recalls the Great Strike of 1928, a workers' rebellion crushed by a police repression that came down like "the roar of a cataclysm" (283). The whole event is washed away by the seemingly endless rain, which lasted "four years, eleven months, and two days" (291). Gone are names and numbers, rebellion and death, in the official version of the event sustained by the government, the media, the police, and the banana company. Like the violence of the slave past narrated by Morrison, the Colombian crisis is a bad dream that should be forgotten: "'You must have been dreaming. . . . Nothing has happened in

Macondo, nothing has ever happened, nothing ever will happen. This is a happy town'" (287). The printed text of history gives the final version, establishing once and for all that "everything had been set forth in judicial documents and in primary-school textbooks: that the banana company had never existed" (359).

In spite of the hyperbolic numbers he provides and the fantastic episodes he narrates, García Márquez says that there is "not one line" in his books that has not been "suggested by reality." The violence that he personally witnessed in Colombia was much broader and killed many more people than the three thousand that the strike's repression kills in the novel. There really was a banana strike and ensuing repression in Colombia in 1928. The worst violence and disruption in the country, however, came with the Colombian civil war—"La Violencia"—which lasted from 1948 to the end of the 1960s and in which "several hundred thousand Colombians" lost their lives.[67] His early writing presented more factual representations of the economic and political life of Colombia, but his work has gradually changed to embrace a broader definition of "reality" that includes the premonitions, visions, magic, and myths of Latin Americans.[68]

For García Márquez, literature is always critical and subversive, going against "the corrupted forms of society."[69] Real art is always revolutionary and iconoclastic, contributing "to the creation of new forms of living, new societies, in one word, to better the life of man."[70] Though she lives in the richer world of North America, Toni Morrison knows that the routine struggles of black people in the United States are in many ways similar to those of peoples in underdeveloped countries. Her mission as a novelist is akin to that of Latin American and other Third World writers. With her storytelling, she can help her people make the transition from a rural to an urban society, understand the continual pressures and conflicts with the dominant powers, and still retain memory and strength. She writes what she calls "village" or "peasant literature," particularly for her people but also for "all sorts of people" whom she can touch.[71]

Besides relating to her Latin colleague in the major themes, characterization, and style of her novel, Toni Morrison's public voice seems to respond affirmatively to García Márquez's call for an active involvement of intellectuals and writers in cultural politics. "Art can be both uncompromisingly beautiful and socially responsible," Morrison believes.[72] In her address to the three thousand writers assembled for the 1981 American Writers Congress, Morrison went beyond concerns with the identity and culture of her "tribe" to claim more freedom and conscience in American literature as a whole. She denounced censorship, stifling publishing standards imposed by profit concerns, and nihilistic literary criticism. "The political consequences for minority writers, dissident writers and writers committed to social change," says Morrison, "are devastating."[73] Literature cannot be alienated from reality, for "a novel ought to confront important ideas, call them historical or political, it's the same thing."[74] The power of such confrontation and the beauty of its writing has given the literature by black authors like Morrison an invigorating freshness that energizes the whole literature of the United States.[75]

García Márquez has called *One Hundred Years of Solitude* the "metaphoric history of Latin America," and one could similarly consider *Song of Solomon* the parable of black America.[76] Both authors combine historical facts, family history, and popular folklore with a background of myth and make a clear, vigorous statement in defense of the interaction of tradition and rebellion, a combination of roots and dreams, a recognition of voices repressed and suffocated by the Western world. By looking South—always deeper South, until her eyes could reach Macondo—Toni Morrison has discovered what readers also realize: that the history of the Americas is "fantastically" similar, the energy of life and culture ultimately draws on the same sources, and the challenges can be better faced if there is union and love. "Am, am, am . . . life, life, life," echoes the valley at the foot of Solomon's Leap. If identity is found and preserved, a new cycle of growth can begin—we can all ride the air.

## The Caribbean as Center: *Tar Baby*

It is not only through the intertextuality in *Song of Solomon* that Toni Morrison has built bridges between the Americas, North and South. Her novel *Tar Baby* brings black and white people from the United States to a very small island in the Caribbean, fictively named Isle des Chevaliers, near the larger and destitute Dominique.[77] The latter name directly evokes French-colonized Haiti, formerly Saint Domingue, a glorious place in the history of the Americas for its early independence, won by slaves led by Toussaint L'Ouverture in 1798. Once "the most beautiful and fertile part of the West Indies and perhaps the world,"[78] Haiti is now the poorest country in the hemisphere, a poignant mirror for the rest of the Caribbean and the poor nations of Latin America. Morrison's *Tar Baby* explores contemporary neo-colonial aspects in the Caribbean islands of her imagination: a poor and black Dominique that works to support the wealthy in Isle des Chevaliers, the United States, and England.

The whites of *Tar Baby* are Valerian Street and his wife, Margaret, owners of the lavish island house named L'Arbe de la Croix. Their closest blacks are their servants Sydney and Ondine Childs, "industrious Philadelphia Negroes—the proudest people in the race" (51). Linking the two races and classes is Ondine's niece Jadine, a beautiful and orphaned "yellow" woman, now twenty-five years old, who is adopted, in a way, by both black and white couples. Two U.S. men, both about thirty years old, are responsible for bringing relationships and feelings to a climax in the novel. One is the Streets' son Michael, always physically absent but constantly present in the memories and conversations of the others. The second is a dark black stranger who calls himself Son and enters the house right before Christmas, throwing the fragile balance of its occupants' relations with one another into disarray. In this novel, the Christmas dinner is the carnivalesque ritual that allows hierarchy and rule to be overturned, hidden emotions to be brought to surface, and repressed anger finally to be expressed.

In the twentieth century, the Caribbean plantation economy has been replaced by a flourishing tourism industry that caters in the same fashion to the pleasures and profits of the upper classes, normally whites of European descent with U.S. birth certificates. The tiny island imagined by Toni Morrison may have been overlooked by colonial greed, but it does not escape the new cycle of foreign occupation. Laborers from Haiti were hired to clear Isle des Chevaliers of its rain forest, "already two thousand years old," destroying animals, flowers, and a river. Civilization marched onto the island in the guise of rich businessmen needing a tropical retreat from long northern winters. Famous architects drew elaborate plans for expensive houses, "the oldest and most impressive" among which is the Streets' L'Arbe de la Croix (8). Isle des Chevaliers is now owned and controlled by similarly retired U.S. expatriates with money.

*Tar Baby* intertextually combines elements of history and mythology. On the other side of the island from the lavish resort area, the ancient and the natural still survive in the black, thick swamp, where the little water left of a "brokenhearted river" went to hide, and in the three wooded "humps of hills" where horsemen roam at night (40). The island received its name from those horsemen, whose origin and race vary from account to account. Among upper-class whites, one version tells of only one French soldier haunting those hills; another of one hundred French horsemen riding one hundred horses. The native population circulate quite a different tale in their separate quarters in Place du Vent, the poor, black sector of the city of Queen of France in Dominique. For them, the horsemen roaming the hills are African slaves who fled from a sinking French ship back in colonial times and "went blind the minute they saw Dominique" (130). The Africans who became only partially blind were taken as indentured workers by French colonists and later had children who also went blind after a certain age. Those who were completely blind went into hiding and still "ride those horses all over the hills," mating with mysterious women who inhabit the swamp trees. According to Gideon, an islander who works for the Streets, his blind wife Thérèse is a member of that race and has the power of seeing beyond the visible "with the eye of the mind" (131). Thérèse shares with seers and healers of African culture the power of a "third eye."[79]

The contrast between the European and the African versions of the story is only one example of the constant play of binary oppositions in the novel and the author's evident concern with the ways in which Western civilization has dominated the physical and cultural landscape of the Americas. For those in power, the stories and the history are those of the conquerors, just as wealth and privilege are still controlled by the white upper class.

Without even knowing the tale of the horsemen-slaves, Son departs from his alienated life to recover its memory. He jumped a cargo ship to reach an island of contradiction and paradox, one side full of magic and blackness, the other oblivious in its carefully sculpted white landscape (5).[80] Toni Morrison makes it clear that, as a writer, she wants to reinforce and pass on the stories told by people like Thérèse and their vision of the world. The legendary swamp women of the island materialize for the reader when Jadine walks by the edge of the forest in what was, for her, "the ugly part of Isle des Chevaliers—the part she averted her eyes from whenever she drove past" (155). The rotten smell and the strangeness of the swamp disturb her nerves; she despairs when she falls in its sticky, stinking mud. The "Diaspora mothers," mythical women of "exceptional femaleness," watch Jadine from the trees, realizing that she is "fighting to get away from them" (157, 248).

The island serves as permanent vacation resort for Valerian Street's retirement. A comfortable haven between the northern civilization and the southern tropics, his beautiful white house and the island become the stage for the continuing conflicts between dominant interests and values and a resisting black culture. His wife, Margaret, hates staying in the place for more than a few months: it is a jungle of heat and strangeness that she, as a porcelain-white and once-Catholic "Principal Beauty of Maine," still cannot master.[81] On their property, the tropical forest has been replaced by a safe greenhouse full of delicate plants from a cooler climate, their growth stimulated by the sounds of classical European music.

Beautiful and well-traveled Jadine typifies a black middle class constantly exposed to Western culture and its judgmental norms. Educated in European art history in France, Jadine has absorbed the convenient hierarchy of cultures established by dominant powers. From that perspective, "Picasso *is* better than an Itumba mask," and all black art shows in the United States and England are mediocre and amateurish (62). Jadine's pride in her own refined good taste blinds her to its predatory quality. For instance, her enjoyment of the beautiful black sealskin coat sent by her European boyfriend, Ryk, as a Christmas present is never shadowed by the memory of the ninety baby seals that went into making it (76). The coat is also evocative of the body of Son, both of them black and desirable to Jadine. For the perceptive reader, both Son and the coat represent species abused for the pleasure and profit of the white, upper-class rule.

The glittery landscape of art galleries and fashion shows is the world that Jadine knows best, but it does not make her happy. Confused by the pressures and demands of her life and career among whites in France, Jadine looks for reassurance and comfort among her relatives in the Caribbean. She feels lonely and puzzled in spite of her success as a fashion model and the degree from a Parisian university. Should she accept the marriage proposal from Ryk? Her black uncle and aunt would not like it, but "white and European . . . was not as bad as white and American" (41). Or does Ryk perhaps expect her to be the "typical" black girl who loves to wear ear hoops, has curly hair, and listens only to jazz? She has none of those characteristics and, in fact, resents standardized signs of "blackness" imposed on anybody with some skin color. "Sometimes I want to get out of my skin and be only the person inside—not American—not black—just me" (40).

At the same time, Jadine feels the lack of African culture in her life, even if she at first does not verbalize it. One unexpected event in Paris completely shakes her self-assurance and dignity: an African woman, dressed in yellow, spits at her in a supermarket. Jadine is perturbed by the powerful look of eyes without eyelashes and the contemptuous spit aimed at her by the very tall woman with "skin like tar." The woman wraps her body in a "canary yellow dress," her hair in "a gelée as yellow as her dress," and her feet in "many-colored sandals." She is a vision of strange, "transcendent beauty" in the middle of a Paris supermarket (38). Awakened by the contrast between her own body and the impressive walk, the large hips, and the full bust of the African woman, Jadine is overcome with a deep sense of inadequacy and inauthenticity. Yet for a long time she is unable to read the messages sent to her by her aunt Ondine, by the African woman in yellow dress who keeps returning in her dreams, and by all the black women holding their breasts out to her in visions. Be a daughter, be a mother, be natural, recover your cultural roots, they say in one way or another, but Jadine's modernity deafens her and hinders her understanding.

Valerian Street is also deaf and blind in his complacent morality. He acts like a benevolent and liberal gentleman, heedless of the neocolonial structure that he helps perpetuate. The origin of the Streets' wealth and power is connected to the history of the sugar monoculture in the Caribbean and its reflection in the present order. The Streets own and operate a sugar-candy industry in the United States, and Valerian's name was given to one of their popular candies. Having manufactured the raw product of the Caribbean and made a huge profit from it, while the islands' workers remain poor, Valerian comes back to enjoy the summer weather and the ocean like a true landlord, without a tinge of awareness or remorse. His butler and cook remain faithful and obedient from a sense of obligation and a fear of the poverty so widespread among blacks. They do not have a place or a life of their own, so the old reality of indentured servitude and slavery seems to have changed only slightly.

When natives come to the house to do any of the cleaning and washing that its idle owners require, they are kept nameless and segregated by both the Streets and the Childs. Gideon and Marie Thérèse Foucault remain "Yardman" and "Mary." If servants are replaced, those nonnames are kept the same to assure ignorance of true identities and faces. The house itself, with its displaced U.S. population, remains a separate island of privilege and difference in the poor Caribbean. Natives are perceived as haughty and uncivilized, despised by the rich white couple, their black butler and cook from Philadelphia, and Jadine. Their gaze repeats the pattern of the first colonial encounters. In the European (now Europeanized) perception, Indians and Africans are brutal creatures without culture or feeling, who can survive only in the shadow of superior white masters.

Like many Caribbeans who leave for the land of the colonizer in search of economic opportunity, the Streets' yardman Gideon experienced a hard immigrant's life for two years in Quebec and for twenty years in the United States. There "money orders, leisure suits and TV abounded," but no stack of dollars could be saved by the poor black Caribbean. He finally returned in humiliation, bringing only a suit and some apples for Thérèse in his pockets (93). He hides his frustration from friends, saying that he came back only because the United States was "a bad place to die in." He is unable to keep hate in his heart, however, and even praises the United States as a place where "they knew how to make money and they knew how to give it away. The most generous people on the globe" (132–33). Forced by poverty and hopelessness to be humble and grateful, Gideon is the eternal outsider to the banquet, unwanted and uninvited to share the prosperity of capitalism.[82] His wife, Thérèse, in contrast, hates the "American Negroes" Ondine and Sydney and refuses to recognize "the presence of white Americans in her world." But she and Gideon welcome Son, who seems one of their own kind. They are black and proud, and it is with pride that they face poverty and rebuild their home after every hurricane that sweeps the island (94). Son has a similar stubbornness and shares Thérèse's rebellious spirit.

In the idyllic unreality of the Streets' home, as in the headquarters of international capitalism, native Caribbeans are kept segregated and poor. The islands are relevant for their supply of sugar and cocoa, but the people exploited in the process remain invisible. The newcomer Son perceives Valerian's contradictions in L'Arbe de la Croix and the repeated cycles of economic domination in the heart of the continent. Valerian paid as little as possible for sugar and cocoa, "as though the cutting of cane and picking of beans was child's play and had no value." He sold them back to the islands in the form of candy and made a fortune. His Caribbean palace was also built by local laborers, and more were hired to do "the work he was not capable of." Like other efficient businesspeople, he paid them "according to some scale of value that would outrage Satan himself," always believing he was a good, "law-abiding man" (174).

Son is critical of people like Valerian Street, makers of waste and thieves of the wealth of the world, who isolate themselves in mansions and behind walls that hide the waste and the destruction of their own creation. Yet Son is no ideal black conscience. Although he differs greatly from Jadine in his criticism of the socioeconomic order, his identity and his life are also distorted by the dominant system. His anger at inequality makes him a rebel who does not see his own inconsistencies and stupidities. A Vietnam veteran whose memories of the war are still painfully repressed, Son uses violence in his personal life against the more vulnerable. In the village of Eloe in Florida, he killed his wife, Cheyenne, by driving his car through the house where she was betraying him with a boy, and has been a runaway outlaw ever since.

Completely alienated from all rites of civilization, on the one hand, and the support of culture, family, and friends, on the other hand, Son assumes seven different documented identities, as well as some invented ones, none of which gives him a sense of who he really is (119).[83] He turns into a solitary wanderer, whose only possible company is that of other solitary figures in the "large and uncounted legion of undocumented men" who refuse to submit to the rules of society and the routine of regular work (142–43). He works on cargo ships, sailing away from "organized territories" in the manner of Huck Finn and Nigger Jim (143). The money orders that he sends to his old father back in Eloe are his only link with any form of family, but he adds no word of love or sign of true connection.

Son's sailor life among foreigners shakes his complacency about his country and himself. Among the solitary men on his last ship was a Mexican ex-convict, who had drawn a ferocious Uncle Sam's mouth on the map of the United States: "a map of the U.S. as an ill-shaped tongue ringed by teeth and crammed with the corpses of children." The United States seemed a "loud, red and sticky" place when seen from abroad through "the international edition of *Time*, by way of shortwave radio and the views of other crewmen." Because the country punished courageous actions against the existing order with death, its fields were "spongy, its pavements slick with the blood of all the best people" (143).[84] But on the ship Son realizes that he was using that same violence when he was ready to smash to death a beautiful and innocent fish that refused to submit to his control, to "cooperate with his hook" and "surrender to his pleasure." He also spilled the blood of his young wife out of blind revenge. The Mexican's perception of truth—*verdad*—showed Son that it was time for this "cierto Americano" to go home and be human (143–44).

Like Jadine, Son feels the urge to return to the place he calls home—in his case, the village of Eloe—to clear up his mental confusion and regain a sense of who he really is. For Jadine, "home" has been transplanted from the eastern United States to the fancy home of the Streets in Isle des Chevaliers, where her uncle and aunt inhabit the separate quarters reserved for them below the kitchen. For Son, home is also a "separate place," simultaneously within and outside the "sticky" country of his birth. The village of Eloe has retained its isolation and its blackness, "presided over by wide black women in snowy dresses," a place "very dry, green and quiet" (144).

In their journeys of reconnection, Son's and Jadine's paths cross when he decides to jump the ship that is revealingly called "large gardens of the king" in one of the Nordic languages—the *Stor Konigsgaarten*.[85] In the waters between islands long dominated by the kings of Europe, Son swims toward the distant lights of the town also ironically called Queen of France. Along the way, however, he climbs aboard a leisure boat that happens to belong to the Streets and which takes him to their house in Isle des Chevaliers, the same "island that, three hundred years ago, had struck slaves blind the moment they saw it" (5).

Black Son arrives just in time for the traditional celebration of Christmas, prepared by the Streets in New England fashion. Margaret Street was especially anticipating the arrival of her estranged son, Michael, to highlight the occasion. The anthropologist Michael actually prefers the company of Indians on the reservation where he works and insists that blacks and Indians should try to rescue their culture and their values from the domination of Western concepts. He keeps away from the comfortable albeit surreal environment of his parents' world just as a black Son "is born" at Christmastime there to shake their complacency and rearrange their lives.

Everyone but Valerian is frightened at the sight of an intruder with eyes like a thief's and the looks of a "swamp nigger" or a "river rat" (136). Son will soon look handsome, however, with newly cut hair and a fashionable attire provided by the condescending white "master," Valerian. He then seems no primitive jungle Negro but their own compatriot, who can play the piano and entertain intelligent conversation, besides knowing how to take care of plants and flowers. Used to impersonations and disguises, Son is able to convince them that he is not looking for sex, when in fact he has desired Jadine from his first sight of her. His violent anger against everything white comes up as he inspects her pictures, her jewels, and her expensive outfits lying around in her bedroom; he calls her a whore. He repeatedly invades her bedroom, but when she is afraid of rape and calls him "nigger," he tells her to stop acting like those white girls "who always think somebody's going to rape you" (103). The distorted heritage of colonialism frames their lives: stronger than desire is the sum of sexist and racist ideas governing the thinking and behavior of both Son and Jadine.

The absence of his biological son, Michael, and other illustrious guests leads Valerian to invite his black servants and the black intruder-turned-guest to the dinner table on Christmas Eve. The fraternal ritual of food sharing is turned into an exchange of violent accusations that pitch servant against master, blacks against whites, and wife against husband, in a way never seen before. Gaiety slides into open hostility with the presence of Son and the dismissal of "Yardman" and his wife from service. Faithful Sydney and Ondine take master Valerian to task; for his part, the liberal patriarch calls them "these people" and Ondine a mere "cook," while Margaret calls their old black friend "nigger bitch," uncovering her rage and contempt for their class and race. Ondine accuses Margaret of physically abusing Michael even as a baby and calls her a bitch and a "white freak." Feeling a terrible menace in the air, Valerian tells the servants to leave forever and orders someone to call the harbor police, as if he were still in command. He now recognizes that by bringing all those people to the dinner table "he had played a silly game, and everyone was out of place" (178–79). In Son's opinion, the whole violent episode could have been avoided if the races had been kept separate, for "white folks and black folks should not sit together" (181). The carnivalesque displacement of hierarchy and order ruptures to reveal bitter undercurrents in racial and class relations.

As racial slurs are exchanged back and forth, Son and Jadine are able to escape from the chaos and hide in her room. Their passion for each other is finally expressed with tenderness, and they decide to flee from the riotous house and leave for the United States. Jadine seems to have found the love and companionship that she hungered for during all her orphaned life. In spite of their differences in education, work, class, color, and attitude toward race, they try a life together in busy, commercial New York and in tiny, nostalgic Eloe.

Unfortunately, they soon realize that one is not happy doing what pleases the other. After a few months, Jadine gets tired of paying the bills and of trying to transform beautiful, black Son into an educated man with ability and sophistication enough to succeed in modern society. Son finds it impossible to work for money and conform to the demands of urban, middle-class life. Still, Son is desperately in love and goes after Jadine when she flies to her relatives in Isle des Chevaliers, but when he arrives she has already left for France. On the island, Margaret now substitutes for the decaying Valerian in the main command of the house, but apart from that slight change, order and hierarchy have been restored to "normal."

The end of the novel offers no easy solutions for the anxious quests of young blacks in modern society. Jadine is a middle-class person who, like all the others she knows, including Ondine and Sydney, wants to "make it" and always plays the game "with house cards, each deck issued and dealt with by the house" (108). Like those others, she performs the role and occupies the space allowed to her by the white-controlled system. The anxieties and contradictions of her mixed self are not resolved by her journey to the island and the proximity of her relatives, Son, or the mythical swamp women. Her experiences there, however, have made her a changed woman. She flees to the heart of Western civilization, the colonizer's France, but she is now willing to face herself and even the old imperial country differently. Paris has whites but also has Africans; Jadine wants to fly to that diversity, meet the woman in yellow who once shook her confidence, and be the free and mature person that she had never been. With the wings of the plane to Paris, Jadine takes off on a personal flight of self-affirmation, returning to Europe aware of the loneliness of her quest but happy to meet the challenge posed to her by all the diaspora mothers of her dreams. She is ready to redesign her space in the world and become a more complete being as she welcomes the African in herself (248–50).

Son, by contrast, has always refused to submit to enclosures and rules and remains a wanderer to the end. He would like to hold onto his "tar baby" Jadine and preserve their love, but it is the all-seeing and all-knowing blind Thérèse who leads him to his destination and fate.[86] Perhaps that destination was written on his face; even Jadine had noticed that "spaces, mountains, savannas—all those were in his forehead and eyes" (135). Thérèse knows the waters of the Caribbean Sea and promises to take him to L'Arbe de la Croix, but she leaves him instead on the other side of the island, where blind slaves once landed to inhabit the forest forever. He cannot see anything, but his guide Thérèse assures him that his place is here, for "they are waiting." Son joins the horsemen and the swamp women who are genuine Africans and free, natural people. For Thérèse, Jadine has forgotten "her ancient properties" and should be left behind in his past (263). Besides, the world as Son knew it offered him no true options: in the dark woods of the island, he would finally be able to make choices (262).[87]

Both Jadine and Son must discover a healthy cultural community where they can belong. Son's journey is also private and lonely, but he needs it to allow the good and the great to surface in himself and to substitute wisdom and maturity for his long uncontrolled anger. He goes away to the deep center of the Earth, where the beginning is and the truth of nature lies, a symbolic retreat into the African cultural past that promises renewal and life. Toni Morrison gives Jadine and Son the same guardian angels: leading the way to freedom and awareness are magic women like Thérèse, their breasts nursing the lost children of today, their hands pointing the way to cultural affirmation and true freedom.

The novel is dedicated to the strong women of Morrison's own family, "Mrs. Caroline Smith, Mrs. Millie McTyeire, Mrs. Ardelia Willis, Mrs. Ramah Wofford, and Mrs. Lois Brooks—and each of their sisters, all of whom knew their true and ancient properties." They are Morrison's great-grandmother, grandmother, and other female relations who were "just absolutely clear and reliable" and always retained an "intimate relationship with God and death and all sorts of things that strike fear into the modern heart." In spite of what they suffered in life, they "retained their dignity" and "had to pass it on."[88] Morrison believes that the problems blacks face in contemporary life are insignificant if compared to their historical plight. Their past courage must be remembered if they wish to retain that pride and that strength today.

Even as it explores the complexity of black identity and reinforces memory, *Tar Baby* does not outline clear-cut positions and does not present heroic conclusions. Morrison admits that she has no ready solutions for the questions of racial understanding and general human relationships that afflict her characters and the people of today. In *Tar Baby*, possibly with the exclusion of the mythical blind Africans and the swamp women, there is no one who is always correct and noble and no one who is always wrong and base.[89] Even Thérèse is not able to see the change that Jadine goes through. The blind woman keeps the magic and the rebellious spirit of African ancestors, but she is unable to admit change and diversification. In this novel, Toni Morrison plays with and problematizes binary oppositions of race and class, avoiding a "monologic discourse on racial authenticity."[90]

*Tar Baby* warns of the violence and inequality brought about by slavery and colonialism, a distortion that can be seen in the poverty of so many black people and their dependence on whites, in the barriers between races, and in the continuing control of the economy and culture by traditional white power. What should be done? The alternatives presented are paradoxical and always incomplete.

There is the anthropological answer suggested by Michael Street, who stays away from the corrupting influence of his rich, white family to dedicate himself to underprivileged minorities and cultures threatened with extinction. Valerian and Jadine find his socialist and ecological concerns too romantic and his dream of black people only making and selling crafts too unrealistic. "He wanted a race of exotics skipping around being picturesque for him," argues Valerian (61). They may be often vain and cynical themselves, but here Valerian and Jadine echo an important contemporary critique of classical anthropology and its desire for a pure, crystallized culture among "Third World" peoples.[91]

There is the solution proposed by Son: racial separatism and complete economic independence from the white order. But that may entail escaping to the forgotten Eloe, to a faraway ship, or to maroonage in the forest. For both Michael and Son, the dominant white culture is an enemy threat to be shunned. Its wrongs are immense and unacceptable; the survival of minorities can be attained only outside the controlling order. Their position may sound too radical, but then again, they often voice a powerful critique of the predatory force exhibited by "modern civilization" against people and nature, while other U.S. characters in the novel retain an uncritical aloofness.

There is the struggle of Jadine, who, a black-and-white woman herself, would like to reach a painless and fair compromise between her two sides but is too deeply influenced by Western culture and values to achieve a perfect balance. The novel depicts this kind of social and cultural blend as a problematic, often undesirable, occurrence. Jadine would like to reconcile the contrasting polarities, while Margaret Street tends to pull her to one extreme or the other, "blackening up or universaling out" her mixed physical characteristics. Jadine gropes for a way in between (54). Gideon, the yardman, believes that all "yellow" people like Jadine almost invariably abandon their African roots (133). But Jadine has simply voiced and lived the culture that she learned in school and at home. Unlike the writer, Morrison, Jadine never had a mother and grandmother telling her stories and reconciling her with her African heritage. Her uncle Sydney and aunt Ondine are isolated from a community and cut off from ties with black culture. Even so, Jadine is a young woman who strives for personal definition and independence. In spite of the difficulties, she must negotiate her identity in a complex, multicultural society where Africanness has long been rejected. Jadine chooses to stay on her own in the familiar European environment of fashion and prestige, but in the end she has gained a new awareness of the strength of her Africanness and of the power to assert herself.

*Tar Baby* presents a conflicting dialogue of individual consciences, not a monological, finished theory about the issues it raises. None of the answers found by Michael, Son, and Jadine is totally wrong or totally right. The questions implicit in the novel go beyond the personal dilemmas faced by individual characters to address major issues related to our time and place in this world: Is social and economic equality impossible to be achieved in the Caribbean and the Americas after almost five centuries of an extended colonial rule? How can different classes and races understand one another? How can one be modern, educated, and economically independent without betraying ancient wisdom and cultural roots? Must blacks always side with blacks, no matter what? And must whites always side with whites, as has been traditional in the history of the continent and the world? Should cultural revolution precede an economic and political turnover? Can one compromise with a social order full of inequality and wrong, or should one fight it? Or is it better to simply withdraw? The questions are endless and the answers are tentative and plural, always provisional and circumscribed by place and moment.

## Conclusion

*Song of Solomon* and *Tar Baby* suggest that black history and myth must inform and strengthen not only a separate "black community" but the people and literature of the United States and the Americas as a whole. The stories told by older generations must be recovered and retold, their suffering and resistance remembered and acknowledged in the texts of this multicultural world. The power and nurturance of the diaspora mothers must inspire and support a black youth tempted by nihilism and violence.

Like Gabriel García Márquez in his later works, Toni Morrison does not indicate that armed rebellion or certain political agendas will bring about the desirable social peace. On the contrary, where García Márquez portrays an endless stream of revolutionaries whose wars promote no change or improvement, Morrison creates radicals who are willing to display indiscriminate violence in revenge for the aggressions committed against their race, even if it accomplishes nothing. The urgent need for change is a constant refrain in their novels, but it will result from a comprehensive process involving culture, the economy, politics, and the individual choices of people.

Both Gabriel García Márquez and Toni Morrison tell stories crafted from poetry, fantasy, and myth but deeply grounded in the history and culture of the Americas. For them, history is a broad term: it upholds not only the wars and the laws and the leaders of a people and a nation but also the pains and the joys experienced in the everyday life of the people, their homes, their dreams, their frustrations and hopes. It is, above all, made up of the stories passed on through generation after generation, giving people roots in the past of their culture and the past of the land. The land and the people are in a dynamic state of flux and forever changing. There is no way to preserve a crystallized Macondo or a beautiful Eloe, safe from the decay of age and the corruption of "civilization." Amid the quests and the struggles of the people and the transformation of their geographical space in time, the stories of Morrison and García Márquez above all reaffirm freedom and love, eternal responses to all human longings.

# 4

## The Dry Wombs of Black Women: Memories of Brazilian Slavery in *Corregidora* and *Song for Anninho*

> A magic woman is creating visions and voices and
>    possibilities.
> —Gayl Jones,
>    *Song for Anninho*

Gayl Jones's works reveal a special interest in Brazilian colonial history and a commonality in style and scope with some Latin American writers, Carlos Fuentes in particular. Unlike Paule Marshall and Toni Morrison, who had direct contact and family ties with "the extended Caribbean," Jones's interest in Brazil was triggered by the historiography on race relations. Characters and episodes of Brazilian slave history have found their way into her imagination and writing. Using Brazil as a foil to realities of race and gender in the United States, Gayl Jones retrieves the African presence in the whole process of the creation of America as a continent. In this chapter, I examine the inter-American bridges to Brazilian history and Latin American literature constructed by Gayl Jones in her novel *Corregidora* and in her narrative poem *Song for Anninho*.[1]

The works of Gayl Jones again ask, "What is an American?" this being of mixed races and different colors, and wonder if there is a future even though the past was so full of pain. Unlike classic accounts that privilege the Colombian saga and the European outlook, Jones's exploration of American history looks for the untold feelings of black people under the oppression of slavery and during its aftermath. In the company of Paule Marshall and Toni Morrison, she seeks connections with and explanations for centuries of black history in the Americas, writing from the perspective of a black woman living in the United States during the second half of the twentieth century. The result is a multivocal narrative where races and cultures intersect in a context of violence, complexity, and ambiguity.

Gayl Jones explains her interest in Brazil within a broad Afro-American framework. She would actually like to write about "the whole American continent" and "of blacks anywhere/everywhere." The experience of the "Brazilian history and landscape," even if "purely literary and imaginative," helped her "imagination and writing" and added a new perspective to her understanding of U.S. history.[2] Jones articulates such cultural and historical connections in an intertextual space "in between" the Americas. Besides her interest in the colonial past, Jones has repeatedly expressed her feeling of kinship with contemporary Latin American writers such as Gabriel García Márquez and Carlos Fuentes, who have directly influenced her "notions of fiction." She especially relates to their moral and social responsibility in describing "particular historical and contemporary nightmares," a commitment that she also sees present in the work of other black and Native American writers from the United States.

Aspects in which Latin American novelists have affected Jones's writing include the blend of history and myth in language and the shifts in time and space allowing for broader and deeper perceptions to be translated into writing. Jones singles out their combination of "different kinds of language . . . and of reality" along with their construction of a "relationship between past and present with landscape" as major influences on her work. She admires their use of language, which is "never flat and one-dimensional," never static or bland, and a technically innovative quality that retains deeply human implications. Her personal response goes beyond mere technique; it involves cultural ties and a sense of trust and solidarity that she also feels with writers such as Zora Neale Hurston, in the black tradition, and N. Scott Momaday, a Native American. Jones shares with Latin American writers the wish to write a new *American* narrative, though recognizing its connections with European literary history. They write in European languages, argues Jones, but try to imagine new ways to express a whole "*American* heritage" (the emphasis is hers) that is also "Amerindian and African."[3]

Like Fuentes and García Márquez, Gayl Jones is first of all indebted to her own "people," in her case, black U.S. writers such as Zora Neale Hurston, Alice Walker, Ernest Gaines, Michael Harper, and Jean Toomer. But she also shares with the two Latin American writers of the "boom" generation an admiration for such writers as James Joyce and Ernest Hemingway; Miguel de Cervantes looms large in their literary backgrounds. Jones relates the storytelling of the Spanish master to "the picaresque Afro-American slave narrative."[4] She studied Spanish language and literature in graduate school during the 1970s, a factor that certainly enhanced her interest in the Spanish author and in the culture of Latin America and that gave her a sense of familiarity with that literature and culture. The polyglot, hybrid nature of her style mirrors the mixture of the people who inhabit the Americas and her text. As a reader of other literary and historical texts, Jones creates an intertextual narrative that is transgressively American.

In addition to the influence of Latin American writers on the scope and style of her storytelling, Gayl Jones's research on slave history in Brazil informs a kind of work that is original and unique.[5] In her first novel, *Corregidora* (1975), as well as in the narrative poem *Song for Anninho* (1981), characters spring directly out of Brazilian history, which, for Jones, is part of the "collective past" of the African diaspora that she attempts to bring into her own stories. Ursa and Almeyda, the respective female protagonists in the two works, are linked to Brazilian slavery. Ursa significantly embodies the ongoing inter-American debate with her unusual combination of a present identity in Kentucky—like the author's—and an ancestry rooted in the Brazilian slave system. Ursa is the great-granddaughter and granddaughter of female slaves and their Brazilian master, Corregidora, whose name is carried on as a sign of oppression by the four generations of women transplanted to the United States. Almeyda in *Song for Anninho* is a seventeenth-century female slave kidnapped from a sugar plantation in northeastern Brazil by runaway male slaves from the Republic of Palmares, the largest and longest-lived Maroon settlement in Brazil and in the Americas.[6] Through Ursa and Almeyda, Jones rewrites historical records long dominated by an upper-class, white, male perspective. The characters bring a black woman's imagination, her dreams and nightmares, into that narrative.

Although Gayl Jones's stories spring out of her interest in Brazilian history and its connections with the North American experience of slavery, they are far from being dry accounts of "what really happened." They are highly personal, psychological explorations that reflect Jones's wish to make "some kind of relationship between history and autobiography."[7] That history, like the autobiography, is in many ways her own, since the drive to understand the relations between blacks and whites and between women and men under slavery motivates her writing as much as her own struggle with the traditional female roles of wife and mother.

Gayl Jones is among the many U.S. writers who have looked beyond the southern borders of this country, particularly toward Brazil, in search of a clearer understanding of the plight and the legacy of Africans in their diaspora.[8] She is an original presence among scholars who have explored Brazilian slavery and its abolition. Her version of history has the point of view and the artistic and cultural specificity of a black woman writer born in 1949 in Lexington, Kentucky; raised and educated until the tenth grade in segregated schools; and later influenced by education and professionalization in two academic institutions in the East, Connecticut College and Brown University. With an identification and a solidarity based on gender and race, Jones brings out of forgetfulness voices of black women abused in the Brazilian past. She joins them with black female voices of today in a single chorus of collective memories. Together, they embrace the struggles and the oppression of black men in the tragedy that slavery and segregation have signified in the history of the continent.

Because of its large size and its position as largest importer of slaves in the *New World*, Brazil has constantly played the role of foil to the U.S. system. Brazil was "by far the largest single participant in the traffic, accounting for 41% of the total" of the approximate number of 9.9 million Africans who "were forcibly transported across the Atlantic," while the United States accounted for only 7 percent of that number.[9] By contrast, the slave population in the United States expanded from the original 600,000 Africans to the approximate number of 4.4 million by 1860, which made the United States "the nation with the largest number of slaves in the nineteenth century," with a very small percentage of free blacks.[10]

Brazil began importing Africans early and stopped doing it late, continuing the slave trade until 1850 and slavery until May 13, 1888, when slavery was at last abolished in the country and throughout the continent. Manumission had occurred with great frequency in Brazil, however, so the actual number of slaves was then lower than the free population of color.[11] Statistical data have been interpreted to support the opposing viewpoints that "corroborate" the goodness of the Portuguese-Brazilian planter who let so many slaves free before abolition and was supposedly less repressive, on the one hand, or the healthiness of the U.S. slave system, which showed much higher survival and reproduction rates among slaves than elsewhere in the Americas, on the other hand.

Since the 1960s, historical scholarship has made a greater effort to demystify the plantation system by placing the Portuguese not a degree higher or lower than other European slaveowners.[12] Studies have shown that the more frequent manumissions in Brazil largely resulted from structural conditions (such as the small number of white settlers). In turn, racial discrimination became more evident as large numbers of white European immigrants were brought in to make up for the loss of slave labor and to help populate (some would say whiten) the Brazilian territory after mid-nineteenth century.

In the last three decades, scholars in the two countries have re-evaluated the economic, political, and social aspects of the system of slavery in its different modalities.[13] The miscegenation and interpenetration of cultures lauded by Brazilian sociologist Gilberto Freyre have not yet brought the desired social and economic equality between the two extremes in the color scale. The loose racial classification adopted in Brazil and Latin America has been the source of heated scholarly controversy: while to some scholars such as Marvin Harris and Carl Degler it seems less oppressive than in the United States, others find it an invitation to hypocrisy and persisting social inequality.[14] Rather than a true sign of multiculturalism, the Brazilian color scale may actually reveal "a painful and deceiving magic," for society keeps denying blacks a desired social mobility and reinforcing their condition of inferiority.[15]

Only in the last two decades has there been a concerted effort by academic spheres to hear marginal voices and face the true reality witnessed by women, blacks, and Indians in Brazil. Former slaves narrate their memories, African descendants retell stories, and black people describe their own experiences with discrimination in the world of today. In the United States, Gayl Jones participates in this revision and rewriting of Brazil and the Americas with *Corregidora* and *Song for Anninho*. Regardless of similarities and differences between slave systems, Jones's own historical research undoubtedly showed her that blacks are oppressed today much as they were yesterday, all over the Americas; and that they have been kept voiceless for too long. Her stories are imaginative accounts of the personal dilemmas encountered by black women under slavery and afterward, an attempt to give them a voice.

## *Corregidora:*
## Bridging the United States and Brazil

The novel *Corregidora* is a disturbing love story that describes the intimate life of Ursa Corregidora, a mulatto woman from Kentucky, from the time of her marriage to Mutt Thomas in December 1947 to their reunion twenty-two years later. When the story begins, Ursa is a beautiful and attractive young woman; by the end, she is almost forty-eight, lonely, hurt, but still attractive, looking younger than her age (174). Mutt is then an older, "solider," and "changed" man, who returns after all those years to confess how much he had missed her and to ask her back. As she says yes, they return to the same Drake Hotel where they had spent the four months of 1948 that their marriage had lasted (182–84).

Thus simplified, the story seems as thrilling and profound as any grocery-store rack romance. Gayl Jones, however, adds to it an immense, almost insurmountable burden of hate and repression, centuries of dark memories passed on from generation to generation of black women—Corregidora's women, all insistently named Corregidora to evoke the pain. Jones connects them to the violence against black women perpetuated in the present, disrupting female identity and sexuality and undermining the possibility of love.

The setting for *Corregidora* is urban Kentucky, often the inside of a bar where Ursa sings the blues, under the greedy eyes of men and the jealousy of husband, Mutt. Her singing job and the men's gaze lead Mutt to alcohol and madness. In Ursa's own words, "He didn't like for me to sing after we were married because he said that's why he married me so he could support me" (3). A patriarchal framework shapes Ursa's life as much as it had shaped her great-grandmother's; the only difference is that now she is legally married and her husband is black. Mutt commands like the Corregidora master: "I'm your husband. You listen to me. . . . I don't like those mens messing with you" (3). Struggling to get away from his violence in one of their angry fights, Ursa falls down the stairs and loses the baby she is expecting. Mutt was drunk and beat her down, pleading later that he did not mean it. The horror of the scene and its consequences are traumatic: Ursa loses the baby, her womb, and the ability to surrender herself to love (4, 6, 25).

Ursa's sense of sterility and loss will remain a constant part of her solitude. Leaving Mutt, she finds it is impossible to return the passion that Tadpole, the owner of Happy's Café and her protector after the fall, expects from her. Neither can she accept the offers of love from two women across the street, Catherine Dawson (Cat) and Jeffrene (Jeffy). All sexual pleasure has been taken from her, much as it had been denied to black women in bondage. "He made them make love to anyone, so they couldn't love anyone" (104). Ursa's search for love takes her across gender boundaries and transgresses conventional heterosexual mores, even in its frustration.

Within this insistent crisscrossing of the boundaries of nations, races, genders, and cultural conventions, Gayl Jones specifically conflates racial and gender subordination and identifies male privilege as a separate axis of power. In the novel, any man is still Corregidora in many ways. Even the usually more gentle and thoughtful Tadpole, Ursa's second husband, reenacts forms of patriarchal domination and is confused with the slaveholder in Ursa's mind (19, 68). Why Ursa should have different sexual needs from his, for instance, is a matter beyond his comprehension. The parallels are closer between Corregidora and Mutt, Ursa's first husband and the man who "dried her womb." Mutt insists that he loves her, but she rejects his dominating and violent ways: "Is that the way you treat someone you love?" (46). Her memories and dreams of Mutt constantly overlap with images of her white ancestor; the old man howls inside her when she thinks of Mutt caressing her body or "bruising her seeds."

In fact, Mutt has inherited the sexist morality established in the Americas by the colonial system: he wants to possess a woman, to control her and brand her as his property. In or out of slavery, women have no names of their own. They always "belong" to men, whose names they take and whose orders they obey. Jealousy is simply a macho war, a question of territorial control over the woman's name, body, and life. From the beginning, Mutt resents Ursa not taking his name when they marry: "*Ain't even took my name. You Corregidora's, ain't you? . . . You ain't my woman*" (61). The pronouns "he" and "him" are often used ambiguously in the novel, suggesting the actual blurring of male figures in Ursa's mind and the generalized ideology of patriarchal society (10, 15, 16).

Ursa's nightmarish dreams bring back Corregidora as a father-lover who also claims her as one of his women. She blames both Corregidora and Mutt for the "silence in [her] womb." Black women had undergone abuse and rape for so long that she feels Mutt should now suffer the burden of guilt that Corregidora did not have: "He got a lifetime of feeling guilt. I don't know how many lifetimes" (34). The madness of slavery is perpetuated through the persisting violence of men and through the parallel obsession running in Ursa and her family, a clan of lonely women dedicated to remembering Corregidora and revenging their past (99).

Gilberto Freyre's well-known book *The Masters and the Slaves* seems to have provided a departing point for characters and episodes in *Corregidora*. The "terrible but fraternizing" system that Freyre describes (very much in the voice of an heir to yesterday's slaveholders) probably represented a major push for Gayl Jones to rewrite that history through Ursa Corregidora. Ursa is the bastard great-granddaughter of "a Portuguese seaman turned plantation owner" named Corregidora and his favorite slave girl, his "little gold piece" called Dorita (10). Freyre argues that the warm climate and languorous nature of Brazil stimulated the frequent physical and cultural encounter of Portuguese men and African slave women, leading to a privileged "absence of violent rancors due to race." Instead of being devoted to whiteness or bound by Christian morality, like the southern U.S. planter, according to Freyre, the Portuguese developed a taste, if not a preference, for the mulatto woman, "at least for purposes of physical love."[16] In Freyre's opinion, the Catholic church stimulated sexuality and resembled African religions. It was "softened" and "lyric," full of "phallic and animistic reminiscences of the pagan cults," quite different from "the hard and rigid system of Reformed countries." Freyre describes Brazil's beginnings in a "milieu . . . of sexual intoxication" in which the master had no scruples in abusing slave women to "increase the herd and the paternal capital."[17] With *Corregidora*, Gayl Jones adds an ironic and tragic twist to Freyre's view of miscegenation as a source of unity and peace.

What were the feelings of the slave woman? Her opinions were not asked, and they did not matter for the dominant society, as Freyre himself realized.[18] How conscious was she of the exploitation? What were its consequences on relationships between blacks? In her ground-breaking study of 1988, Brazilian historian Sonia Giacomini could find no data providing concrete answers to those questions.[19] Gayl Jones probably faced similar concerns as she sorted through the controversies among the several comparative historians who have elaborated studies of the Brazilian slave system.

As Jones pondered over Freyre and other established historians (normally male and white) during her graduate studies at Brown University in the 1970s, the lost memories of slave women and the unwritten history of their plight found form in *Corregidora* and *Song for Anninho*. "Writing is a very responsible thing," Jones argues, and it is necessary to connect "oral traditions and written documentation," as she attempts in her work, "to counteract the effects of false documentations," particularly regarding the histories of black peoples and Native Americans.[20] She sides with Paule Marshall and Toni Morrison in her commitment to the history of her race in the *New World*.

Jones imagines the underside of history, "the picture not taken" of slave women and their bastard daughters. Unlike most historians and sociologists, she decides to explore the more intimate and complex aspects of slavery. Yet her focus on the sadism and the disruption caused by slavery in Brazil recalls the pervading description of such aspects in the work of Gilberto Freyre. Even though Freyre ultimately places strong emphasis on the positive consequences of the master–slave interaction and miscegenation, he also provides graphic reports of the sadomasochistic quality of those relations and the disruptive effects of slavery on the colonial psyche. He portrays both slave and master as victims of a cruel system: the slave was physically deformed and turned "pathogenic," but the master was also led to insanity by the brutal and depraved system. Divided between true affection for his black nurse, his childhood friends, and his *mucama* lover, on the one hand, and the unchecked power that he had over them all, on the other hand, the slavemaster was shattered by internal conflicts, which he frequently expressed in sadism and violence against blacks and which reflected in his own physical and mental deterioration. An unequal and disturbing reality of sadomasochism characterized the relations between the European man and the Indian or African women under his control.[21]

Gayl Jones focuses on the brutal show of power by slaveowners and by men in general over women. Sadism, violence, and incest are part of the obsessive heritage brought down to her character Ursa from the Brazilian and entire American past. Ursa's name may vary, from U.C. to Ursa Corre or Corregidora, but in all cases, she carries the past in her identity and in those names, a past that her mother, her grandmothers, and she herself were unwilling to "unname" and forget (4–8). Hate should be kept burning, for the evil had been too great; they could never let go of this man who had abused their bodies for his pleasure and profit, for generation after generation (9).

The Corregidora women refused to discard the hateful name and the tragic past, never assuming a new, proud identity under an African name, as many Black Nationalists have done, or even adopting the names of their husbands, as the majority of women in the Americas still tend to do. Rather, the Corregidora women preferred to keep a fierce hold on the memory of their master and that of their own victimization. The consequences are contradictory and paradoxical, because their oppression is intensified and prolonged in their form of resistance, yet their memory preserves a story otherwise left untold. It gives effective testimony against the fires that burned facts about the Africans and the slave trade, the useful forgetfulness upheld by the system, and the lies told in the history that the dominant order eagerly generated. Ursa makes specific reference to the burning of slave-trade documents that was ordered in 1891 by the minister of finances in Brazil, Rui Barbosa: "When they did away with slavery down there they burned all the slavery papers so it would be like they never had it" (9).[22]

Without an organized front of anti-abolitionist slaveowners, Brazilian emancipation was characterized by the overwhelming intellectual and popular support made possible by the lateness of its occurrence and by the very formation of the population. In *Corregidora*, Gayl Jones imagines an ex-slave account of the happy celebration of freedom in Brazil. Ursa hears about Princess Isabella (Isabel in history) signing the decree passed by the legislature in 1888, outlawing slavery forever. People celebrate it by dancing in a Carnival in the streets.[23] Her women characters contrast the remembered Brazilian event with the tragic Civil War in the U.S. South: *"They signed papers, and there wasn't all this warring like they had up here. You know, it was what they call pacific. . . . People was celebrating and rejoicing and cheering in the street, white people and black people"* (78).

In *Corregidora*, the memories, hearts, and especially the wombs of women are archives. In the face of the continuing denial of rights and history to African descendants, these personal archives are the living records of the women's past. The burning of papers in Brazil is symbolic of the pillage and destruction done throughout the continent against the memory of Africans and their descendants. A new, reverse burning is needed now to destroy the influence of white colonialists: *"We got to burn out what they put in our minds, like you burn out a wound. . . . That scar that's left to bear witness. We got to keep it as visible as our blood"* (72). Great Gram had determined that the role of her female descendants should be the preservation and embodiment of truth to counter the erasure of their history. She passes on the mission: *"'I'm leaving evidence [of what they done]. And you got to leave evidence too. And your children got to leave evidence, we got to have evidence to hold up. That's why they burned all the papers, so there wouldn't be no evidence to hold up against them'"* (14).

Gayl Jones problematizes the ideal of motherhood and the traditional reliance on the bond between mother and child as the foundation of most cultures in the world. There certainly has been a premium put on procreation in West Africa, so one could argue that the option *not* to have children goes against memory and against "black traditions."[24] Ironically, procreation was also extremely valued by slaveowners in colonial times. Ursa explains to Catherine the heroic mission of the Corregidora women, their need to "make generations" to keep alive the memory of the past. Her friend is not as convinced of the validity and ethics of their vows. Although the Corregidora women have insisted that procreation is a form of resistance and power against the oppressor, Cat knows that it is a weapon for the oppressor as well, "a slave-breeder's way of thinking" (22). Such contrasting arguments reflect the ambiguities and paradoxes that Gayl Jones approaches in this complex novel.

Catherine perceives the contradiction behind the revenge set up by the Corregidora women, just as she finds Ursa's determination only to "see what I need to see" excessively restrictive and blinding (35). Those women allow no man to really enter their lives, because they are dedicated to the memory and the picture of their master. Their icon is grotesque, and his cult is prolonged in the name of hate: *"That's what evil look like"* (12). Corregidora's portrait resembles the syphilitic, decadent, and mad Portuguese planter described by Freyre: he went mad, as *"they all do"* (99).[25] When his health deteriorated, Corregidora firmly believed that his slaves had worked some black, evil magic against him.[26] Great Gram thinks he simply *"had a stroke or something,"* although he certainly deserved any amount of evil (11). In the photograph they keep of him, to "know who to hate," he appears "tall, [with] white hair, white beard, white mustache, a old man with a cane and one of his feet turned outward." He looks devilishly mad, with "neck bent forward like he was raging at something that wasn't there" (10).

In the stories that she passed on to her family, Ursa's Great Gram still recalled the younger Corregidora, "*a big strapping man*" with "*hair black and straight and greasy*" that made him look like a Creek Indian. He was very conscious of the class difference separating Indians from Europeans, however, and "*if you said [it] he'd get mad and beat you*" (11). Jones echoes historical accounts by Freyre and others that have emphasized the mestizo color of the Portuguese, in contrast with the purely European Anglo-Saxons.[27] Corregidora is described as a sea captain from Portugal who received "lands . . . slaves and things" from the king. He was an indolent and sickly man who had no scruples in commercializing the bodies of slave women to pay for his leisure and pleasures (23).

The mad abuse of women in slavery is told over and over, from daughter to daughter, repeated like a refrain throughout the novel, a tale that Jones wants to have remembered by all readers and Americans. Ursa wants to bear responsibility for her part in passing on the tradition, but her seeds were "wounded forever" by Mutt. They were "burned" like the Brazilian documents and can no longer testify. Was this an accident? Catherine thinks so, but Ursa cannot forgive Mutt (45, 41). She feels guilty and ashamed for not fulfilling her role as a Corregidora woman; she wants or has been taught to want "to make generations" (22). Only very gradually does Ursa admit to herself that their pledge may not be completely right. The cult of fertility was a major element of African religions, but their tradition of honoring the dead and praying to the gods for fertility did not have that burden of hatred and revenge. The African tradition of it could not make sense in a sterile and hostile world.[28] Ursa's conflicts and contradictions in *Corregidora,* including those over the issue of childbearing, have much to do with the social pressures on blacks and on women at the time the novel was written. They also bear a close relationship with Gayl Jones's own life. Ursa's relationships, says Jones, "could be 'translated' into details in [her] own life," and Corregidora, beyond the historical intertext, "is really a metaphor for things in [her] own experience." "Making generations" was a conflict for Gayl Jones before it materialized in her novel: "Since I was twelve I decided that I wasn't going to ever get married and have children. . . . But then I realized that when you make that kind of decision, you're not making it for yourself, you're making it for your mother and your grandmother . . . and your great-grandmother."[29] By asking her "What about the generations?" Gayl Jones's mother disturbed her resolution not to bear children and left her with a sense of guilt and ambivalence. Jones makes her character Ursa face similar dilemmas, as she wonders whether the lives and the children of Corregidora women have simply remained controlled by the white master or whether she is betraying the memory of her oppressed ancestors by thinking that way. Ursa's sterile womb allows her to escape that domination and that obsession after all. There is actually no choice or decision on Ursa's part, and the novel's dramatic ambiguities constantly undermine classic dichotomies of good and bad, black and white, love and hate. Ursa wavers between a loyalty to the women of her family and a wish to be finally free: "I *am* different now. . . . I can't make generations. And even if I still had my womb, even if the first baby had come—what would I have done then? Would I have kept it up? Would I have been like *her,* or them?" (60).

Ursa's personal experiences often echo the past that she would like to forget. Her marriages recall stories told by her women ancestors. When still a child in the Portuguese colony of Brazil, Great Gram had been a favorite for Corregidora: "*She was the pretty little one with the almond eyes and coffee-bean skin, his favorite . . . his little gold piece . . . Dorita.*" Such favoritism made her life no easier. The "gold piece" was abused both for the master's sexual gratification and for the pleasure—and the money—of other landowners (10, 124). Ironically, Mutt repeats the expression "my little gold piece" to describe Ursa's sex decades later, thus reinforcing and blending together crippling memories (60). The signing of papers to divorce Tadpole also provides Ursa with an ironic connection between her and the abolition; she "was a free woman again, whatever that meant" (173).

Why did Gayl Jones depict a Portuguese rather than an English planter as the hateful "whoremonger and breeder" of her novel? Freyre's early studies on comparative slavery certainly helped spread the idea that sexual intercourse between the male slaveholder and his female house servants was much more common in Brazil than in the United States. Such wider miscegenation in Brazil would explain the higher degree of cultural and social pluralism in that country. All

Portuguese men in the northeast of Brazil had children with their slaves, according to Freyre: "Bastards, natural sons—what sugar planter did not have them in large number?"[30] In Brazil, as in the Caribbean, the practice of concubinage was largely institutionalized.

Historiography has long confused the practice of interracial relations with its acceptability. Along Freyrean lines, Stanley Elkins contrasts the "closed and circumscribed" social system in the United States and the complete "disciplinary authority" of its masters with the "confusing promiscuity of color" in Spanish-Portuguese colonies, "such as would never have been thinkable in our country." According to Carl Degler, sexual contact between whites and their slaves did occur in the South, though the practice of using female slaves as prostitutes and a source of income for the master was "virtually unknown" there.[31] Eugene Genovese argues that in the U.S. South there was also "ostensible seduction and imposed lust" but not the harem imagined by "abolitionist fantasies." Marriage vows and moral rules were strongly enforced among whites in the United States, while Brazilian Portuguese males would "sow their wild oats with happy abandon" and not feel the "psychic agony and social opprobrium" that a U.S. southerner would feel if he took black "wenches" for pleasure.[32]

With or without guilt, in hiding or in the open, the white man sought the bodies of black women. Pierre L. van den Berghe, among many other scholars, insists that although concubinage was more acceptable in Brazil than in the United States, "there is no indication that miscegenation was relatively more common in Latin America than in the English colonies" during the colonial period.[33] More recent scholarship has tended to avoid generalizations about sexual life and childbearing based on nationality and country. It prefers to focus on specific variations of demographic patterns even within the same country and region on the basis of plantation size, proportional number of male to female slaves and blacks to whites, and the kind of work performed by slaves.

The patriarchal environment of sadism and violence often pitted white women against black slave women on both southern U.S. and Brazilian plantations. Violent treatment of slaves was common. The slave woman carried the triple burden of enforced labor, sexual abuse, and breeding "little niggers for Massa," and in addition, she would often be brutally abused by the mistress, as Jacqueline Jones found to have been the case on U.S. plantations. Because of jealousy of the real or suspected infidelity of their husbands and "to vent their anger on victims even more wronged than themselves," mistresses attacked slave women "with any weapon available—knitting needles, tongs, a fork, butcher knife, ironing board, or pan of boiling water," which often resulted "in the mutilation or permanent scarring of their female servants."[34]

The black slave woman thus suffered twice for a sexual encounter that she did not pursue. In Brazil as in the United States, she was stereotyped as a strong, lascivious being, ready for sexual contact. In the U.S. southern mentality, she was often perceived as a Jezebel "governed almost entirely by her libido . . . the counterimage of the mid-nineteenth century ideal of the Victorian lady."[35] Judgment was passed on the basis of the nudity, polygamy, and religious ceremonies in her African background, all of which were associated by Europeans with lewdness, lust, and promiscuity. She was the evil serpent that tempted good white men out of their righteous tracks. By contrast, the black woman's capacity for breeding was especially prized by the southern slavery system; the use of breeders seems to have been more common in the United States than in Brazil. According to historian Deborah Gray White, "American slavery was dependent on natural increase of the slave population," which was stimulated through "numerous incentives" and proper conditions for breeding.[36]

Gayl Jones's *Corregidora* decries the sacrifice of so many black women, brutalized and animalized by the cruel patriarchal slave system. Jones is not interested in establishing a clear-cut line of distinction between Brazilian and U.S. southern conditions or in providing support to statistics. As a black woman, she identifies with the generations of slave women abused by European men in the colonial past, and she attempts to rescue their feelings and sorrows. She associated the oral history learned from her family with her own observations and her reading of historians and sociologists who emphasized the pathological effects of slavery on blacks and whites. The setting of her novel is Brazil, but the sacrifice of young women happened everywhere. She writes in her novel, "How many generations had to bow to his genital fantasies? . . . And you with the coffee-bean face, what were you? You were sacrificed. They knew you only by the signs of your sex. They touched you as if you were magic" (59).

Great Gram and Corregidora symbolize three centuries of the "peculiar institution" in different regions of Brazil, with their several economic cycles rooted in the exhaustion of male and female black bodies. He is the archetypal colonizer and master, a sea captain turned planter of coffee and sugarcane (10–11, 124), with properties surrounded by other plantations of cane, cotton, coffee, and tobacco and by mines for gold.[37] Raped by the master and other men, Ursa's great-grandmother embodies all slave women exploited by masters throughout the "extended Caribbean."

In Brazil as elsewhere, the landowners manipulated the lives of slaves as they pleased, regardless of their feelings, their married state, or the existence of children.[38] In Gayl Jones's novel, the master Corregidora ruled over the bodies and the lives of his slave women. None of them was allowed to sleep with black male slaves (124, 127). Great Gram's sons were sold, a memory so painful for her that it could not be talked about (61). The master's violence was indiscriminate in the fields, in the houses, and in bed. Jones describes it as a sadistic sex show that abused blacks for the entertainment of bored whites: "All them beatings and killings wasn't nothing but sex circuses, and all of them white peoples, mens, womens, and childrens crowding around to see" (125). The novel depicts prostitution as a carefully organized activity that made distinctions between prize women and the average ones, all of whom were at the mercy of the master's whims. While the common whores were "trash" to be "sent . . . into them" in one room, the favorite ones had private rooms and were given only the "cultivated men" (124).

In the understanding of Great Gram, sex came to mean rape by a white despot while black feet ran away, hunted by hounds and mobs in the fields (128). In her memories, a black woman lived only for the service and pleasure of white men. Ursa's grandmother much later replays the role that her race had been given in Brazil, as if she has incorporated the spirit of those times. In her own home in Kentucky, she powders her nakedness and lifts her breasts under the startled observation of her son-in-law Martin. She consciously caresses her body and provokes him, and then cruelly, with the spirit of Corregidora, she spurns his black presence from the room and from her daughter's life. "You black bastard . . . what you doing watching me? . . . You ain't had no right messing with my girl" (130).

Similar echoes of racism and sexism absorbed from the colonial rule recur in the novel, many times in a displacement of anger turned by blacks against blacks. Frantz Fanon's arguments regarding the domination of the hegemonic ideas of the colonizer over the colonized and peoples of color seem to reverberate in the story. Ursa's feelings of loss and failure for not being able to bear children any longer have to do with the pledge to tell the truth to future generations, but they may also reflect the incorporation of the breeding role traditionally imposed on women by the dominant society, inherited from colonial times when women were valued for their capacity to procreate (127). Because Ursa has no womb, she wonders, "Now, what good am I for a man?" (25).

Nineteenth-century writer Silveira Martins said that "Brazil is coffee, and coffee is the Negro." At an earlier period Brazil was sugar, "and sugar is the Negro."[39] Coffee and sugar mix together, and the sweet blackness in the coffee cup is gulped down with unthinking pleasure by the whole plantation society, the inner bitterness disguised and transformed. Gayl Jones insistently remarks on the coffee-bean color of the matriarch Great Gram, and also scatters the seeds and grains of exploitation throughout her story.

In the twentieth century, pretty black women are still kept as house servants and whores, having their coffee blackness appreciated only for sexual pleasure. When Catherine's employer, Thomas Hirshorn, tries to touch her with the sweet talk that "nigger women is pretty," she spills coffee grounds on the floor of the kitchen. Like a modern planter, Hirshorn does not hesitate to call her "clumsy nigger" when his wife comes into the room (65–66). Today, as before, the black woman is perceived as having no feelings, an easy target of the lust and the violence of the dominant society. For centuries, the black woman has been sexually abused and then blamed as sinful, hot-blooded, and lustful.

As a counterpart, the sexual drives of white Christian wives have long been repressed and denied. The early and frequent deaths of European women in the Portuguese colony point to the other side of the same coin of male domination. Such illnesses and deaths have been traditionally justified by the hardships of the climate, an explanation that the novel seems both to uphold and to contradict. In the stories told by Great Gram in *Corregidora*, the white wife was both victim and abuser, a grotesque, sad woman who spills her revenge on the black woman slave but also sleeps with her (13). Weak and sickly, the wife dies early; she was able to breed only "a little sick rabbit" that barely survived one day (23). In *Song for Anninho*, the white mistress who silently smiles as she watches the bleeding of

Almeyda also carries a baby who sucks at her breast all the time; the mistress is as cruel as she is lifeless and sickly (*SA*, 29). According to historical records, white mistresses often used slave bodies for their own convenience, sexual or commercial. In *Corregidora*, some are even said to have promoted slave prostitution so that they could have some money for themselves (*C*, 23).

The picture that Gayl Jones creates of the past is violent and grotesque, a tale of machismo and decadence where abuse is the norm. Corregidora's wife exemplifies the forms of extreme sadism that took over the white woman in the colony, maddened by solitude and envy, herself a victim who takes revenge on those below her. Her violence is again disruptive to herself, because she hurts exactly the woman who could be ally (and lover, in Jones's novel) against the domination of the common master. As often is the case told in journals and history books, the master in the story despises his wife and is almost as violent with her as with the slaves. The wife's repressed anger and shame spills over Great Gram's body and she tries to hurt Great Gram with "hot prongs" between her legs. As Corregidora caught her in the attempt, he *"knocked the prongs out of her hands and then he started beating her."* The wife *"went crazy"* and died shortly afterward (172).

All the stories and memories make Ursa dread the white man that she carries in her mind and in her face. She needs only to look at a picture of herself to realize the shadow of Corregidora under her eyes. She suffers the dilemma of the mulatto who rejects what she is, her name, her long hair, her "evil" soul, for they were imposed on her race by a slaveholder (42). Ursa would never admit that some of her beauty might have come from him (46). She would like to deny her mulatto condition and all that it symbolizes. She had hoped to be "different," less Corregidora, but the past is inescapable: "When I saw that picture, I knew I had it. The mulatto women" (60).

Would Ursa feel the same conflicts if she had been raised in Brazil? The historiography familiar to Gayl Jones would probably say no. Even if both countries privilege light skin, they treat people of mixed color differently. In the United States, the white part in Ursa is considered legally "invisible," even if her face shows evidence of the mixture of different bloods.[40] It is revealing that Gayl Jones makes Ursa look like an Hispanic person, a *morena*, as Audre Lorde was once described in Mexico, and that Ursa should describe herself as "American." She is indeed a hybrid and thoroughly American, mixing two races, two hemispheres, and several continents in her memory and her blood:

> "What are you?" he asked.
> "I'm an American."
> "I know you a American," he said. "But what nationality. You Spanish?"
> "Naw."
> "You look like Spanish." (71)

Ursa struggles between past and present, between her own painful memories and the darker memories of her ancestors, between the bloods that she carries in herself; an identity in search of peace and definition. The burden of American history weighs heavy on her: "Shit, we're all consequences of something. Stained with another's past as well as our own. Their past in my blood. . . . My veins are centuries meeting" (45–46). In a similar way, Almeyda in *Song for Anninho* asks, "Am I a woman, or the memory of a woman?" (*SA*, 35).

Almost as much as she rejects Corregidora, Ursa rejects the thought of loving Mutt after all his violence. Still, her dreams keep bringing Mutt back in a mixture of resentment and desire. Can she hate and at the same time love? Ursa's dreams revolve around that paradox. Release comes only through her singing of the blues: "When do you sing the blues? Every time I ever want to cry, I sing the blues" (*C*, 46). The songs have come out of the tales of oppression and sorrow hummed by Grandma, from the "pages of . . . suppressed hysteria" in the lives of black women (59). Ursa's mother hid her own sorrow in the Christian comforting messages of a Baptist church, but the tales she passed on to her daughter come translated from the past as sad "devil's music" (54).

For Ursa, the blues help explain what she "can't explain" (56). She wants to put the painful conflicts of her own life and of the lives of all black women in song, and the blues seem exactly "a song branded with the new world." (59). In a voice that comes out "strong and hard but gentle underneath," like the "callused hands" of her people in the fields of America, her music reflects the paradox that she feels about Mutt and that her ancestors may have felt toward Corregidora: "hurt you and make you still want to listen" (96).

The blues also translate Ursa's own mixture of Europe and Africa and allow her to express the sorrow of the mulatto woman split between a white world that either denies or exploits her and a black world that distrusts her (69). In the United States, as in Brazil, a beautiful mulatto woman is still associated with adultery and lust, both by whites and blacks. In the novel, Ursa is perceived as a threat by women in the black Baptist church of Bracktown, where Mama lived. The ghost of Mrs. Corregidora seems to lurk behind the ugly voices of black women coming out of church and wondering if Ursa is "some new bitch from out of town going to be trying to take everybody's husband" (73).

*Corregidora* explores the ironies of the mulatto stereotype through the character Ursa. Rather than making Ursa a lustful woman, her conflicting, mixed heritage robs her (as well as her mother and grandmother) of the enjoyment of natural sexual drives. The self-denial and frigidity of the Corregidora women, Gayl Jones suggests, are a consequence of the old and persisting abuse of black women in the Americas. In a patriarchal society, men have traditionally brought violence and disruption into women's lives and sometimes destroyed even their wish to remain alive. As a child, Ursa heard from her Gram that she "ain't never known a woman take her life less it was some man" (133). Her "experienced" school friend May Alice fails to show her a pleasant side of sexuality. In her account, women simply give in to male sexual drives, regardless of their own needs: "You wouldn't feel you had any right to tell them to stop," says May Alice (140). Women's role to give pleasure and submit to male demands has not changed with the modern age.

Lesbianism is introduced in the novel as a possible alternative to frustrating heterosexuality, but it proves just as prone to violence and deceit. After she becomes pregnant, the teenager May Alice suggests that sexual relationships with other women would be harmless and safer (141). It may also be more fulfilling, Ursa's friend Cat Lawson will add years later. May Alice's description of the paradoxical mixture of pain and pleasure, rejection and attraction, in heterosexual relationships will resonate in Ursa's adult mind as she tries to understand contradictions in her own (and her ancestors') life (156, 163).

French anthropologist Roger Bastide has said that "the mulatto in Brazil sets the picture of the black mother in the kitchen, and, in the place of honor in the living room, the portrait of the white father."[41] In *Corregidora*, Gayl Jones explores the ambiguous possibilities of mirrors and portraits. It is Corregidora that Ursa sees in her reflection in the mirror. A picture of the master Corregidora and a piece of classic colonial furniture are the palpable items marking the cultural heritage brought from Brazilian slavery. The only concrete relic that the Corregidora women keep from that country, besides the photograph of the master, is "an expensive dark-mahogany" china cabinet "imported from Brazil" (123; the first time Brazil is named in the novel). The cabinet is kept sparkling and immaculate, as in the old plantation houses, a piece of the "casa-grande" described by Gilberto Freyre. But what has happened to the African religions and deities, the drums, the herbs, the music, and the dancing so common in Brazil? In *Corregidora*, Jones disregards African retentions and influences, choosing to emphasize the cultural vacuum created by slavery, the confusion of identities, and the psychological rupture. Only in *Song for Anninho* does she turn to "the world that Africans made" in Brazil and their legacy for America as a whole.[42]

Slave rebellions of an individual or a collective nature were common occurrences in Brazil, but for the Corregidora women such forms of resistance seemed out of the question. In Brazilian colonial history, slaves many times ran away, rebelled in large armed revolts, or killed their masters, but horrible punishment was certain to come if they were caught alive by the "mob and hounds" that hunted them. Many *quilombos*—villages of runaway Negroes, hidden in the mountains or forests—existed in several states from beginning to end of the institution of slavery, but Corregidora's slaves had heard of only one such village, Palmares.

Concerned with emphasizing the oppression of slavery, Gayl Jones focuses *Corregidora* on the hopelessness and fear of women slaves; escape was always more difficult and rare for them. A woman's revenge would have to be private, done in bed, such as cutting off the master's penis, even if the punishment for the act was twice as bloody as the act itself (67). Great Gram's young black friend at the plantation dreamed of "running away and joining the renegade slaves up in Palmares," but she knew that the *quilombo* had long been destroyed. For the young man, however, Palmares was a symbol that nourished his own courage and strength: "Palmares was way back two hundred years ago, but he said Palmares was now" (126). A central symbol for the history of people of African descent in Brazil and the Americas, Palmares gains more relevance and exclusive space in Jones's *Song for Anninho*.

Unlike the rebels of the *quilombos*, Corregidora's slave women were frightened and dominated by the system. Their relationship with the master was full of ambiguity, a complex mixture of hate and (repressed) desire. Ursa's Great Gram stayed with Corregidora, as many slave women in reality did, *"even after it ended."* When she escaped, it was not out of rebellion but out of fear for her life, because she had done something mysterious *"that made him wont to kill her"* (79). She somehow reached Louisiana in the United States and went back to Brazil in 1906 to pick up her daughter who had been left behind on the plantation. Free from the constraints of social realism, Gayl Jones creates imaginary traveling between the hemispheres to allow for a broader exploration of racism and oppression.

Slavery had finally ended when Great Gram returned to Brazil, but not the prostitution of young black bodies that it had established as a regular fact of life. Grandma, then a young girl, was being abused by Corregidora just as her mother had been (79). Still, as Grandma looks back on that time, she suspects that Corregidora had developed some strong attachment to her mother, in spite (or because) of the mysterious "thing" that she had done to him. Corregidora would probably have liked to keep both women, the mother as well as the daughter, then pregnant with his child.

Paradox marks the reaction of Corregidora's slave women. Thinking back, Grandma believes that she really hated him and was awfully glad when her mother came to rescue her from his domination. But she sometimes doubts her own memory of what really happened and seems to voice Jones's own thoughts on representation and storytelling. Stories are being constantly transformed by new tellers and listeners, and memories are never crystallized into unchangeable truths. *"It's hard to always remember what you were feeling when you ain't feeling it exactly that way no more,"* Grandma realizes (79). The complexity and contemporaneity of Jones's version of history remind the reader that distinct, black-and-white accounts are plain simplifications. Gayl Jones introduces paradox and ambivalence in her narrative and is not surprised when the novel is called ambiguous by a critic: "I wanted it to be. I always like it when there are a lot of different possibilities."[43]

Ambiguity and paradox follow the Corregidora women of Jones's novel in their journey across the American continent. Transferred to the United States for their twentieth-century saga, the two former slaves move from Louisiana to Kentucky in search of better jobs (with Grandma already carrying another Corregidora child, Ursa's mother). They remain divided between the wish to live in the present and the promise to remain faithful to a past symbolized by a picture and a name.

As part of their contradictory heritage, the older Corregidora women also share in the manipulation of history. They eliminate the name of Ursa's father, Martin, from their stories and convince Ursa's mother to do the same, "closed up like a fist" in the furious loneliness of her private memory (101). She insists that she had never wanted a man, so since the beginning she "wouldn't let [herself] feel anything." She "gave him nothing" for two years, until in madness he left her (117–21). Her later memories are mixed with attraction and repulsion—"two lumps on the same camel"—much like her ancestors' relation to Corregidora, no matter how fiercely they denied it. Those women had banished Martin because he confronted their most profound and repressed dilemma, the one that creates the major tension and contradiction throughout the novel: "He had the nerve to ask them . . . how much was hate for Corregidora and how much was love" (131).

In economic terms, Kentucky did not offer the expected better life. Black people seem still left with the occupations that nobody else wants, struggling under an anonymous rule that retains traditional castes. Women can be housemaids and go on working in "white women's kitchens," as Ursa's Great Gram, her grandmother, her mother, and Cat Lawson have done (30, 108). They can still sell their food, again as Mother and Cat have done; be prostitutes (38, 79); work night shifts in factories ("ain't much different from a kitchen"), like Lorene, Jeffy's mother (29–30); straighten black women's hair (105); or become blues singers, like Ursa and Vivian (who inherited Ursa's place at Happy's and the love of Tadpole Mc-Cormick), always "fighting the night" and the deep loneliness of the urban ghetto (97). Men can own cafés where other solitary black people, like Tadpole, come to hear the blues, or they can do odd jobs, like Martin. In other states it is no different: black men can still labor under the sun on tobacco farms, as Mutt does in Connecticut (183).

Together with the twentieth-century lives of the Corregidora women, the testimonies of Cat Lawson, Mutt Thomas, and Tadpole McCormick about their ancestors allow Gayl Jones to explore the ironic reality of freedom for a black person in the United States and to connect the two biggest slaveholding societies in America. Mutt's memories go far back into southern slavery, when, worse than taking land, the law took his great-grandfather's wife away from him and back into slavery. He had "worked as a blacksmith, hiring himself out," and had bought their freedom. But when he got into debt, "the courts judged it was legal" for his creditors to take his wife, because "he had bought her, and so she was also his property, his slave" (151). As property she passed from hand to hand.

Hard work sometimes permitted a black man to buy "a little piece of land" in the free South, as Tadpole's father did, but the legal books had their pages torn and ownership by blacks was erased from the records. Hopes for a better economic future and a piece of land of their own kept being crushed by the racist capitalist order. Manipulation of facts and records to suit the dominant power echoes the destruction of the slave documents in Brazil. "They ain't nothing you can do when they tear the pages out of the book and they ain't no record of it. They probably burned the pages" (78). Legal rights have distinct meanings for whites and blacks, as the word said by one has a different value from that said by the other. What blacks affirmed and showed did not matter, only the reality created by official history (170). Ursa learned as early as childhood that crimes against blacks did not count for the police, especially in the case of women. The death of a black woman was ignored, buried forever "in the nigger *woman* file" (134).

Later in the twentieth century, Ursa and her mother live in loneliness and isolation, still burdened with the tales of women treated like breeding animals, priced according to the quality of their genitals and their bellies (132). In spite of the maddening past, they sometimes wonder if perhaps it is possible to overcome fears and allow themselves a new freedom. "Why do you keep fighting me? Or is it yourself you keep fighting?" (132). Martin and Mutt seem to sound alike, coming out of dreams and repressed memories to pull mother and daughter away from the Corregidora chains. The past had been terrible, and the present has enormous difficulties for blacks, especially women, but history cannot be held static. "Whichever way you look at it, *we* ain't *them*," Mutt insists. But for Ursa, as for her mother, past and present are bound together as their identities repeat Gram and Great Gram (151, 184).

Gayl Jones's narrative raises questions about the control and use of power in public and personal spheres, issues largely related to contemporary conditions in the larger society and within black communities. Ursa suggests that, in spite of the oppression of patriarchal tradition, no race or gender has the monopoly of domination and no country or time has the key to happiness. Can slavery and oppression be left behind for a new life to begin? Mutt symbolically abandons the job he held on the tobacco farms of Connecticut to become a singer at age fifty-eight. He joins Ursa in the world of the many black musicians that he loves: Thelonius Monk, Ray Charles, and Billie Holiday (169). He is just as weary as Ursa of reminders of bondage, of the smell of the dead: "I just got tired of tobacco, I got tired of the smell" (183). But he continues to identify himself with his ancestors, even at the moment when he comes back to Ursa. He felt as if he were going crazy without her, just like his great-grandfather when his wife was taken away (183–84).

At the end of the novel, Ursa is still trying to discover and capture the kind of power that her great-grandmother once had over Corregidora. She would like to reenact with Mutt that same mysterious bond and perhaps understand what had tied her black-and-white past together for so long (184). Exhausted with a burden too heavy to carry, she seems to have forgiven the white devil to a certain extent, placing him closer to mortals. Ursa realizes that all human beings hurt one another, blacks and whites, men and women, she and her women ancestors as much as Mutt and Corregidora. She also realizes that Corregidora's power had far exceeded his time: the women of her family had remained faithful to his memory and his control for more than a century. Perhaps it is time to let him go.

But even after twenty-two years, Ursa has not really forgiven Mutt; nor is she free of Corregidora and Great Gram. As Ursa and Mutt reunite in the same hotel room where they once lived, a circle of their life closes and coincides with her ancestors'. Performing oral sex on Mutt gives her a clue to the power that Great Gram once had over Corregidora. "It had to be something sexual," she realizes. "In a split second of hate and love [she] knew what it was." Reenacting that "moment of pleasure and excruciating pain at the same time" helps Ursa understand the dangerous proximity of life and death, of loving and killing (184). The tension and the conflict remain for Ursa and Mutt in spite of the tenderness. At the end they hold on tight to each other, aware that they can kill but are also hungry for comfort and tenderness, and they agree:

"I don't want a kind of woman that hurt you."
"I don't want a kind of man that'll hurt me neither." (185)

Based on imaginary elaborations and rewritings of the historical records, *Corregidora* is a unique novel in its combination of the most disruptive aspects of slavery in the Americas. Characters take on a symbolic quality in the circular, recurring pattern that is enriched by their collective memory. That narrative device reveals Jones's concern with the persisting realities of sexual and racial domination and recalls the similar style of Latin American writers Carlos Fuentes and Gabriel García Márquez. Like them, Jones also combines historical accounts, dreams, obsessions, and the stories of mothers and grandmothers to create her own tale. Recalling the use of ambiguity and paradox in Fuentes, Jones is interested in several different but complementary dimensions of reality and in open-ended stories that keep bringing the past back into the present. Indeterminacy for Jones and for the Latin American writer is not simply a matter of aesthetic choice but a strategy that allows them to address a contingent and indeterminate world.

Fuentes and Jones share a similar freedom from traditional requirements of social realism and "historical" fiction. Both writers problematize history and reinvent it in their play of portraits and mirrors and their cycles of violence. Their characters inherit the burden of that history: they are often obsessed with grotesque memories and still involved by violence and solitude in their present. The aesthetic strategies similarly adopted by Gayl Jones and Latin American "magical realists" correspond to the complex sociohistorical processes and the grammars of opposition inscribed in their works.

*Corregidora* does not reach a clear resolution. The constant identification of personalities and times suggests a persisting pattern of sadomasochism in human relations. However, Gayl Jones never meant to provide a "final statement" to the "American dilemma." The novel raises doubts and asks "questions that have been there all along" in our complex history.[44] As such, it is an effective and powerful statement about the disturbing conditions and effects of slavery, exposing its combined load of sexism and racism.

Gayl Jones transforms barrenness into art, and Ursa bears testimony by the telling of her story in song and in prose. Described by the author as "a blues novel," *Corregidora* laments the suffering of women and men in the notes and cries of its songs. The blues express the inexpressible, as the novel also tries to do. In Ursa's voice, the novel retells stories of pain and confusion, echoes sounds of hate and of love, of whiteness and blackness, all mixed in a woman who ironically looks "Spanish" to eyes trained to see only in black and white.

In slavery as in freedom, black people in the novel are isolated by color and class boundaries, largely keeping the condition of a "pariah group" in the United States of the twentieth century. Like the blues, Gayl Jones's characters are North American; Brazil is, in the novel, a museum piece of furniture, a portrait, memories of oppression that find resonance in the new environment of the United States. For the North American Gayl Jones, Brazil is a geographical and historical intertext that can perhaps help a better understanding of what it means to be black in Kentucky and in the United States. It is a place that contains pieces of history and fragments of memory that may complement and illuminate the questions and dilemmas of the present in the northern nation.

## Song for Anninho:
### An Epic Poem for Palmares

Brazilian history and the indictment of violence, racism, and injustice are again taken up by Gayl Jones in *Song for Anninho,* a long poem recited by the runaway slave woman Almeyda in memory of her husband, Anninho. The reflective, meditative quality of its narrative style allows Jones to explore issues of authenticity and origin in culture, matters of intense interest for black writers and activists. Unlike some of them, Jones does not defend the going back to pure roots for the reconstruction of a black identity. She is interested in the continuous process of cultures meeting, clashing, and sometimes combining in redefinitions and adaptations, and she is suspicious of a search for "the truth" in a glorious, static past.

Language as a vehicle and repository of culture, in the same way, cannot be preserved intact along the migrations, the wars, and the shifting powers in the development of history. Almeyda's grandmother regrets the loss of the language and culture that she had in Africa, but Almeyda realizes that it is useless to dream of an unchanging world when, in fact, there is no "origin" or "beginning" to be recovered. She says:

> "My grandmother always talked about how we
> lost our language here,
> but she was speaking Arabic when she

came here, so she had already
lost her original one generations before." (47)

As much as she wants to remember Africa, Almeyda knows that
culture is endlessly built through contact and interaction.[45] A new
language is created as *"new words"* are put *"in the place of the old ones"*
(47). At the same time, when processes of domination rob the dominated peoples of their language, their narratives also disappear. Anninho plans to write a new history of Palmares as lived by the rebels
themselves, for the Portuguese had corrupted facts to suit their own
purposes: "You see how they transform heroes into villains, and noble actions into crimes, and elevated codes into venality?" (60). As
she composes her own chronicles, Almeyda decides to erase the
names of the Portuguese—"the military chieftains," the governors—
in revenge against their violence and against the namelessness of
Africans in their world and texts. Almeyda wants to record only the
names of her people, such as Anninho and Zumbi and even Ganga
Zumba, the black traitor who helped destroy Palmares. Anninho reminds her, however, that unnaming the whites will repeat the oppressor's act, not eliminate it. Paradoxically, "in denying their
names," Almeyda would "have given them names" (61).

*Song for Anninho*, like Toni Morrison's *Tar Baby*, allows the writer
the opportunity to explore the natural beauty of the American continent and lament the destruction of a wealth of resources and marvels
perpetrated by centuries of greedy colonization. Almeyda carries the
memory of "a greener past" in Africa; at the same time she struggles
for recognition and love in the Brazilian Alagoas, where she now
belongs. She feels part of the *New World* even if the Portuguese colonizers deny it. The granddaughter of an African, she knows that

> this is my place. My part of the world
> The landscape and tenderness,
> the wars too and despair,
> the possibilities of some whole living. (17)

Language of whatever kind is often inappropriate and limited for
the articulation of our deepest feelings and dreams. The difficulty of
communicating and sharing one's thoughts and desires through
words is a recurring point in *Song for Anninho*. In a story told by
Almeyda's grandmother, a man and a woman keep so long without
speaking to each other that they simply forget how to use words and
communicate. Men and women do not share common vocabularies

anymore, but there is still the possibility of "saying" things and connecting through touch and love:

> And those words became the
> words that men and women do not
> say to each other. The words
> ceased to be words and became tenderness. (48–49)

Jones discusses writing and history by constructing her *Song* as a multivocal account about the creation of writing itself. Like Carlos Fuentes and, even earlier, William Faulkner, Jones makes use of different layers of "reality" and different voices narrating them. Using a black woman as narrator, as the site of struggle and repository of memory, she empowers the muted voices of history more directly than does Fuentes, whose protagonists are normally men who ascend to the upper class. At the same time, she also experiments with the surreal and the nonlogical in her works, in the manner of *lo real maravilloso*. It is in her second novel, *Eva's Man* (1976), however, that the coexistence of "fantastic" and "real" are explored to a greater extent.

Gayl Jones's narrative technique often recalls the Fuentes of *The Death of Artemio Cruz*.[46] Fuentes constructed Artemio Cruz's story in three different narrative voices: I, You, and He. They come in varying print styles to help the reader sort out fragments of different times and places filling up Artemio's memory as he is about to die and to distinguish the voice of the narrator from the stream of consciousness of Artemio Cruz. Jones also adopts various print modes, indicating different times and voices, in *Corregidora* and *Song for Anninho*. In *Corregidora*, Gayl Jones is a chronicler of the personal, playing with different levels of perception. The "sense of an intimate history" of Ursa's narrative provides a sharp contrast with conventional historical writing as well as with the "almost impersonal history of Corregidora."[47] *Song for Anninho* is completely based on Brazilian history, but it is again made intimate and personal in the point of view of the young, fugitive slave woman Almeyda.

Originally planned as a novel titled *Palmares*, the narrative ended up in the form of a "song," a dramatic-narrative poem that sounds like a ballad. *Corregidora*, in turn, which in its first version was a kind of ritual song, resulted in "a blues novel." For Jones, as for Fuentes and García Márquez, writers are free to play with forms and genres as much as with points of view and with fragmentations and reconstitutions of time and space. They share a dream of creating a new language and new forms, both in history and in textuality, out of the knowledge and the memory of the old. Where there was silence, let there be a voice. The language of the master may be used to signify new meanings, as Almeyda longs for:

> *Think about language. We will*
> *make words out of words.*
> *We will use the same words,*
> *but they will be different.* (47)

A similar blend of collective and personal history was attempted by Carlos Fuentes in *The Death of Artemio Cruz*. Mixing times, places, and narrative voices in his stories, he aims at a more complete and "total" narrative in his investigation of individual and national identity. For his protagonists, Fuentes seems particularly interested in mixed-blood men whose identities are split between allegiance to the abused, dark mother and dedication to the power structure embodied by the white, absent father and the *patria* he controls—as the word indicates from its Latin root *pater*, it is the "fatherland." Artemio Cruz is the illegitimate child of a plantation master and his mulatto servant. Thomas Arroyo, the protagonist of *The Old Gringo* (1985), is the bastard son of another *Señor* and an Indian servant. Within their olive skins and their aggressive virility, the divided souls of such men reveal the conflicts and barbarities of Mexican history and their reverberations in contemporary times. Past is present and future, with history going around in circles. The power structure is able to maintain itself by abusing the dark and the poor.

But ambiguity and contradiction tend to become inevitable facts in Fuentes's as well as in Jones's version of history, independent of the race and color of the people portrayed. In Fuentes, Cruz and Arroyo are rebels and patriots but also exploiters (Cruz already is, and Arroyo tends to become one). Even as they resist domination, the women in Jones's *Corregidora* inadvertently perpetuate oppression. In *Song for Anninho*, the first Negro leader of Palmares, Ganga Zumba, is portrayed as a man corrupted by power (Palmares and black history recover their heroic stature under the leadership of Zumbi).[48]

As Carlos Fuentes and Gabriel García Márquez have done in their narratives, Gayl Jones explores the paradoxes and ambiguities in language itself and the traps implicit in the idea of any "true" account of events.[49] First of all, there is the question of power and control of information and language, which goes hand in hand with the control of history itself. In *Corregidora*, there are repeated instances of "truth" being held by the white man and only his voice being heard in U.S. society: "If a white man hadn't told them, they wouldn't have seen it. If I come and told them they wouldn't've seen it," says Ursa. Being the one who tells and is heard also means being the one who possesses and dominates. The major example of that is America itself, registered as European: "They say Columbo discovered America, [but] he didn't discover America" (*C*, 170). Like other writers of the continent, including Toni Morrison and Paule Marshall, Gayl Jones insists on the creation of a counter-narrative through the characters and the tales she imagines. The confluence of history and myth in their language rescues the America that had been marginalized and obliterated for centuries. "To invent a language," says Carlos Fuentes, "is to say all that history has muted."[50]

In *Song for Anninho*, Almeyda and Anninho are imaginary runaway slaves from the Republic of Palmares, a large Maroon "country" actually established by fugitive slaves in the heart of Brazil—now the state of Alagoas—from the end of the sixteenth century to 1695. The point made by Anninho and Almeyda about the need to produce their own version of history becomes poignant when we remember that there is no account left by any of the inhabitants of the eleven villages, or *quilombos*, that constituted that remarkable republic. Ironically, whatever is known of Palmares today is based on documents left by those who wanted to destroy it. "The Negro Republic will always be seen from a distance," says Brazilian historian Décio Freitas, "and only slightly will we ever glimpse at its inside."[51] Trying to tread closer than the historian can, Gayl Jones's imagination comes inside Palmares and records the joys and cries of the people.

Brazil and the colonial time do not make space for love. *"This is the wrong time for a man and a woman,"* says Almeyda, for "this is a country that doesn't allow men to be gentle. White men or black men" (46, 38). Almeyda's voice reverberates with Jones's own anxieties in the twentieth century and with a despondency that is very much our contemporary. As Carlos Fuentes often does in his fiction, Gayl Jones travels back and forth in history and weaves her narrative as a past story still very much present.[52] In *Song for Anninho*, Jones explores the idea of the circularity and repetition of historical cycles.

Almeyda realizes that *"Everything happens again. There is nothing / in this world that doesn't happen again"* (66). The oppression hovering over Almeyda and Anninho is similar to the traumas that befall the *Corregidora* women in slavery and continue to dominate Ursa's life and relationships in the mid-twentieth-century United States.

In the two works by Jones analyzed here, childlessness has to do both with personal choice and the violence of the times. Jones seems to transpose her own exchanges with her mother and grandmother to *Song for Anninho*, where Almeyda's grandmother disapproves of a woman who mutilated herself to avoid sex and procreation. "She had done it, because she didn't want / any man at all, not the black ones or the white ones," because she was horrified by the discovery of "how they could use her" (44). It was no time for love and certainly *"the wrong time for a man,"* a refrain echoing in Jones's stories to decry the impossibility of love amid cruelty. "I cannot give myself / over to a man in this season. And besides, / I would not be giving. There is / no such thing as giving these days" (53). The woman refused to be valued by the numbers of new slaves she could produce: in that culture, "a woman / is worth nothing if her body can't / produce for them, or bear the burden / of their flesh" (55). Even if she could not alter the system, she felt that she had gained a control over her own body that the other women did not have.

Almeyda is mystified by the power and magic of the woman's story, which even the masters seem to have respected: "Why was it that the master hadn't killed her? / What was her story? / What was her charm?" (56). The other women in Jones's imagined community were both fascinated by and afraid of the woman's evil courage; but some who disapproved of her would themselves abort as soon as they became pregnant. Having children was a privilege seldom achieved by the overworked and exhausted bodies of women in Brazilian sugarcane plantations. Historical records show that the infant mortality rate was extremely high among slaves, with 70 to 80 percent of the babies dying at the moment of delivery. Abortion was a common procedure practiced by slave women to prevent their own offspring from suffering the same life under slavery.[53] "They think I have mutilated myself," says the dark, scarred woman in Jones's book, "but I have kept myself whole" (57). Right and wrong are very ambiguous terms in a world where "vices and virtues are confused" (51).

Almeyda's grandmother gives voice to the women in Gayl Jones's own family who believed that self-mutilation harmed a woman's spirit as well as her flesh. "Even in a time of hardness," the older wise woman says in the poem, it is impossible to understand "why a woman would let the bird go." A woman is "part past" and "part future, too," so she is the sum of herself, her ancestors, and her children (54). Without children, a woman's identity is incomplete. If becoming sterile is a bitter form of protest, having children is like continually telling the story; it is, albeit paradoxically, also an act of resistance and courage. In Gayl Jones's tales, the bodies of both Ursa and Almeyda are dried of their "seeds" and "juices" by the violence of the times. Bitterness "sucked [her] womb dry," but Almeyda still dreams of a happier future where love can exist:

I wanted my womb to grow deep for you, Anninho,
even in a time like this one,
in spite of the time. (64)

As Anninho and Almeyda dream of a New Palmares where the memory of King Zumbi would reign in glory and peace, Anninho plans to write the chronicles of their wars against the Portuguese. He wishes to narrate the heroism of their feats to counter official accounts. Almeyda, however, has a more focused history in mind. She promises Anninho that she will write *his* chronicles: through her narration and Jones's imagination, the story of Anninho, a lesser hero, a common if brave man in Zumbi's kingdom, comes to life (60). Unlike the scope of male chroniclers, including Anninho's plans for his own narrative, Almeyda's tale is not concerned with the facts of war or the feats of commanders: "It's not the actions I wish to capture, / but the spirit!" (60). In that process, she actually privileges her own memories and feelings. The narration, the point of view, the crisscrossing of relationships presented, and the anxieties and conflicts exposed all turn *Song for Anninho* into *her* chronicles.

Almeyda's book, passed to us through Gayl Jones, makes only slight mention of the treason of Ganga Zumba against his fellow Palmaristas or his reconciliation with the Pernambuco police and government in 1678. The great Zumbi, who succeeded Ganga Zumba as leader of the Republic of Palmares, is honored in the book as he has been even in the official chronicles of the Portuguese, but he is not the central focus of *Song for Anninho*. Almeyda held him in awe for his strong spirit, his "religious and secular" command, "his solemn intelligence" (59). Almeyda is a simple, quiet woman among "the thousands who lived in the quilombos," one among many around the great Zumbi. Anninho takes part in the central government of the republic as a member of the council and "in charge of trading and reconnaisance expeditions" for Zumbi. He is not jealous of Almeyda's dreams of the great chief because he "loved him dearly" himself and considered Zumbi a sun that "must shine" (59). Gayl Jones is not afraid to deal with ambiguous, split devotions, feelings that do not become clearly defined. It is in the hearts and minds of people like Anninho and Almeyda that Jones centers her story.

Sharing a tradition with slave narratives written by women, Almeyda's first-person account departs from the typical male focus on "external social grievances" to privilege "very delicate and complex interpersonal relationships."[54] Almeyda recalls her former life as slave on a sugar plantation and in a shoemaker's shop before she was stolen away by "the men of Palmares" (29). Her memories of her slave life come back as she flees from other Portuguese in the forest. Images of violence and sadism will haunt her forever: the shoemaker's wife always watching Almeyda with jealousy and the master spanking her with "the heel of a shoe until it bled," while his wife smiled in relief (28–30).

Almeyda flees from violence and cruelty like many other slaves of the Americas who joined with Maroons throughout the "extended Caribbean." In Brazilian history, the escape of so many slaves to Palmares and the number of free people of all colors who joined them only enraged the colonial power more and more, especially when the prosperity of Palmares contrasted with the decline and poverty of the colony. Soldiers encroached on the rebels and tried successive attacks against their fortifications, but the Palmaristas were expert guerrillas. They always managed to escape and hide in the surrounding forest before the damage was done. For Anninho and the men of Palmares, the struggle for freedom was interminable, and though they avoided direct fighting and killing, they did kill in raids and in self-defense "when it was necessary" (29). They did not wish to destroy the system; they only hoped to be left in peace. "Why can't they let us stay in this place we have made for ourselves?" (37).

The day the Palmaristas decided to change tactics and respond to attacks from within their walls, they lost the battle. The number and the force of the government army outdid all their expectations and efforts. In Jones's book, Almeyda tells of their immense suffering through the chaotic persecution and the mutilation of Palmares Negroes by the barbaric soldiers, led by Domingos Jorge Velho. It took place in the hills of the Barriga Mountains in the southern part of the province (*Capitania*) of Pernambuco, during the final years of the seventeenth century. In her sorrowful litany, Almeyda recalls the destruction of the village by the soldiers and her separation from her lover during their troubled escape into the dense forest. The spirit of the times is graphically represented in the narration of atrocities committed against the body of Almeyda, a ravaged geography in the hands of conquerors. The desperate but lyrical poem narrates how, during her flight in the forest away from the falling Palmares, her breasts are violently cut off by the persecuting soldiers and thrown away in the river. Although she was then counted among the dead, she survives through the magic wisdom and the healing powers of Zibatra, who is also the listener to her story in the poem.

The bodies of men and women are a terrain of recurring violence in Gayl Jones's work: a site of dismemberment in *Eva's Man;* sexual mutilation and decapitation in *Song for Anninho;* and torture, rape, abortion and sterilization in *Corregidora.* The body is branded by the cruelty and paradoxes of the times, yesterday and today. Though the physical torture may seem detailed and obsessive at times, Jones in fact almost minimizes the actual violence perpetrated in history. In the case of the destruction of Palmares and the killing of Zumbi, for instance, the records reveal atrocities much greater than those that Jones describes.[55]

After its one hundred years of resistance, Palmares had become a shame and a stain for the powerful. Killing Zumbi was the ultimate dream of the Pernambuco government and the Portuguese rulers. Furtado de Mendonça, a member of Velho's band also named in Jones's text, convinced the captive Palmarista Antonio Soares to reveal Zumbi's hiding place and stab him with a knife. The end came on November 20, 1895. Zumbi's body was carried to the neighboring township of Porto Calvo, where authorities proceeded to record the historic deed so that no doubt would remain about his (previously often-rumored) death. The official history is more brutal than any imaginative account of Zumbi's death: "The examination of the corpse revealed 15 bullet perforations and countless numbers of stabs by cold steel weapon; after death, the Negro general had been castrated and his penis had been tucked into his mouth; they pulled out one of his eyes and chopped off his right hand."[56]

After he was recognized and confirmed as the real Zumbi, his head was cut off in front of all the officials, then salted and taken to Recife, the capital of the *Capitania* of Pernambuco. It was stuck on a post in the most public and visible place in the city in order "to satisfy the offended ones and those who had just complaints, and to frighten the Negroes who in their superstition believed him immortal." The Portuguese crown declared the slave rebellion finally controlled and eradicated, after honoring and rewarding Jorge Velho, Antonio Soares, and other agents of betrayal and destruction. As if to confirm Anninho's indictment of official interpretations, the Portuguese king freed Soares, forgave him for his earlier stay in Palmares, and recommended his name among "the great benefactors of Pernambuco's history."[57]

In spite of the celebrating and the rejoicing among soldiers, government officials, and landowners, the dense forest would continue to protect runaway slaves and other poor in the colonial era for many years to come, and hundreds of other *quilombos* would spring up in hills and forests throughout the slave regions of Brazil. In *Song for Anninho*, Jones retells the resistance and reaffirms the continuing strength of Zumbi's spirit:

> "They put him in a public place
> so that we would forget he was immortal.
> They thought we would believe as they believe,
> that with the stroke of a knife a man
> would lose his immortality." (56)

In Almeyda's dreams, King Zumbi reassures her that, in spite of all the violence, "flesh and blood and spirit continues in the world" (59). Three hundred years after Zumbi's death, this poem contributes to spreading his dream and his struggle around the world.

Gayl Jones draws on intense historical research to write *Song for Anninho*, reinterpreting facts and echoing others as she chooses. She recalls historical information regarding the political and social organization of Palmares and the strong king elected and honored by his people. She evokes the strong and brave men who made Palmares the terror of the colonial power and registers the republic's prosperity; the trade done with neighboring villages and farmers; and the snatching of women, other slave men, and the necessary goods from cities and plantations by raids of Palmaristas. She reaffirms the knowledge of the forest held by the residents of Palmares, their physical strength, and their superiority over the Portuguese whenever they resorted to guerrilla warfare. She recounts the similarity of Brazil and Africa, the greenness of the landscape and the harsh weather. And she remembers Palmares as a community of Africans that welcomed diversity.

Even if its population was originally composed of runaway slaves, Palmares grew into a society open to all races and creeds and to all "the persecuted and disinherited from the colonial system."[58] Indians, free blacks, and whites came freely or were brought to the settlement. Like Zumbi himself and many others, Anninho had been a free Negro who came to Palmares by choice (37). Zumbi's principal wife was a white woman "with light skin and fair hair . . . the daughter of some forest dweller" (69). Oral tradition maintains that Zumbi was married to a white woman named Maria, who followed him of her own will after an incursion by Palmaristas on a plantation.[59]

In *Song for Anninho,* Gayl Jones depicts Zumbi drawing a picture of the woman of his desire; she has the long hair of the white queen, but Almeyda's "dark skin and eyes" (79). Strong and admired, he can have all the women he wants but seems to wish for one with all races in herself. Jones plays with the idea of incest, a recurring theme in *Corregidora,* in her depiction of Zumbi's ideal woman: "*It was mulatto women he wanted. . . . It was his own daughter he wanted then?*" (79). The white queen decides to make her skin darker with the sun, trying to embody in herself all the women he could want. It is not a daughter he desires, perhaps, just a symbolic Total Woman as in "the legends of enchanted Moorish women bathing in fountains" (79).

Anninho fantasizes about Moorish women much in the same way as Zumbi or the Portuguese planters of Brazil. In his study of the Portuguese character, Gilberto Freyre mentions "the enchanted Moorish woman" as a favorite erotic fantasy for Portuguese men since earlier times, when wars and conquests brought Portugal closer to Africa and the Orient. The charmingly hybrid figure was "brownskinned, black-eyed, enveloped in sexual mysticism, roseate in hue, and always engaged in combing out her hair or bathing in rivers or in the waters of haunted fountains."[60] Freyre connects that fantasy to the later "glorification of the mulatto woman, the cabocla or Indian woman, the brown-skin or brunette type," in the Brazilian lyrics of the twentieth century. Gayl Jones extends the fantasy to men in general, blacks as well as whites.

The white color of Zumbi's wife is a matter of constant puzzlement for Almeyda. As her memory blurs together stories and facts of her life, that white woman mixes with other images of white women jealous of the love that black women inspire in men. The episode allows Jones to speculate on the appropriation of African beauty by the white culture (here represented by Queen Maria) without a corresponding admiration and respect for black people. The queen, brought from Portugal in Jones's tale, *"had made herself dark like"* Almeyda, even though *"she hated the dark women"* (83–84).

Gayl Jones relates her explorations of race and color to questions of gender. She elaborates on the differences between men and women and the "truths" that the genders must realize about themselves and each other. In her poem, only women are truly capable of mixing with other races and integrating the spirit of Palmares: "The women are different, the men tell us, / the women become a part of whatever people / they come among." Ironically, by endowing women with a superior sense of adaptation, the black men justify their taking of white and Indian wives: "It does not matter if / the woman is blanca or negra, women are different, / they become wherever they are" (69). The confused strains of memory in Almeyda's narrative may make it hard for the reader to distinguish between times and points of view, but the irony is clearly emphasized. The apparent praise coming from the men disguises manipulation and a constant disregard for women's feelings:

> *The women are different. We know about the women.*
> *It does not matter. Women are always to be taken*
> *in wars of liberation. Call her the Reina Blanca.*
> *It does not matter with a woman. They are always*
> *captured when there is the need. They forget*
> *where they were and become where they are.*
> *Not true.*
> *Tell me what then.* (70)

Even if they had been brought to Palmares through kidnapping, as black, white, and Indian women often were, Jones imagines a healthy environment and a strong support group for the common women in that society. They get together to share old troubles and celebrate the dignity now achieved. The older women help the new ones, and they share together in joys and sorrows as much as in work, "mending straw mats, and cutting down forests." In a circle, they talk and share feelings, all except the upper caste of "Zumbi's women," bound together in grief and in celebration (72).

Gayl Jones rereads the lives of Palmares Maroons from the perspective of a modern woman living in an advanced society where increasing attention is paid to sexual harassment and rape, as well as to healing rituals and communities of women gathering for their mutual empowerment. The strong Muslim orientation of Black Nationalists in the United States, may, in addition, have influenced Jones to make Almeyda's lover, Anninho, and her grandmother Muslims, when Muslims were not common in the Palmares republic (14). Although Palmares had people from different areas of Africa, it was predominantly influenced by the Bantu language and culture of Angolan slaves.[61] Syncretic forms of verbal communication and religious ritual were created in Palmares to accommodate peoples of different languages, races, colors, and creeds. The language spoken combined Portuguese and African languages, as well as Indian languages, to a lesser degree. Chapels had images of African deities as well as of Jesus, Mary, and the Catholic saints.[62]

A "syncretic" figure himself, Zumbi was born in Palmares but was captured and taken away by soldiers while still a baby. He was raised by the priest Antonio Melo in a district near Palmares, baptized as Francisco, taught to read and speak Portuguese and Latin by the time he was ten, and trained to be an altar boy. He was never a slave; on the contrary, Francisco/Zumbi and Father Antonio apparently had sincere affection and respect for each other. The priest praised his ingenuity and Christian faith in letters to Portugal and was shocked when the boy of fifteen ran away to Palmares. Zumbi came back many times to visit the priest, bringing gifts and telling him about his new name and life. The name Zumbi, or Zambi, as it appears in Portuguese documents, may have been inspired by the Congo deity Nzambi.[63]

In her book, Gayl Jones makes Almeyda the Catholic granddaughter of a remarkable African slave woman who was strong enough to have fought against both the Portuguese and the Dutch who took over and controlled Pernambuco from 1630 to 1654 (13). The grandmother was intelligent enough to hide her Islamic faith from the Jesuits with whom she enjoyed "exchanging viewpoints" (35). Almeyda resembles her grandmother in her beauty and dignity, and walks with the majesty of the women in the African village of her forebears. They had learned to balance with grace the burden over their heads, whether it was a physical burden or some huge psychological weight (38). As in *Corregidora*, the narrator in *Song for Anninho* identifies with her female ancestor and incorporates "all her words and memory and fears" in the present:

She said, You are the granddaughter
of an African, and you have
inherited a way of being.

As the two communicated, Almeyda recalls, "I became my grandmother and she became me" (32–33). Almeyda's grandmother was
wise and sensible, a strong survivor of a series of wars and disruption. She had brought from the African culture the ability to send
away evil spirits and to divine future events. Almeyda is amazed at
the powers of her grandmother, but she herself is not endowed with
the same.

Almeyda is symbolic of the whole martyrdom and perseverance of
generations of slave women in the Americas. She constantly emphasizes how she can feel centuries in a moment and has "the blood of
the whole continent running in [her] veins" (12). While Ursa has
inherited the burden of being a Corregidora and is constantly tor-
mented by that thought, Almeyda's memory insistently recalls her
African grandmother's strength and independence. The possibility of
a European ancestor is only suggested and never becomes an obsession: a Dutch mapmaker in Recife bought her grandmother as a
young and beautiful woman at the beginning of the seventeenth century (16). But Almeyda's color and eyes are her African grandmother's.[64]

The healer Zibatra treats Almeyda after the ravaging destruction
done by the Portuguese troops. She speaks to Almeyda in untranslat-
able words, but also in Portuguese and in the Indian language Tupi
(11). She describes herself as "a mystic and biblical scholar . . . an
enchantress and a mixer of herbs" (13). She speaks in tongues and is
both in time and timeless, evoking the magical properties of Gabriel García Márquez's Melquíades, Toni Morrison's Pilate and
Thérèse, and Paule Marshall's Lebert Joseph. With a deep knowledge
of the body, she rubs turtle oil on Almeyda's wounds with her healing hands, singing holy chants in mysterious tongues and traveling
through past and future with her "third eye":[65]

"I know places where the visible
and the invisible meet,
where the human and the divine come together. . . .
I have seen with a third eye,
and a fourth one, and yet another.
I have spoken in tongues, and beyond language." (13–14)

The visible and the invisible also meet in Gayl Jones's account of the escape of "brave Palmaristas" from the cannons and weapons of enemy troops. Historians describe how, cornered by the massive attack on the cliffs of steep mountains, some five hundred men of Palmares fell or jumped into the abyss.[66] Jones's narrative evokes African myths and the flying men depicted by Toni Morrison in *Song of Solomon*: the men from Palmares "could have become birds" as they fled from oppression, just like Morrison's Solomon. Trusting the powers that "the god" can grant, Almeyda is always watching out for birds, "hoping it's some Palmarista!" (36).

In the manner of Zibatra, Gayl Jones plays with different languages in *Song for Anninho*. She occasionally inserts Portuguese words in the narrative, mostly names of animals, plants, and trees (*jaboti, caneleira, ipecacuanha*), besides Brazilian words for "healer" (*macumbeiro, curador*). The names of characters in *Song for Anninho* may be words adapted from the Portuguese, like Anninho and Almeyda (the latter taken from Governor de Almeida).[67] Jones also refers to historical figures such as Zumbi, Ganga Zumba, Domingos Jorge Velho, and "Furtado do Medoça" (*sic*). Occasionally, Jones's study of the Spanish language interferes with her word choice. Almeyda says the people of Palmares call Zumbi's white wife "Reina Blanca," for instance, when the Portuguese form should be "Rainha Branca." For *Corregidora*, Jones also adapts the Portuguese word *corregedor*—a former judicial title and function corresponding to that of today's judges—giving it the feminine Spanish form.[68] In spite of a few inconsistencies, Jones's use of such words and names reinforces her poem and novel as cross-cultural works challenging the barriers of language and nationality in the Americas.

As García Márquez has so often stated in relation to his own work, Gayl Jones feels that her novels are ultimately optimistic and that her message is one of understanding and love, in spite of the display of brutal violence in the texts. What they suggest, Jones says, is "the alternative to brutality, which is tenderness."[69] In *Song for Anninho*, she keeps the promise and pursues the possibility of "love in times of cholera," as García Márquez would also do in his work. The times keep denying lovers the proper conditions for their personal lives to grow and their love to flourish. Still, the sad reflection of Anninho is a cry of hope and love in spite of it all:

*That was the question, Almeyda,*
*how we could sustain our love*
*at a time of cruelty . . .*
*look at each other with tenderness.*
*And keep it, even with everything.*
*It's hard to keep tenderness*
*when things all around you are hard.* (32)

While several themes of *Corregidora* are woven into the narrative of *Song for Anninho*, there is in the poem a departure from the obsession with the name and the world of the colonizer. If Palmares was an impossibility in the earlier novel, now it is brought to the forefront with its epic reality and its powerful meaning for all the dark peoples of America in their resistance to oppression. As Gayl Jones reconstructs Almeyda's tale through imagination three centuries after its historic counterpart, she echoes and reaffirms the resistance and endurance of all African slaves across time and space. "This earth is my history / none other than this whole earth," says Almeyda to Anninho. "We build our houses on top / of history" (11). Jones brings into the literature of the United States a history of black rebellion whose importance in the Americas "is second only to the Haitian revolt" and which has been compared by even conservative historians to the Trojan epic in the *Iliad*.[70]

Since the 1960s, the importance of Palmares has been explored in plays, songs, and intensified historical studies in Brazil.[71] The anniversary of Zumbi's death on November 20 has been adopted as the National Day of Negro Conscience in Brazil, and his name is a major inspiration for hundreds of black groups organized in the last decades. In 1985, the location of the central village of Macaco in the Republic of Palmares—Serra da Barriga, now in the state of Alagoas—was established as a historic area to be preserved. Yet for black men and women in Brazil and elsewhere, the New Palmares of peace, equality, and love dreamed by Almeyda and Anninho is yet to come.

In *Corregidora*, Ursa and Mutt withdraw from any hope of social change to concentrate on their personal relationship. The final scene shows the pursuit of sexual gratification and of individual power over each other's body and mind, even as the two try to begin anew and live with more tenderness. *Song for Anninho* narrates an epic journey for love and understanding, in spite of the hardness of the times. There is no idealized future of happiness and equality for all; on the contrary, the struggle is constant and cruel.

Colonialism does not end with Brazil or the Americas becoming officially independent. Almeyda's grandmother, in her clairvoyance, could predict cycles of exploitation of Africans—"others with the same flesh and blood and dreams"—going on and on. "It was not true that / there would come a time when the hardness would / be over," she foretold. "There would not come such a time, / never in her lifetime and not in mine and not / in the lifetimes of those that come after us" (44–45). Yet in spite of the pain and the sorrow that she had seen in her lifetime and could foresee in other times and places, Almeyda's grandmother never lost her strength. She fought and ran with her body and was brilliant in her mind, but most of all she had faith in the spirit. This was stronger than any fist or law of the oppressor, for only the spirit "is a match for cruelty" (45).

Instead of the strong physicality of *Corregidora,* the final scenes in *Song for Anninho* show the almost disembodied and mystical dialogue between Almeyda and her memory of Anninho. Even if defeated, separated, and destroyed by those in power, the two reaffirm hope in the new times of tenderness that the dreamers and the brave can bring to life. The search is still one for true companionship and understanding between man and woman, "the ways a man must be with a woman, the ways a woman must be with a man" (81), and the creation of new voices and roads that may be conducive to that. The message of endurance and understanding comes across with clarity and directness in Almeyda's tale, in a language reminiscent of the "new mestiza" writer Gloria Anzaldúa and the Spanish poet Antonio Machado:

"It is a long journey, Almeyda. . . .
You must create the roads as you travel them." (71)[72]

## Conclusion

Even as she weaves myth and magic in her narrative, Gayl Jones is careful not to make her tales less cruel or more picturesque by resorting to colorful folk sayings and stories from Africa. Perhaps she also shares with Carlos Fuentes a certain distrust of folklore as a sugary substitute for history and culture. Fuentes sees a "great cultural farce . . . in disguising the past and presenting it clad in the bright colors of folklore."[73] Jones uses no mask for the suffering and the oppression that black women and men have experienced in the creation of the *New World*. *Corregidora* develops and ends with the tragedy of the past still weighing on the present and preventing freedom. As she wrote *Song for Anninho* in 1981, Jones had moved toward a stronger affirmation of power and a clearer focus on the resistance of Africans and their descendants in the Americas.

Rather than responding to the monologic text of history with an idealized tale of unified African origins, Jones probes into that history with bitter sensitivity and joins in the creation of a new narrative and a new voice for our continent. The connection of her work with Brazilian history, particularly the memory of Palmares, as well as with the literature of Latin American writers such as Carlos Fuentes and Gabriel García Márquez celebrates difference as it recognizes the strengths of diversity in the process of our cultural formation. The multivocal space of Gayl Jones's stories inscribes a complex play between submission and transgression, song and war, signs of the literature and the history of the continent.

# 5
# No Final Chord: The Music of Morrison, Jones, and Marshall

Oh, I got the blues,
but I'm too damn mean
to cry.*

"Captive people have a need for song," says a woman writer from the Caribbean, the Jamaican Michelle Cliff.[1] In a new American narrative, the plural voices and multifocal perspectives of U.S.-born writers Toni Morrison, Paule Marshall, and Gayl Jones record and explore that captivity, that need, and the songs that the two have created throughout the making of the *New World*. The stories of these women are individual and collective, local and general, autobiographical as well as national and continental. The urgency in their telling connects them to the works of Latin American writers such as Gabriel García Márquez and Carlos Fuentes, with which they may also have intertextual relations. By so doing, the works of Morrison, Marshall, and Jones depart from a tradition of estrangement between a "developed" North, perceived as white, and the "Third World" of South and Central America and the Caribbean, normally represented as dark, different, and alien in U.S. narratives.

Literary criticism has traditionally emphasized a canon that cir-

---

*This is "perhaps the most familiar line in all of the blues"; it appears in several anthologies of old black folksongs. See Lawrence W. Levine, *Black Culture and Black Consciousness* (Oxford: Oxford University Press, 1977), 260.

cumscribes "American literature" within white and, preferably, male borders. It discredits not only the literature of the rest of the continent but also the writings of black men and women within the country. Along with blacks, other "different" peoples have been marginalized by the rigidity of established norms governing society and reflected in the hierarchy of cultural forms. Toni Morrison has decried the ethnic segregation persisting in the field of literature and criticism up to today. She says, "There is something called American Literature that, according to conventional wisdom, is certainly not Chicano literature, or Afro-American literature, or Asian-American, or Native-American, or . . . It is somehow separate from them and they from it."[2]

The literary and critical establishments reveals the same binary opposition between center and margins existing in society at large. Paule Marshall, Toni Morrison, and Gayl Jones are among a remarkable group of black women writers who, in recent decades, have contributed to denounce social inequality and undermine traditions that have often left "others" invisible and silent.[3] Without belonging to any literary clique or subscribing to a common style, each writer has told stories that recreate the nation and the culture. More than that, these women rewrite the continent: they, too, are "Americans." When the myth of the United States as a white nation of blond northern Europeans comes to an end, the perception of a radical difference between North and South America and their literatures also loses ground.[4] In their stories and their songs, Morrison, Jones, and Marshall join other writers whose many hands, voices, races, genders, and colors are putting forth a new face and a new text for the American continent.

The works of these three writers associate socioeconomic and historical facts with myths and dreams of past and present in stories that crisscross the geographies, times, and histories of the American people. At the same time that the African presence in the continent is rescued from the stereotypical representations or the oblivion in official narratives, that history is investigated in struggles and dilemmas persisting today in the life of the continent. The past is scarred by the tragic Middle Passage across the Atlantic, the exhaustive labor of men and women in the houses and fields of plantations, and the sexual exploitation of slave women by white masters. The land and the bodies were drained of their strength by the abuse and the greed of colonialism.

Reflecting that past, the present revolves around renewed cycles of economic and cultural dependency that are reinforced by a national and international order still controlled by similar concerns. The land and the bodies are ravished geographies in the works of Morrison, Jones, and Marshall, and their books are acts of rebellion crying against centuries of exploitation and oppression. They reinforce the commonality of a slave past and the search for an "extended Caribbean" cultural identity that is African even if deeply marked by the European colonizer.

In spite of the varying degrees of suffering and resistance that they inscribe and the different perspectives they open, the writings of Morrison, Marshall, and Jones all target awareness and change. For them, as for García Márquez and Fuentes, writing is itself a revolutionary act in its affirmation of a new subject and a new language against forgetfulness and erasure. Moreover, in its narrative beauty it can be a subversive statement denouncing the unequal and unjust patriarchal order established in the Americas since the time of Christopher Columbus.[5] The past can spell out lessons and hopes of a brighter future at the same time that it reminds of continuing patterns of injustice and pain. In the three women writers, memory of history and of myth stands out against chaos. Empowerment for oppressed black women and men lies exactly in the recuperation of the songs, the dances, the stories, the dreams, the pains, and the struggles that inform cultural identity.

Morrison, Marshall, and Jones do not offer a monolithic representation of "the black experience." The very meaning of "blackness" is problematized in the number of colors, hues, and class positions comprising that classification in the United States and interacting in their multiracial works. The meaning of "America" is revised and expanded. America is the native who was here before all others; it is also Africa, and Europe, and Asia. In different ways, the works of Morrison, Jones, and Marshall explore the complexity of social and cultural structures in parts of the continent where the number of Africans was significantly high from the beginning. Their works problematize the colonial legacy of racial prejudice and the social contempt for the "tragic mulatta" in those areas, along with the attendant cultural ambiguity of the mixed individual.[6]

Born of a white father and a black mother who is either slave or socially inferior to the male, Gayl Jones's Ursa Corregidora and Paule Marshall's Merle Kinbona hate the oppressive history that they carry in their genes. Twentieth-century whites and blacks in Jones's novel still tend to regard the "mestiza" Ursa as an oversexed woman, hungry for men.[7] In Toni Morrison's *Tar Baby*, light-skinned Jadine Childs is also a displaced person, seen with suspicion by darker blacks and always as an "other," however beautiful and exotic, by pure whites. Jadine, Ursa Corregidora, and Merle Kinbona negotiate their mixed heritages under pressure, searching for their place in a modern America that is both similar to and different from the old. This *New World* must finally assert its Africanness in history and in culture and at the same time come to terms with its multiculturalism. In the stories of these women, the black-and-white dichotomy is explored and broken apart in its many hues and nuances. The ambiguities and contradictions of the characters and the attendant tensions in the narrative are emblematic of a wide range of paradoxes that marks America itself.

The works of Morrison, Jones, and Marshall provide different articulations of the heritage of the slave past and African origins. In Jones, for instance, every individual character and each successive generation rework bits and pieces of memory. Gender, age, time, and place interfere with one's definition of the self and the culture. The Corregidora women react differently to the same history from one generation to the next. The perceptions of one person also shift as time and distance interfere between now and "what really happened." The new resembles the old in many ways, and yet past and present refuse to be fixed in an unchanging frame of crystallized "truth."

The three women writers show varying responses to specific events and circumstances of black history and culture, privileging the mythical past (Morrison), the heroic slave resistance (Marshall), or the personal feelings of black women (Jones). But each writer also varies in style and theme from one work to the other. Gayl Jones's later piece *Song for Anninho*, for instance, is more focused on the world created by the slaves than is *Corregidora*, a novel that dwells on the disruptive power of the slaveholder. Morrison's *Tar Baby* stages the interaction among blacks, whites, and "yellas" in the interrelated spaces of Europe, Africa, the United States, and the Caribbean. *Song of Solomon*, however, almost draws a line around the black "nation" in the United States, within which the different characters negotiate their relation to modern capitalism and the peasant cultural heritage of African ancestors. Marshall shows a materialist approach in *The Chosen Place, the Timeless People* and a political focus in *Daughters* that contrast with the culturalist bent of *Praisesong for the*

*Widow.* Even if all of Marshall's novels positively emphasize renewal and change, the first highlights economic empowerment and historical awareness of (neo)colonial exploitation (both within and between countries), whereas *Praisesong* emphatically turns to personal and cultural empowerment through the recuperation of stories, songs, and dances of one's "nation" in Africa.

Differences among the three authors exist side by side with many commonalities. The first major link between the works analyzed here is the negotiation of black identity in the cultural and historical reference of the United States. A second common point is the concern with the dilemmas inherited by women from the (still) oppressive patriarchal order. Finally, another major bridge between their works is their contextualization within a larger American space, their connection with the history and the culture of the Caribbean and Central and South America. Besides these major thematic linkages, the novels can often be compared in terms of narrative strategies.

The works of Toni Morrison and Gayl Jones are intertextually connected. The two writers have expressed an interest in and identification with each other's texts on different occasions, recalling a similar cross-reference between García Márquez and Fuentes. As senior editor at Random House, Morrison was Jones's editor for *Corregidora* and made several suggestions about the novel before its publication.[8] Morrison has commented on the lack of "a sense of joy" in Jones's writing as an exception to the rule in black women's writing. She has, however, praised Jones's ability to take "a large idea," the burden of slave history, and bring "it down small." In Morrison's view, that characteristic gives *Corregidora* "a universality and a particularity which makes it extraordinary."[9] Several critics find similarities in the women depicted by Morrison and Jones. Robert Stepto has commented on a connection between Morrison's *Sula* and Jones's emasculating/emasculated women; Keith Byerman has pointed out the similar complexity and grotesqueness of several of Jones's and Morrison's female characters.[10] The sterility, the violence, and the distortions presented are textual ways to probe into the actual lives of women yesterday and today.

The insistent questioning reaches no complete answers in the narratives of Morrison, Marshall, and Jones: characters and readers must go on exploring the meaning of racial identity and the complexity of its construction in the United States and throughout the continent. Each book is never a closed, definitive statement. As Toni

Morrison says of her works, they contain openings for the reader to fill in, invitations for a reimagining and a rewriting that should be the responsibility and the privilege of us all.[11] Morrison wants her stories to reproduce the beautiful and emotional open-endedness of black music. In jazz, she says, "there is no final chord"; its sounds have "a quality of hunger and disturbance that never ends."[12] Even if in other instances the writers' statements suggest closure, their characters and stories move between the authors' intentionality and the diverse readings allowed by the texts. Deeply immersed in the history of the Americas, the multiplicity of voices and languages points to the striking ethnic polyphony of our *New World*.[13]

The complex legacy of racism and sexism for a black woman in the United States and throughout the Americas is approached by Morrison, Marshall, and Jones on the basis of their own experiences and the stories passed on by their communities and their families. Even as they dramatize the ambiguities and indecisions of modern individuals, Marshall's major novels emphasize collective solidarity through the quests of the female protagonists Selina, Merle, Avey, and Ursa. Morrison embodies salvation and rebirth in strong mythical women such as Pilate and Thérèse and explores the paradoxical inner world of individual women in their relationships with other women or men. Jones's *Corregidora* and, to some extent, *Song for Anninho* probe into the possibilities and dilemmas of female sexuality and motherhood. Mothers and daughters are also problematized in Marshall's novels, from *The Chosen Place, the Timeless People* to *Daughters*. Marshall and Jones are willing to examine homosexuality as a viable alternative for both sexes. Interracial sexual contact is also more visible in Marshall and Jones; Marshall treats it as a possibility in spite of the historical exploitation of blacks by whites, but for Jones and Morrison, the legacy of racial separation often seems insurmountable.[14]

In the works of all three writers, female protagonists are complex and intriguing but normally do not eclipse male characters. Although their central characters are often women, Jones and Morrison have rejected the idea that their work is primarily feminist or gender-centered. Morrison finds "feminist or women's" literature confining. "I write without gender focus," she says, and she admires women writers who "write as people—like Eudora Welty and Flannery O'Connor—not about and for women only."[15] Gayl Jones also dislikes categorization. "I'm not really sure I know what a feminist is," she says, although she writes about "independent women." Jones is interested in the human being, regardless of gender: "The storyteller's vision as I see it shouldn't sacrifice the wholeness of anyone, man or woman."[16] Marshall and Jones are particularly concerned with the human need for healthy love relationships and urge the equality of men and women in war as in bed. Their fictional spaces are filled with men and women of different places, colors, and backgrounds, even as they record their own memories and the specificities of their communities in the United States.

While Marshall's fictional world is basically the Bajan (Barbadian) immigrant community in New York and its roots in the Caribbean, Morrison and Jones are culturally and historically indebted to the U.S. experience of slavery and segregation in the U.S. South. Like García Márquez, Fuentes, and other Latin American writers, Morrison and Jones feel a connection to the best known writer of that region, Mississippian William Faulkner. Beyond their common admiration for his style and the fact that he is another writer from the "extended Caribbean," the reasons for that connection may vary.[17] The sense of a multidimensional present, the layering of many voices and perspectives, and the emphasis on particular places and people created in the images of the writer's own life history and birthplace characterize not only Faulkner but also García Márquez, Fuentes, Morrison, Jones, and Marshall.[18]

"And what you is? . . . What's your nation?" demands Lebert Joseph of Avey Johnson in Paule Marshall's *Praisesong for the Widow*. The woman hesitantly answers that she is simply a tourist from the United States—New York, to be more specific.[19] In one way or another, in direct evocation or implied reference, the works of Marshall, Jones, and Morrison attempt to respond to the broader meaning behind such questions. The quest for individual and cultural identity unfolds as part of the process of formation of a nation or nations in America.[20] The music echoing in the different works bears signs of each nation and also reflects the multicultural reality of the *New World:* the blues in *Corregidora;* the blues and spirituals in *Song of Solomon;* the jazz, blues, and protest songs in *Daughters;* the calypso and the samba in *The Chosen Place, the Timeless People, Praisesong for the Widow,* and "Brazil"; the folksongs and dances in *Song of Solomon* and *Praisesong for the Widow.* The music is both memory and creation, both Europe and Africa, crossroads signs of the *New World.* The memory of African drums and dances and the memory of old

slave songs and ring shouts, whether or not they are directly re-
trieved in these stories, filter through the sounds of the continent.[21]
The history and culture of the nation and the continent are recreated
in Marshall's, Jones's, and Morrison's storytelling. As in other attempts at asserting independent collective identities, here "liberation
is necessarily an act of culture."[22]

Literary historian Barbara Christian, among other critics, has
pointed to the connection of folk forms and women's history in contemporary writings by black women. According to Christian, their
"exploration of new forms based on the black woman's culture and
her story" has revitalized the novel in the United States, altering "our
sense of the novelistic process."[23] The specificity of the race-gender
inscription on the novelistic genre can be associated with a general
concern for the rewriting of culture from an oppositional standpoint,
another feature of contemporary women writers such as Morrison,
Jones, and Marshall. The critical reinvention of culture connects the
three writers not only to other major black women writers of today,
such as Alice Walker, Ntozake Shange, and Toni Cade Bambara, but
also to related developments in contemporary literature of the United
States and Latin America. As we have seen, through intertextuality
Toni Morrison and Gayl Jones have built bridges with Latin American novelists Gabriel García Márquez and Carlos Fuentes, two best-
selling authors of the Latin American "boom" of the 1960s and early
1970s, both of them male and white-skinned. Linking the works of
these four writers, despite their differences, is a commitment to the
rewriting of the history of the *New World*. In the context of "minority" writing in the United States and the development of literature in
the continent, Morrison, Jones, and Marshall have constructed
works that are important intertexts. Bridges that crisscross and
touch, they connect races and cultures and approximate geographies
and histories.

Racism in areas of the African diaspora is associated with other
crucial contradictions and tensions of past and present: male sexual
domination, economic exploitation of the lower classes, the persisting poverty and dependence of poor communities and nations, the
imperialist control of the United States over the continent. Such socioeconomic aspects are explored in the works of the three writers.
For Latin American novelists García Márquez and Fuentes and for
U.S. writers Morrison, Marshall, and Jones, fiction and poetry are
above all acts of personal and cultural reflexivity. Their works dig

into history and the cultural past to explore questions of national identity—be it as members of a "Black Nation," the United States, Colombia, or Mexico—and reach out beyond specific racial and national boundaries to absorb a region or a continent.

The elaboration of personal and collective identity often entails antagonism and dichotomy: *we* and *they,* the oppressed and the oppressors, the people and the conquerors. The writings of Morrison, Marshall, and Jones often repeat common strategies in "narrating the nation" but may also blur divisions and turn them into ambiguities and contradictions, in a constant rearticulation of identity and culture. Their exploration of the dilemmas and paradoxes of black culture in the United States is complicated by their own ambivalent positions in relation to the dominant culture of the country: often apart and antagonistic, they nevertheless negotiate a place in it and effectively work for its transformation.[24]

I have repeatedly used the notion of "extended Caribbean," borrowed from Immanuel Wallerstein, to bind together the characters, themes, settings, and intertexts articulated by Paule Marshall, Gayl Jones, and Toni Morrison. With its music, its stories, and its rituals, the "extended Caribbean" of their works stretches north and south along the Atlantic and spreads its influence beyond the core plantation-slave region. Like the blues and the calypso, the Caribbean islands are symbolic of the polyphonic variety of the region and contain centuries of celebration and sorrow in their collective memory.[25] The novels of Paule Marshall, Toni Morrison, and Gayl Jones are full of the music of the continent and perform a role similar to that of the islands. Even as they retain their specificities, they relate to one another and connect the hemispheres. Like the Caribbean islands, their novels are bridges between North and South America; between colonial history and contemporary dilemmas; and between Africa, Europe, and America, linking *us* and *them.* In the historical and literary intertextuality of their novels, in their critical commentary, and through the geographical bridges that they create, Morrison, Marshall, and Jones help undermine the parochialism of traditional literary studies. At the same time that they join other writers and critics in the contemporary effort to redefine the literature of the United States as polyvocal and multicultural, they insert it within a larger American context, in the company of other cultures and writers from the continent of America.

This study of Morrison, Jones, and Marshall has attempted to interrogate the complex tensions in their narratives. They draw on roots and traditions but at the same time suggest the need for renovation and change. They are deeply grounded in U.S. history and culture but at the same time invite openness to peoples below the southern borders. They address the empowerment of black people and culture but also reveal the hybrid nature of their history and of the culture of the American continent.

Works without final chords and definitive interpretations, the writings of these women allow for a variety of readings that enrich and transform the critical debate. My own response returns their gaze from below the border and inscribes their inter-Americanness in the critical foreground. Barbara Christian has said that "writing disappears unless there is a response to it."[26] Each response, however, constructs that writing in different ways, in a constant discovery of new meanings and significances. This one is a reaffirmation of the beauty and complexity of literature by black women in the United States—and of the many bridges connecting it to "the extended Caribbean" beyond the country's southern borders.

# ABBREVIATIONS

C     Gayl Jones, *Corregidora* (Boston: Beacon, 1975)

CPTP    Paule Marshall, *The Chosen Place, the Timeless People* (New York: Harcourt, Brace & World, 1969)

PW    Paule Marshall, *Praisesong for the Widow* (New York: G. P. Putnam's Sons, 1983)

SA    Gayl Jones, *Song for Anninho* (Detroit: Lotus, 1981)

SOS    Toni Morrison, *Song of Solomon* (New York: New American Library, 1977)

# NOTES

## CHAPTER 1
### Stepping-Stones between the Americas:
### The Works of Paule Marshall, Toni Morrison, and Gayl Jones

1. "American" disciplines tend to be focused entirely on the United States, and American Studies programs have no "Central American or South American texts" (Barbara Harlow, *Resistance Literature* [New York: Methuen, 1987], xvi). This "exclusionary practice" in U.S. literary studies disregards "the history, cultures, and discourses of the Americas as a totality" (José David Saldívar, "The Dialectics of Our America," in *Do the Americas Have a Common Literature?* ed. Gustavo Pérez Firmat [London and Durham, N.C.: Duke University Press, 1990], 63).

2. I borrow the term from Brazilian critic Silviano Santiago in "O entre-lugar do discurso latino-americano," *Uma literatura nos trópicos* (São Paulo: Perspectiva, 1978), 11–28.

3. Gordon K. Lewis, *Main Currents in Caribbean Thought* (Baltimore: Johns Hopkins University Press, 1983), 2.

4. Immanuel Wallerstein, *The Modern World System*, vol. 2: *Mercantilism and the Consolidation of the European World Economy* (New York: Academic, 1980), 103. I borrow the term "alibi" from Gayatri Spivak, *The Post-colonial Critic: Interviews, Strategies, Dialogues*, ed. Sarah Harasym (London: Routledge, 1990), 77.

5. Stuart Hall, "Cultural Identity and Cinematic Representation," *Framework* 36 (1989): 78.

6. "Afroamerica" is "the black zone . . . situated basically on the Atlantic coast of the two continents," extending "from north to south,

from the North-American state of Virginia to the city of Rio de Janeiro" (Julio Le Riverend, "Afroamerica," *Casa de las Americas* 6 [May–Aug. 1966]: 23–31). Charles Wagley applies the terms *Afro-America* and *Plantation America* to the space going from the U.S. South to middle Brazil (in *The Latin American Tradition: Essays on the Unity and the Diversity of Latin American Culture* [New York: Columbia University Press, 1968], 14).

7. Ethnic autobiography and autobiographical fiction "serve as key forms for explorations of pluralist, post-industrial, late-twentieth century society" (Michael Fischer, "Ethnicity and the Post-modern Arts of Memory," in *Writing Culture: The Poetics of Ethnography,* ed. James Clifford and George Marcus [Berkeley: University of California Press, 1986], 195). Though not strictly autobiographical, the works of Morrison, Jones, and Marshall approach the complex process of inheriting and reconstituting ethnic and gender identity that is described in Fischer's article. Carlos Fuentes has pointed out the proximity between fiction, poetry, and anthropology in "modern Hispanic-American" novels that try "to invent or recover" myth (in *La nueva novela Hispanoamericana* [Mexico: Joaquín Mortiz, 1969], 20).

8. David W. Noble, *The End of American History* (Minneapolis: University of Minnesota Press, 1985), 7. The appropriation of *America* is also discussed in Sacvan Bercovitch, "The Problem of Ideology in American Literary History," *Critical Inquiry* 12 (Summer 1986): 631–53, and Benedict Anderson, *Imagined Communities: Reflections on the Origin and Spread of Nationalism* (London: Verso, 1983), 64. Gabriel García Márquez has expressed the Latin American feeling: "It bothers me that the people of the United States have appropriated the word *America* as if *they* were the only Americans" (quoted in *Ourselves among Others: Cross-cultural Readings for Writers,* ed. Carol J. Verburg [Boston: Bedford-St. Martin's, 1991], 531).

9. Wagley, *Latin American Tradition,* 1–2; Richard M. Morse, *New World Soundings: Culture and Ideology in the Americas* (Baltimore: Johns Hopkins University Press, 1989), 1, 134, 165; Octavio Paz, "Reflections: Mexico and the United States," *New Yorker* (Sept. 17, 1979): 137–53.

10. The term is from Oscar J. Martinez, *Troublesome Border* (Tucson: University of Arizona Press, 1988).

11. *Flying Down to Rio* is "the only film of the 1930s" to avoid the usual negative stereotypes of Latin Americans. National and private interests (to win markets and war allies, to a large extent) motivated it, and "sensitivity for the Latin character" was soon "studio policy" at RKO, then controlled by the Rockefellers (Allen L. Woll, *The Latin Image in American Films* [Los Angeles: University of California, Los Angeles, Latin American Center Publications, 1980], 58).

12. Raymond T. Smith, "Culture and Social Structure in the Carib-

bean," *Peoples and Cultures of the Caribbean,* ed. Michael Horowitz (Garden City, N.Y.: Natural History, 1971), 463.

13. For the construction of the "dark" difference in the European imagination and its consequences in history, see Edward Said, *Orientalism* (New York: Vintage, 1986). For a detailed analysis of the complementary myths of the Caribbean "cannibal" and the "noble" savage, see Peter Hulme, *Colonial Encounters: Europe and the Native Caribbean 1492–1797* (London: Methuen, 1986).

14. Winthrop R. Wright, Café con Leche: *Race, Class, and National Image in Venezuela* (Austin: University of Texas Press, 1990), 26–28.

15. Eugene D. Genovese, *The World the Slaveholders Made* (1969; reprint, Middletown, Conn.: Wesleyan University Press, 1988), 13.

16. José Martí, *Our America: Writings on Latin America and the Struggle for Cuban Independence,* ed. Philip Foner (New York: Monthly Review, 1969), 89–90, 313.

17. Ibid., 359.

18. Barbara Christian, "The Race for Theory," *Cultural Critique* 6 (Spring 1987): 56.

19. Debating "Latin American Culture and Identity" in a 1987 colloquium in Mexico, Juan Nuno said that the "touching stone," the contrast, the "other" for Latin America is always Anglo-Saxon America: "It seems impossible to treat Latin American themes without the mandatory referent of the contrast with the 'other' America" (Juan Nuno, "Latino América: Variedad y divergencia," *Vuelta* [March 1988]: 56–57; my translation). Black Nationalists in the United States tend to construct the dominant U.S. culture "under the sign of Mother Country," with black communities as "colonies." See Elliott Butler-Evans, *Race, Gender and Desire: Narrative Strategies in the Fiction of Toni Cade Bambara, Toni Morrison, and Alice Walker* (Philadelphia: Temple University Press, 1989), 28–29.

20. A major factor in personal, racial, and communal identity, (un)naming is constantly evoked by black writers in the United States such as Alice Walker, Toni Morrison, Gayl Jones, Audre Lorde, Ishmael Reed, and LeRoi Jones. See Kimberly W. Benston, "I Yam What I Am: The Topos of (Un)naming in Afro-American Literature," *Black Literature and Literary Theory,* ed. Henry Louis Gates, Jr. (New York: Methuen, 1984), 151–72.

21. Quoted by Wendy S. Tai, "Black Out? African-American Gaining," Minneapolis *Star Tribune,* 28 Feb. 1989, 1, 8B. John Wright was chairman of the Department of Afro-American and African Studies at the University of Minnesota at the time.

22. Elisa Larkin Nascimento, *Pan-Africanism and South America: Emergence of a Black Rebellion* (Buffalo, N.Y.: Afrodiaspora, 1980), 2–3.

23. Melville J. Herskovits, "Problem, Method and Theory in Afro-american Studies" (1945), in *The New World Negro,* ed. Frances S. Herskovits (Bloomington: Indiana University Press, 1966), 4.

24. Henry Louis Gates, Jr., "The Blackness of Blackness: A Critique of the Sign and the Signifying Monkey," in *Black Literature,* 299.

25. Langston Hughes, "I, too," in *Selected Poems* (New York: Alfred Knopf, 1968), 275.

26. My focus on three black women writers to the apparent exclusion of other black women, black men, and other writers of color is largely due to the time and length limitations of this work and is in no way meant to signify that they are of lesser importance in rewriting a plurivocal and multicultural America.

27. Exclusive idealizations in black feminism are discussed by Hazel V. Carby, *Reconstructing Womanhood: The Emergence of the Afro-American Woman Novelist* (New York: Oxford University Press, 1987), 7.

28. Octavio Paz, *The Labyrinth of Solitude* (1961; reprint, New York: Grove, 1985), 219–20.

29. Barbara Smith, "Introduction," in *Home Girls: A Black Feminist Anthology,* ed. Barbara Smith (New York: Kitchen Table Women of Color, 1983), xxxii, liv; idem, "Toward a Black Feminist Criticism," in *Feminist Criticism and Social Change,* eds. Judith Newton and Deborah Rosenfelt (New York: Methuen, 1985), 3–4. Smith echoes Frantz Fanon's caveat about the inexistence of a privileged "oppressed" viewpoint and of a clear dividing line between the culture of the dominant groups and the culture of the dominated.

30. Alice Walker, *In Search of Our Mothers' Gardens: Womanist Prose* (New York: Harcourt Brace Jovanovich, 1983), 36, 209–12. Walker's positive assessment of Cuba's racial reality contrasts with earlier criticism by Black Nationalist John Clytus and Black Panther Eldridge Cleaver, who blamed the Cuban government for repressing black organization and protest against inequality. See also Leslie B. Rout, Jr., *The African Experience in Spanish America, 1502 to the Present Day* (Cambridge: Cambridge University Press, 1976), 311. Rout overgeneralizes about Latinos of all nations and centuries when he concludes that because Fidel Castro is "first and foremost a Latin," his concepts of race "may differ very little from those of Simon Bolívar"(312).

31. Leonardo Boff, *Teologia do cativeiro e da libertação* (Petrópolis, Brazil: Vozes, 1987), 115.

32. Luiz Castaneda, quoted in Wendy S. Tai and Mark Brunswick, "Civil Rights Unit Seeks Power to Investigate Minneapolis Police," Minneapolis *Star Tribune,* 9 Feb. 1989, 21A.

33. Frantz Fanon, *Black Skins, White Masks* (New York: Grove, 1967), 109.

NOTES

34. Audre Lorde, *Zami: A New Spelling of My Name* (Trumansburg, N.Y.: Crossing, 1982), 154–56. Lorde's parents, like Paule Marshall's, immigrated to the United States from the Caribbean in the 1920s. Her mother's memories of the island of Grenada contrast with her impressions of the United States: there "everybody had a song for everything"; but not so in Harlem, "in this cold raucous country called america" (11). In the 1920s, her mother defined herself as "spanish" so that she could get a job: "American racism was a new and crushing reality that my parents had to deal with every day of their lives once they came to this country" (69).

35. Jack Kerouac's novel *On the Road* shows a sympathetic view of Mexicans but still emphasizes difference. The white protagonists feel like intruders in the magical and ancient Mexican mountains, like the soldiers and outlaws from the United States who had walked that route before. The dark Indian girls seem so different from them; even their sweat, which looks like "heavy oil, and always there," is different from "the kind of sweat we have." Their dark eyes seem innocent and saintly but also alien and impenetrable: "They stared unflinchingly into ours. We rubbed our nervous blue eyes and looked again. Still they penetrated us with sorrowful and hypnotic gleam" (Jack Kerouac, *On the Road* [London: Andre Deutsch, 1958], 298).

36. Langston Hughes, *In the Hispanic World and Haiti*, ed. Edward J. Mullen (Hamden, Conn.: Archon, 1977), 39. The emphasis given by Cuban poet Nicolás Guillén to a mulatto or mestizo heritage was a point of view "impossible for Langston Hughes to conceive in the United States, where notions of white supremacy and segregation" were strictly enforced amid bitter racial conflict (Martha Cobb, *Harlem, Haiti and Havana: A Comparative Critical Study of Langston Hughes, Jacques Roumain and Nicolás Guillén* [Washington, D.C.: Three Continents, 1979], 140).

37. Ntozake Shange, "Bocas: A Daughter's Geography," in *A Daughter's Geography* (New York: St. Martin's, 1983), 22–23.

38. Saldívar in "Dialetics," 78. The term *Third World* is controversial. I adopt Fredric Jameson's definition: "a range of other countries which have suffered the experience of colonialism and imperialism." Jameson uses "other" to mean neither from the capitalist First World nor from the socialist bloc, but the term commonly refers to nations and people within nations (like blacks in the United States) who are perceived as different in traditional Western narratives. See Fredric Jameson,"Third-World Literature in the Era of Multinational Capitalism," *Social Text* 15 (Fall 1986): 67.

39. Ntozake Shange, "A Weekend in Austin: A Poet, the People, and the KKK," in *See No Evil: Prefaces, Essays and Accounts 1976–1983* (San Francisco: Momo's, 1984), 57.

40. Toni Cade Bambara, *The Salt Eaters* (New York: Vintage, 1980), 65–68.

41. Gloria Anzaldúa, *Borderlands/La Frontera: The New Mestiza* (San Francisco: Spinsters-Aunt Lute, 1987), 194–95. Anzaldúa also supports no frontiers in women's sexual orientation and behavior and makes that evident in both *Borderlands* and *This Bridge Called My Back,* ed. Gloria Anzaldúa and Cherríe Moraga (New York: Kitchen Table-Women of Color, 1981).

42. Spivak, *Post-colonial Critic.* Similar views are expressed by Trinh T. Minh-ha, *Woman Native Other: Writing Postcoloniality and Feminism* (Bloomington: Indiana University Press, 1989).

43. Toni Morrison, interview with Thomas Le Clair, *New Republic* 184 (21 March 1981): 29. Alice Walker's novel *The Temple of My Familiar* (New York: Pocket Books, 1989) also bears resemblances to Latin American "magical realism"; see Claudia Dreifus, "Interview with Alice Walker," *The Progressive* (Aug. 1989): 29–30. Walker's novel has additional inter-American elements, such as the character Zedé, an Indian woman from an "old country in South America" who "floated into" the United States. The novel mixes centuries and continents, not limited to the "extended Caribbean" region.

44. Gayl Jones, interview with Michael Harper, in *Chant of Saints: A Gathering of Afro-American Literature, Art, and Scholarship,* ed. Michael Harper and Robert B. Stepto (Chicago: University of Illinois Press, 1979), 365–66; interview with Roseann Bell, "Gayl Jones Takes a Look at *Corregidora,*" in *Sturdy Black Bridges: Visions of Black Women in Literature,* ed. Roseann Bell (Garden City, N.Y.: Doubleday, 1979), 283–84.

45. Walter Benjamin, "The Storyteller," in idem, *Illuminations: Essays and Reflections,* ed. Hannah Arendt (New York: Schocken, 1968), 83–109.

46. George Lipsitz, "Myth, History, and Counter-Memory," in *Politics and the Muse: Studies in the Politics of Recent American Literature,* ed. Adam Sorkin (Bowling Green, Ohio: Bowling Green State University Popular Press, 1989), 162.

47. Gabriel García Márquez, "La revolución Cubana me libro de todos los honores detestables de este mundo," interview with Manuel Pereiro (*Bohemia,* La Habana, 1979), reprinted in *García Márquez habla de García Márquez,* ed. Alfonso Renteria Mantilla (Bogota: Renteria, 1979), 208. He literally considers remapping the Americas on the basis of African influence: "It wouldn't be a bad idea [to change Brazil's place in the map]" (my translation).

48. Quoted in Barbara Christian, "Paule Marshall," in *Dictionary of Literary Biography: Afro-American Fiction Writers after 1955,* ed. Thadious M. Davis and Trudier Harris (Detroit: Gale Research Co., 1984), 33:167.

49. Toni Morrison, "Writers Together" (Keynote address to the American Writers Congress, October 1981), *The Nation* (24 Oct. 1981): 397, 412.

50. García Márquez's and Fuentes's novels, along with pioneering cinema in Latin America, have influenced the development of an international "Third Cinema" concerned with collective memory, expression, and liberation. See Teshome H. Gabriel, "Third Cinema as Guardian of Popular Memory: Towards a Third Aesthetics," in *Questions of Third Cinema,* ed. Jim Pines and Paul Willeman (London: BFI Publishing, 1989), 53–64. Anti-Marxist writers and critics in the United States and England, however, have downgraded Latin American writers and deplored their influence. For instance, Karl Shapiro has blamed the decline of poetry in U.S. universities on the influence of South American Marxist poets and their "large doses of angst, warmed-over surrealism, anti-American hatred, and latino blood, sweat, and tears" (quoted by Gene H. Bell-Villada, "Northrop Frye, Modern Fantasy, Centrist Liberalism, Antimarxism, Passing Time, and Other Limits of American Academic Criticism," in *Reinventing the Americas,* ed. Bell Gale Chevigny and Gari Laguardia [Cambridge: Cambridge University Press, 1986], 288). In 1972, Earl Shorris found it difficult for the United States to respect Latin American literature (except that of Jorge Luis Borges) because of the Latino stereotypes common in this country and the nationalist-leftist ideology of most Latin American writers. García Márquez was perceived as the most dangerous of all, "for he is an enemy of history, a converter of the straight line of Western progress into the mythical circle of older civilizations, a telegrapher sending back to us the metaphysics of the formerly vanquished" (Earl Shorris, "Gabriel García Márquez: The Alchemy of History," *Harper's Magazine* (Feb. 1972): 98.

51. Fanon, *Black Skins,* 226–32.

52. Quoted by Alejo Carpentier, *La novela Latinoamericana en visperas de un nuevo siglo* (Madrid: Siglo XXI, 1981), 251. The translation is mine.

53. Fanon, *Black Skins,* 172.

54. Martí, *Our America,* 90–92.

55. Susan Willis, *Specifying: Black Women Writing the American Experience* (Madison: University of Wisconsin Press, 1987), 96. Willis links Morrison's *Song of Solomon* to Mario Vargas Llosa's *La casa verde* and to a general Third World tradition of allegorical writing, which helps expose the contradictions of capitalism. Novelists usually included in the so-called Latin American boom are, besides Gabriel García Márquez, the Argentinean Julio Cortázar, Mexican Carlos Fuentes, and Peruvian Mario Vargas Llosa; earlier names are Alejo Carpentier and Miguel Angel Astúrias. Willis calls the group "modernist" and situates the boom between the Cuban Revolution and the death of Salvador Allende in

1973. The period and the classification vary among critics. Kumkum Sangari, for instance, describes García Márquez's style of "marvelous realism" as a nonmimetic, polyphonic, non-Western narrative mode, neither modernist nor postmodernist ("The Politics of the Possible," *Cultural Critique* 7 [Fall 1987]: 157–86.

56. Timothy Brennan, "National Fictions, Fictional Nations," in *Salman Rushdie and the Third World: Myths of the Nation* (New York: St. Martin's, 1989), 7–17; Anderson, *Imagined Communities*, 74–77.

57. Willis, *Specifying*, 3.

58. For Peruvian liberation theologian Gustavo Gutierrez, "The concept of 'rereading of history' can appear to be an exercise for intellectuals, unless we understand that it is the result of a remaking of history." For Gutierrez, to remake history means "to 'subvert' it . . . make it flow not from above but from below" (*The Power of the Poor in History*, trans. Robert R. Barr [Maryknoll, N.Y.: Orbis, 1983], 201–2).

59. Hortense J. Spillers, "Afterword," in *Conjuring: Black Women, Fiction, and Literary Tradition*, ed. Hortense J. Spillers and Marjorie Pryse (Bloomington: Indiana University Press, 1985), 249. Spillers lists three novels by Morrison, two by Jones, and two by Marshall among the fourteen major works published by black women writers in the United States between 1965 and 1983, a time of "relatively unprecedented development" and prestige for writings by black women (257).

60. I here echo Antonio Gramsci, as well as Gayatri Spivak in her influential, if controversial, essay "Can the Subaltern Speak?" in *Marxism and the Interpretation of Culture*, ed. Cary Nelson and Lawrence Grossberg (Urbana: University of Illinois Press, 1988), 271–313.

61. W.E.B. DuBois wrote the essay "A Negro Nation within the Nation" in 1935, describing the "peculiar position of Negroes in America" and their obvious segregation and arguing for "a new economic solidarity" among Negroes and control of their own education and industries (in *A W.E.B. DuBois Reader*, ed. Andrew G. Paschal [New York: Macmillan, 1971], 69–78).

62. Important recent U.S. publications involving women as authors and objects of study include Deborah Gray White, *Ar'n't I a Woman? Female Slaves in the Plantation South* (New York: Norton, 1985); Barbara Bush, *Slave Women in Caribbean Societies* (Bloomington: Indiana University Press, 1990); Filomina Chioma Steady, *The Black Woman Cross-culturally* (Cambridge: Schenkman, 1981); Jacqueline Jones, *Labor of Love, Labor of Sorrow: Black Women, Work, and the Family, from Slavery to the Present* (New York: Vintage, 1985); Rosalyn Terborg-Penn, "Women and Slavery in the African Diaspora: A Cross-cultural Approach to Historical Analysis," *SAGE: A Scholarly Journal on Black Women* 3, 2 (Fall 1986): 11–15.

63. Paula Giddings, *When and Where I Enter: The Impact of Black Women on Race and Sex in America* (New York: William Morrow, 1984), 314–24.

64. The term "social dramas" is used by anthropologist Victor Turner, "Social Dramas and Stories about Them," *Critical Inquiry* 7, 1 (Fall 1980): 141–68. Turner and others focus on festivals and rites as forms of interaction and plural reflexivity in John J. MacAloon, ed., *Rite, Drama, Festival, Spectacle: Rehearsals toward a Theory of Cultural Performance* (Philadelphia: Institute for the Study of Human Issues, 1984).

65. Ethnographer Renato Rosaldo discusses the radical reorientation within ethnography concerning the definition of culture, the role of the informant, and the position of the ethnographer. Questioning within the discipline sprang from the general revisions going on in the United States in the 1960s and 1970s, along with the "potent historical conjuncture of decolonization and the intensification of American imperialism" (Renato Rosaldo, *Culture and Truth: The Remaking of Social Analysis* [Boston: Beacon, 1989], 35). Ethnographers have lately become increasingly "interdisciplinary," connecting fieldwork with history, economy, political science, and psychology. See John Van Maanen, *Tales of the Field: On Writing Ethnography* (Chicago: University of Chicago Press, 1988), 129.

66. From statements by Paule Marshall in "Return of a Native Daughter: An Interview with Paule Marshall and Maryse Condé," *SAGE: A Scholarly Journal on Black Women* 3, 2 (Fall 1986): 52–53.

67. Chapters of the book first came out in *The Anglo-African Magazine* in 1859 and again in *The Weekly Anglo-African* in 1861–1862, but the entire text reached book form only in 1970: Martin Delany, *Blake, or the Huts of America,* with an introduction by Floyd Miller (Boston: Beacon, 1970). According to Miller, the book is "the most important black novel of this period" and focuses on major issues of the 1850s, which are still important today: the institution of slavery, southern interest in the Cuban annexation, the possibility of slave revolution, and psychological liberation through collective action (xii).

68. Term quoted is from Walker, *In Search of Our Mothers' Gardens.*

## CHAPTER 2
### From the Natives' Point of View:
### The Ethnographic Novels of Paule Marshall

1. Ethnography in a contemporary sense is the subjective description of how people use culture to make meaning for themselves. See James Clifford and George E. Marcus, eds., *Writing Culture: The Poetics and Politics of Ethnography* (Berkeley: University of California Press, 1986); and George Marcus and Michael M. J. Fischer, *Anthropology as*

*Cultural Critique: An Experimental Moment in the Human Sciences* (Chicago: University of Chicago Press, 1986). The idea of ethnography as a busy intersection rather than a microcosm of culture is from Renato Rosaldo, *Culture and Truth: The Remaking of Social Analysis* (Boston: Beacon, 1989).

2. Michael Fischer argues that "ethnic autobiography and auto-biographical fiction can perhaps serve as key forms for explorations of pluralist, post-industrial, late twentieth-century society" ("Ethnicity and the Post-modern Art of Memory," in *Writing Culture,* ed. Clifford and Marcus, 195).

3. Paule Marshall's major works, in order of publication, are *Brown Girl, Brownstones* (New York: Avon Books, 1959; reprint, New York: The Feminist Press, 1981); *Soul Clap Hands and Sing: Four Novellas* (1961; Washington, D.C.: Howard University Press, 1988); *The Chosen Place, the Timeless People* (New York: Harcourt, Brace & World, 1969); *Praisesong for the Widow* (New York: G. P. Putnam's Sons, 1983); and *Daughters* (New York: Atheneum, 1991). References to specific pages of these works are made in parentheses directly in the text.

4. The title of the collection is adapted from a line in the second stanza of W. B. Yeats's famous poem "Sailing to Byzantium" and refers to the old men portrayed in the stories: "An aged man is but a paltry thing, / A tattered coat upon a stick, unless / Soul clap its hands and sing."

5. Barbara T. Christian, "Paule Marshall," in *Dictionary of Literary Biography,* ed. Thadious M. Davis and Trudier Harris (Detroit: Gale Research Co., 1984), 33:163.

6. Marshall uses the spelling "Guiana."

7. The word is misspelled "Café Sinho" in the book.

8. The mixture of attraction and repulsion inspired by the show is no doubt connected to other, similar encounters (the European versus the Caribbean/Caliban, discussed here in Chapter 1, p. 5–6) and the reactions of white performers and audiences in "black" minstrel shows. See Nathan Irvin Huggins, *Harlem Renaissance* (New York: Oxford University Press, 1971), 253–54.

9. Rob Nixon, "Caribbean and African Appropriations of *The Tempest,*" *Critical Inquiry* 13 (Spring 1987): 557–78. The play is used to counterattack European domination in the Caribbean by Barbadian writer George Lamming, *The Pleasures of Exile* (1984), and by poet Edward Brathwaite (1969) among several other works; it is evoked by Martinican Frantz Fanon in *The Wretched of the Earth* (1961) and *Black Skins, White Masks* (1952); reworked in Aimé Césaire's *Une Têmpete* (1969); and converted into a national and hemispheric symbol by Cuban Roberto Fernández Retamar in "Cuba hasta Fidel" and *Calibán: Apuntes sobre la cultura en nuestra América* (Mexico: Editorial Diogenes, 1972).

10. From Roberto Fernández Retamar's translated work "Caliban: Notes toward a Discussion of Culture in Our America," *Massachusetts Review* 15, 1–2 (1974): 24.

11. Barbados is a tiny island of 166 square miles, with a total population estimated at 256,000 in 1989: 42 percent urban, 99 percent literate, 70 percent Anglican. Its ethnic composition is 80 percent African, 16 percent mixed, and 4 percent European. About the symbolic role of Caribbean islands according to Martí, see p. 7.

12. Barbados was proclaimed independent from British rule in 1966 but remains within the British Commonwealth with Queen Elizabeth still as head-of-state. A governor general represents her on the island and appoints a prime minister and the cabinet, and both the governor and prime minister choose the twenty-one members of the Parliament Senate. Only the twenty-seven members of the House of Assembly have been elected by popular vote since 1981. General information on Barbados in this chapter is from F. A. Hoyos, *Barbados: A History from the Amerindians to Independence* (London: Macmillan Caribbean, 1978), 32–80.

13. Barbados shares most of the general characteristics of West Indian colonization: a monocrop leading to economic vulnerability; late independence; mercantile exploitation (raw materials in exchange for overpriced manufactured goods from the "mother country"); political colonialism, with the central government located abroad; education controlled from abroad with "imposition of curricula, texts and examinations"; class stratification, with the darker-skinned forming "the mass of the proletariat" and the lighter-skinned "the bulk of the controlling class," often with mulattoes (descendants of white fathers and black mothers) in intermediate positions. See Michael M. Horowitz, "Introduction," in *Peoples and Cultures of the Caribbean*, ed. Michael M. Horowitz (Garden City, N.Y.: Natural History, 1971), 3–5.

14. Development projects sponsored by international organizations or multinational companies have multiplied in the Caribbean and Latin America over recent decades. Many of these projects are dissociated from the local cultures and bound for failure: Haiti, for instance, "is a cemetery of projects" (Marcelo Grondin, *Haiti: Cultura, poder e desenvolvimento* [São Paulo: Brasiliense, 1985], 92).

15. Rosaldo, *Culture and Truth*, 35.

16. According to some historians, slavery in Barbados was harsher than in other sugar colonies. Slaves outnumbered whites by four to one by the end of the seventeenth century. Many slave uprisings took place in opposition to their inhuman living conditions. The great rebellion of 1675 was meant to set Cuffy as king of the island. Conch shells sounded like trumpets to announce that canes should be lit to start the fire and the uprising. Betrayal by a woman led to failure; seventeen leaders were immediately executed, six burned alive and eleven beheaded, their

bodies dragged through the streets to warn other conspirators. Another big insurrection took place in 1812, when many plantations were again burned by insurgents. But the British crushed the rebellion; 176 slaves were killed in battle and 214 were executed after trial by court-martial. See Hoyos, *Barbados*, 32–80, 90–94.

17. Allon White, "Hysteria and the End of Carnival: Festivity and Bourgeois Neurosis," in *The Violence of Representation: Literature and the History of Violence*, ed. Nancy Armstrong and Leonard Tennenhouse (London: Routledge, 1989), 163.

18. I have in mind "classic" narratives of America—Columbus's, Captain John Smith's, Daniel Defoe's, Shakespeare's, etc.—analyzed in Peter Hulme, *Colonial Encounters: Europe and the Native Caribbean, 1492–1789* (London: Methuen, 1986); and also the recurring representation of Carnival sites in European and U.S. mass media, especially Hollywood. In *Main Currents in Caribbean Thought* (Baltimore: Johns Hopkins University Press, 1983), Gordon K. Lewis attributes the coincidence of a Catholic base in major Carnival centers (Rio, Port of Spain, New Orleans) to the smaller degree of puritanism and higher tolerance of Catholic missions in those cities, as opposed to a "harsher" Protestant mentality.

19. Umberto Eco, "Frames of Comic Freedom," in *Monica Rector, Umberto Eco, V. V. Ivanov: Carnival!* ed. Thomas A. Sebeok (New York: Mouton, 1984), 6.

20. Mikhail Bakhtin, *Rabelais and His World* (1965; Bloomington: Indiana University Press, 1984), 10, 49.

21. Keith Q. Warner, *Kaiso! the Trinidad Calypso: A Study of the Calypso as Oral Literature* (Washington, D.C.: Three Continents, 1982), 70.

22. On Caribbean Carnival, see John W. Nunley and Judith Bettelheim, eds. *Caribbean Festival Arts: Each and Every Bit of Difference* (St. Louis: St. Louis Art Museum, 1988); Errol Hill, *The Trinidad Carnival: Mandate for a National Theatre* (Austin: University of Texas Press, 1972). On Brazilian Carnival, see Roberto da Matta, *Carnavais, malandros e heróis: Para uma sociologia do dilema brasileiro* (Rio de Janeiro: Zahar, 1978) and "Carnival in Multiple Planes," in *Rite, Drama, Festival, Spectacle: Rehearsals toward a Theory of Cultural Performance*, ed. John MacAloon (Philadelphia: Institute for the Study of Human Issues, 1984), 208–40; Victor Turner, "Carnival, Ritual, and Play in Rio de Janeiro," in *Time Out of Time: Essays on the Festival*, ed. Alessandro Falassi (Albuquerque: University of New Mexico Press, 1967), 74–90; Monica Rector, "The Code and Message of Carnival: Escolas de Samba," in *Monica Rector*, ed. Sebeok, 37–152.

23. The rigid English rule in Barbados gradually relaxed to allow slaves some weekend time for dancing, drumbeating, and cockfights. Planters came to believe that those activities were harmless and even

contributed to higher productivity and general tranquility. See Hoyos, *Barbados,* 32–80. Those drums and dances continue in today's Carnival celebrations and in the popular culture of the island and reveal a similar pattern of tolerated transgression.

24. Carnival in Trinidad has "survived despite the efforts of colonial authority and the wishes of the upper class." Since the 1962 independence, bands have used more African themes and traditions and carnival has changed from "a rowdy festival of the urban lower class" into a true "cement of society," providing "an invaluable catharsis for all" (Nunley and Bettelheim, *Caribbean Festival Arts,* 92, 113). More pessimistic about samba parades in Rio de Janeiro, Ana Maria Rodrigues argues that black music and dance have been incorporated by whites as a result of authoritarianism and domination (*Samba negro, espoliação branca* [São Paulo: Huciter, 1984]). Victor Turner confesses his own enthusiasm for the Brazilian Carnival but acknowledges the critiques of Brazilian Marxists, on the one hand, who see Carnival as a tropical "opiate of the masses" and the bourgeoisie, on the other hand, who find it "vulgar and violent." The high clergy characterizes it as "immoral and pagan" (Turner, "Carnival," 75).

25. Edward Brathwaite sees Marshall's depiction of Carnival as less typical of the Bajan traditions of Barbados and more similar to the masquerades of those other two islands ("The African Presence in Caribbean Literature," in *Africa in Latin America: Essays on History, Culture and Socialization,* ed. Manoel Moreno Fraginals [New York: Holmes & Meier, 1984], 134).

26. Patrick Taylor, *The Narrative of Liberation: Perspectives on Afro-Caribbean Literature, Popular Culture, and Politics* (Ithaca, N.Y., and London: Cornell University Press, 1989), xi.

27. Maroonage was a form of slave resistance "where large numbers of slaves, men and women, ran away from plantations, frequently before they had been 'seasoned' into plantation life, and established free autonomous 'maroon' communities" (Barbara Bush, *Slave Women in Caribbean Society 1650–1838* [Kingston: Heinemann; Bloomington: Indiana University Press; London: James Currey, 1990], 63). The Brazilian *quilombos,* described by Gayl Jones in her works, are similar communities. Like the *quilombistas,* Maroons carried out guerrilla warfare, incited slaves to rebel, and participated in large slave uprisings.

28. Michael Fischer describes the bifocal enterprise of ethnography anticipated here by Marshall: "seeing others against a background of ourselves, and ourselves against a background of others," in a "reciprocity of perspectives" that "has become increasingly important in a world of growing interdependence between societies" ("Ethnicity," 199).

29. Marshall's novel shows a critical attitude about the United States

that has been typical of the West Indian community in New York since the early twentieth century. See Calvin Holder, "West Indian Immigrants in New York City 1900–1952: In Conflict with the Promised Land," in *Emerging Perspectives on the Black Diaspora*, ed. Aubrey W. Bonnett and G. Llewellyn Watson (Lanham, Md.: University Press of America, 1990), 57–77.

30. The novel does not completely clarify the relationship between Merle and the English "protectress." Hortense J. Spillers provides an illuminating discussion on the dynamics of power possibly underlying that relationship in *"Chosen Place, Timeless People*: Some Figurations on the New World," in *Conjuring: Black Women, Fictions, and Literary Tradition*, ed. Hortense J. Spiller and Marjorie Pryse (Bloomington: Indiana University Press, 1985), 151–75.

31. Emigrations such as Vere's are common for the unemployed or underemployed poor of Latin America and the Caribbean. They will go on "as long as the structural disparities between countries with a relative 'surplus population' and countries with comparatively high minimum wages continue to exist." The poor will flee to "the 'promised land,' even if it means permanent discrimination and the risk of deportation." The uprootedness of indigenous people and blacks is directly related to "the closure of the international capitalist cycle" and the "direct economic (as well as political and military) interventions of the U.S. in the Caribbean" (Remco van Capelleveen, "Caribbean Immigrants in New York City and the Transformation of the Metropolitan Economy," in *The Caribbean and Latin America/El Caribe y America Latina: Interdisciplinary Colloquium at the University of Berlin 1984*, ed. U. Fleischmann and Ineke Phaf [Frankfurt-am-Main: Verlag Klaus Dieter Vervuert, 1987], 202).

32. "Shades of colour, degrees of blackness, are the most serious criteria in colonial societies such as the Barbadian, in that common interests and a common cultural background are denied, in order to further one's own imagined favourable position in society" (Jurgen Martini, "'Hell wit' the Canal': The West Indies and Panama in Eric Walrond's *Tropic Death*," in Fleischmann and Phaf, *Caribbean and Latin America*, 187.

33. Michelle Cliff defines *backra* as "white; white-identified. Probably from the West Indian *mbakara*, he who surrounds or governs. Some Jamaicans believe the word derives from back-raw, the conditions of a slave's back after whipping" ("Glossary," in *No Telephone to Heaven* [New York: Vintage International, 1987], 209).

34. "Because they are labor-intensive and capital-poor sectors, backwardness and conservatism are in fact characteristic" of Caribbean peasantries, long controlled by an alien colonial power. "Research workers in Caribbean societies have been struck by the relative absence of community-based activity in daily life" (Sidney W. Mintz, "The Caribbean as a Socio-cultural Area," in *Peoples and Cultures*, ed. Horowitz, 31–38).

35. Marshall emphasizes the Bantu origins of her protagonists in *Chosen Place* and *Praisesong*. The Bantus came from the southern coast of Africa, today's Zaire and Angola; cf. Katia M. de Q. Mattoso, "Slave, Free, and Freed Family Structures in Nineteenth-century Salvador, Bahia," *Luso-Brazilian Review* 25, 1 (Summer 1988): 74. The famous sculpture produced in the kingdom of Benin, also evoked in the passage, is a reminder that many of the slaves brought to the New World came from the area near the Bay of Benin in West Africa.

36. W.E.B. DuBois, among other early twentieth-century black intellectuals, connected the suffering of Jews and Africans. In 1943, DuBois said of the Holocaust, "It is a case of race prejudice on a scale unknown and unconceived since the Emancipation Proclamation" (from a syndicated column in the *Amsterdam News*, quoted in Manning Marable, *How Capitalism Underdeveloped Black America: Problems in Race, Political Economy and Society* [Boston: South End, 1983], 232).

37. Cooperation over trade led newly independent Caribbean governments to organize under CARIFTA (Caribbean Free Trade Association) in 1968; the organization evolved into the bigger and broader CARICOM (Caribbean Common Market and Community) in 1973. Cooperatives also developed within individual countries. See James Ferguson, *Far from Paradise: An Introduction to Caribbean Development* (London: Latin American Bureau, 1990).

38. Edward Brathwaite, "West Indian History and Society in the Art of Paule Marshall's Novel," *Journal of Black Studies* 1, 2 (Dec. 1970): 226.

39. Paule Marshall, interview with Daryl Cumber Dance, *Southern Review* 28, 1 (Winter 1992): 19.

40. The idea of a transformative, creative process rather than a crystallized identity to be "discovered" is a point strongly made by Frantz Fanon in *The Wretched of the Earth* (1961) and echoed by Stuart Hall in "Cultural Identity and Cinematic Representation," *Framework* 36 (1989): 68–81.

41. Marshall finds her own writing more positive than that of other contemporary black women writers from the United States. She sees a way out of struggle and pain and refuses to portray women and blacks as mere victims whose lives are as much "in disarray" as the dominant culture would assume. She avoids showing rape, incest, and other violence as the pattern in black life, even if that is what the market expects (Paule Marshall, interview with Sabine Bröck, "'Talk as a Form of Action,'" in *History and Tradition in Afro-American Culture*, ed. Günter H. Lenz [Frankfurt: Campus-Verlag, 1984], 196–202).

42. Paule Marshall, interview with Maryse Condé, "Return of a Native Daughter: An Interview," trans. John Williams, *SAGE: A Scholarly Journal on Black Women* 2, 2 (Fall 1986): 52.

43. Migration has been a characteristic of Caribbean life from the time of the "brutal and forcible transplantation" of Africans to the later migration movements. Caribbeans began entering the United States at the end of the nineteenth century mainly to work in agriculture; the flow almost ceased during the 1930s but increased again in response to the need for labor during World War II and later under the more liberal Immigration and Naturalization Act of 1965. In the 1970s, 10.7 percent of total legal immigration to the United States was from the Caribbean, excluding the high numbers related to Cuba and the uncounted illegal entrances. Most of the immigrants are concentrated in New York City. See van Capelleveen, "Caribbean Immigrants," 261–62.

44. Marshall, interview with Bröck, 199.

45. Younger writers from the Caribbean such as Michelle Cliff (from Jamaica) and Jamaica Kincaid (Antigua) relate to Marshall in their focus on immigrant life and conflicts, being themselves immigrants to the United States. Describing middle-class Jamaicans living in Brooklyn, Staten Island, or Manhattan, Cliff remembers Marshall: the ones who did not "pass" as whites were "not unlike the Bajans in Paule Marshall's *Brown Girl, Brownstones*—saving, working, investing, buying property. Completely separate in most cases from Black Americans" (Michelle Cliff, "If I Could Write This in Fire I Would Write This in Fire," in *Home Girls: A Black Feminist Anthology*, ed. Barbara Smith [New York: Kitchen Table Women of Color, 1983], 17).

46. Marshall, interview with Bröck, 197.

47. In a parody of Western civilization, the boat illustrates the glorification of French and European culture and the legacy of court hypocrisy and fastidiousness. Dessert is called "Peach Parfait à la Versailles," wall tapestries depict court scenes, and the Versailles Room glitters in its "Louis XIV decor and wealth of silver and crystal on the damask-covered tables" (46–49).

48. *Webster's New International Dictionary of the English Language*, 3d ed. (1966), s.v. "avatar."

49. Spirit possession involves five distinct steps: preparatory ritual baths and other ceremonies; induction into a trance state, particularly by the use of percussion instruments; possession itself, accompanied by a variety of unusual or "socially inappropriate" forms of behavior normally associated with childishness or illness; recovery; aftereffect, with the experience articulated and possibly providing a basis for action. See Irving I. Zaretsky and Cynthia Shambaugh, *Spirit Possession and Spirit Mediumship in Africa and Afro-America: An Annotated Bibliography* (New York: Garland, 1978), xiv-xvi. The authors draw on Vincent Crapanzano and Vivian Garrison, eds., "Introduction," in *Case Studies in Spirit Possession* (New York: John Wiley & Sons, 1977), 1–40.

50. Grenada and Carriacou also occupy an important space in the personal and cultural definitions of U.S. black woman writer Audre Lorde. The daughter of Grenadan immigrants, Lorde perceived "the root of [her] mother's powers" in the swinging walk and the "arrogant gentleness" of the women of Grenada, "the country of [her] foremothers." Stories she heard in childhood told of boat trips to Carriacou and the loving relationships among women on that island. Carriacou became a magic "home" for Lorde, although she had never been there. See Audre Lorde, *Zami: A New Spelling of My Name: A Biomythography* (New York: Crossing-Trumansburg, 1982), 9–14, 256.

51. The ring shout is "the most important African ritual in antebellum America." The circle, usually moving slowly in a counterclockwise direction, with its wavelike dance, drumbeating, and rhythmical singing recalls similar African ring-dance ceremonies "directed to the ancestors and the gods." Church clapping and dancing in the U.S. South often resemble those rituals (Sterling Stuckey, *Slave Culture: Nationalist Theory and the Foundations of Black America* [New York: Oxford University Press, 1987], viii–15). African origins are a vital quest for some black intellectuals and activists and also an increasing concern in recent historiography. The Arada came from the Bight of Benin, and inhabited coastal Dahomey-Togo in western Africa. Other African nations cited in *Praisesong* (166–67) are among the many different groups transplanted during the slave trade. They are the "Old Parents": the "Moko" (or Moco, northwest Bantu), the "Manding" (or Mandingue, from Senegambia), the Chamba (from the Bight of Benin), the "Cromanti" (or Coromanti, from the Gold Coast), the "Yarraba" (Yoruba, from Benin), the "Banda" (Bandia or Bandja, from the Gold Coast), and the Temne (from Sierra Leone). See Philip Curtin, *The Atlantic Slave Trade: A Census* (Madison: University of Wisconsin Press, 1969), 192–98.

52. Marshall, interview with Condé, 53.

53. The linguistic variety of the Caribbean islands has often been cited as an impediment to communication and cooperation among them. In *Daughters*, young Primus Mackenzie sees that problem in Triunion, where some in the North District refuse to speak English, "behaving like they're still maroons fighting the French"; the people in southern Spanish Bay speak Spanish; and the majority speak the official language, English (144). Primus does not know any Spanish but speaks the Morlands Creole "when the spirit moves [him]"(28).

54. Marshall, interview with Dance, 5. Marshall's close acquaintance with Haiti, the Dominican Republic, and the English-speaking islands helped in the creation of imaginary Triunion. Her Haitian mother-in-law inspired Mis-Mack, the angry shopkeeper with a cane (13).

55. Marshall, interview with Dance, 6. Marshall acknowledges West

Indian historian Lucille Mair and U.S. writer Angela Davis as good bibliographical sources on the rebellion of slave women and men.

56. Marshall, interview with Dance, 2. Ursa's name evokes the constellations of Ursa Major and Minor, the first being "the most conspicuous of the northern constellations," located "near the north pole of the heavens," and the second containing Polaris, the North Star (*Webster's New Collegiate Dictionary* [1979], s.v. "Ursa Major" and "Ursa Minor"). Chapter 3 of *Daughters,* totally dedicated to Ursa, is titled "Polestar." The name Ursa Beatrice or Ursa Bea honors Ursa's two grandmothers, Ursa Louise (Wilkerson) Mackenzie and Beatrice (Bea) Harrison. Coincidentally, Ursa has the same name as Gayl Jones's protagonist in *Corregidora.*

57. This dilemma connects Estelle to other imaginary women in Toni Morrison's *Beloved* and Gayl Jones's *Corregidora* and *Song for Anninho.* It also stresses the "unnaturalness" of racial and social violence that has lasted since colonial times and the terrible choices that women often face.

58. Marshall, interview with Dance, 8–10.

59. Ibid., 5.

60. Primus's father, like a U.S. southern plantation owner, always dressed in white suits and white shoes. He also had a keep-miss, to the rage of his wife, the fearful and big "Mis-Mack." A pretty woman when young, Mis-Mack grew fat and nervous in her frustration with her husband and life. She hoped her son Primus would treat a woman differently (155, 161).

61. Marshall, interview with Dance, 7.

62. Paule Marshall had Viney choose that name to honor the great U.S. black singer (considered the best interpreter of spirituals), actor, and political activist Paul Robeson (1898–1976), whose socialist ideas find echo in Marshall's works. He described (U.S.) Afro-America as "a kind of nation" and defended the union of all Negro cultures in the struggle for their own liberation in the United States, the Caribbean, Latin America, and Africa. The poets Pablo Neruda (Chile) and Nicolás Guillén (Cuba) hailed Robeson's important message for all the oppressed and supported his view of art as a revolutionary weapon for change. Against the capitalist order, Robeson saw the primacy of class over race, in the manner of W.E.B. DuBois and Jomo Kenyatta. Ostracized by more provincial black leaders and by the dominant culture because of his radical outlook, he lived and worked in Europe for many years. See Stuckey, *Slave Culture,* 323–52.

63. This point is discussed in Chapter 1, pp. 10–13.

64. Paule Marshall, interview with Sylvia Baer, "Holding onto the Vision," *Women's Review of Books* 8, 10–11 (July 1991): 24.

## CHAPTER 3
### The Redefinition of American Geography and History:
### Toni Morrison's *Song of Solomon* and *Tar Baby*

1. By order of publication, Toni Morrison's novels are *The Bluest Eye* (New York: Washington Square, 1970); *Sula* (New York: Knopf, 1974); *Song of Solomon* (New York: New American Library, 1977); *Tar Baby* (New York: New American Library, 1981); *Beloved* (New York: Knopf, 1987); and *Jazz* (New York: Knopf/Random House, 1992). I use these editions for comments and quotations in the text.

2. Morrison could not find enough crafts made by slaves and instruments of restraint or torture used against them in the museums of the United States. In her research for *Beloved,* she "got a lot of help" in Brazil, where "they've kept everything" (Toni Morrison, interview with Walter Clemons, "The Ghosts of 'Sixty Million and More,'" *Newsweek* (28 Sept. 1987): 75. Brazil is indirectly recalled in *Tar Baby* (p. 54), when the beauty of the female protagonist Jadine is compared to that of (supposedly Brazilian) Eurydice in the 1961 Franco-Brazilian movie *Black Orpheus*. In 1990, Morrison reportedly told a friend that if she had to pick a second country, Brazil would be her choice, "Nobel—Lirismo e Denúncia" (*Veja* 13 [October 1993]: 103).

3. *New York Times* critic John Leonard is emphatic about those links in his review of *Song of Solomon*, "To Ride the Air to Africa," 6 Sept. 1977, 37. He goes so far as to say that the book "may be foolishly fussed over as a Black Novel, as a Women's Novel, or an Important new Novel by a Black Woman" but is in reality "closer in spirit and style to *One Hundred Years of Solitude* and *The Woman Warrior*." Jean Strouse makes reference to the Latin American "taste" of Morrison's "magical" style in "Toni Morrison's Black Magic," *Newsweek* (30 March 1981): 57. Her work also has "a Latin American enchantment" for Thomas LeClair (Toni Morrison, interview with Thomas LeClair, "The Language Must Not Sweat: A Conversation," *New Republic* [21 March 1981]: 25). Susan Willis compares the historical focus and the problematization of the past in *Song of Solomon* to the modernism of Mario Vargas Llosa's *La casa verde* and other novels of the Latin American boom ("Eruptions of Funk: Historicizing Toni Morrison," *Black American Literature Forum* 16, 1 [Spring 1982]: 38). Dorothy H. Lee notices that Morrison's archetypal South reminds one of Macondo ("*Song of Solomon:* To Ride the Air," *Black American Literature Forum* 16, 2 [Summer 1982]: 68). José David Saldívar analyzes "lo real maravilloso" in García Márquez, Morrison, Alejo Carpentier, Maxine Hong Kingston, and Ron Arias in "Claiming the Americas: Contemporary Third World Literature" (Ph.D. diss., Stanford

University, 1983). Vera M. Kutzinski explores Afro-American myths and history in García Márquez's fiction in "The Logic of Wings: Gabriel García Márquez and Afro-American Literature," *Latin American Literature Review* " (Jan.–June 1985): 133–47. More recently, Gayl Jones has attributed to Morrison's novels "some of the magic reality—the sense of fluid possibilities" present in the work of García Márquez. She remembers Carlos Fuentes in the historical power of Morrison's characters and the possibilities of their transformation (Gayl Jones, *Liberating Voices: Oral Tradition in African American Literature* [Harmondsworth, England: Penguin, 1992], 173–76).

4. Morrison, interview with LeClair, 29. On an earlier occasion, Morrison expressed admiration and admitted envy of "Márquez, Miguel Astúrias, and other Latin Americans" but denied any conscious reference to their work in her own texts (Toni Morrison, interview with Mel Watkins, *New York Times Book Review* [11 Sept. 1977]: 50).

5. Mikhail Bakhtin, *Problemas da poética de Dostoiévski* (Rio de Janeiro: Forense-Universitária, 1981); Umberto Eco, *Pós-escrito a "O nome da rosa,"* trans. Letizia Zini Antunes and Alvaro Lorencini (Rio de Janeiro: Nova Fronteira, 1985); Julia Kristeva, "Word, Dialogue, and Novel," in *The Kristeva Reader,* ed. Toril Moi (Oxford: Basil Blackwell, 1986).

6. Enrique Hernández, "The Seductive Life of García Márquez," *Village Voice,* 3 July 1984, 45. In García Márquez's boastful words, "Every time I hear my leftist friends complain about North American penetration in Latin America I laugh into my coat lapels because the real cultural penetration is that of Latin America into the United States." García Márquez was the writer most widely translated and sold in the boom of translation and publication of Latin American novels from 1960 to 1980.

7. According to Charles Michener et al., "Latin American Laureate," *Newsweek* (1 Nov. 1982): 31.

8. Robert G. Mead, "For Sustenance, Hope," in *Critical Essays on Gabriel García Márquez,* ed. George McMurray (Boston: G. K. Hall, 1987), 29. Critics are split over whether the vitality and maturity of those novels won over the international markets or whether the popular novels simply met the requirements of those markets. Sara Castro-Klarén and Héctor Campos argue that the publishing boom in Latin America and the wide sales in the United States by García Márquez and others were exceptions to the rule and do not signify the creation of markets for Latin American literature in general ("Traducciones, tirajes, ventas y estrellas: El 'boom'," *Ideologies and Literature* 4, 17 [Sept.–Oct. 1983]: 319–38). Tim Brennan adds that boom writers are popular in the First World because they give a taste of the Third without threatening the complacency of the liberal bourgeoisie ("Cosmopolitans and Celeb-

rities," *Race and Class* 31, 1 [1989]: 1–19). The publishing phenomenon
of black women writers in the United States has undergone similar critiques. Bell Hooks argues that publishers tend to concentrate on best-
selling black women writers ("Black Women Writing: Creating More
Space," *SAGE: A Scholarly Journal on Black Women* 2, 1 [Spring 1985]:
44–46). Arthur P. Davis sees a combination of popular themes and publishing circumstances in the black literary upsurge since the 1960s
("Novels of the New Black Renaissance (1960–77): A Thematic Sur-
vey," *CLA* (The College Language Association) *Journal* 21, 4 [June
1978]: 457–90. As with other phenomena of literary history and popular culture, artistic merit and cultural relevance are not dissociated from
the interests of cultural industry.

    9. Such applause comes from critics as different as Alastair Reid
("Basilisks' Eggs," *New Yorker* [8 Nov. 1976]: 176) and Ivan Ivask
("Freedom of Imagination Regained," *Books Abroad* 47, 1 [Winter 1973]:
8). As was pointed out in Chapter 1, writers included in the so-called
Latin American boom are, besides the Colombian García Márquez, Argentinean Julio Cortázar, Mexican Carlos Fuentes, and Peruvian Mario
Vargas Llosa. Older writers such as Alejo Carpentier, Miguel Angel Astúrias, and Juan Rulfo have received renewed attention, and younger
ones such as Manuel Puig and Isabel Allende can also be seen as part of
the boom's sweeping currents.

    10. Gene H. Bell-Villada, "García Márquez and the Novel," in *Critical
Essays,* ed. McMurray, 218.

    11. Joseph Epstein, "Anti-Americanism and Other Clichés," *Commen-
tary* (April 1983): 61.

    12. John Barth singles out Italo Calvino and Gabriel García Márquez
as examples of a possible "post-modern synthesis" ("The Literature of
Replenishment," in *The Friday Book: Essays and Other Nonfiction* [New
York: G. P. Putnam's Sons, 1984], 204–5). "Surfiction" writer Raymond
Federman takes the epigraph of his novel *Smiles on Washington Square*
(New York: Thunder's Mouth, 1985) from *Hundred Years.* Critic Gene H.
Bell-Villada ("García Márquez," in *Critical Essays,* ed. McMurray, 217)
sees the influence of García Márquez's mixture of the fantastic and the
prosaic in the work of John Nichols and Robert Coover. By contrast,
Susan Willis labels the "great novels of the Latin American boom" as
"modernist texts" (*Specifying: Black Women Writing the American Experience* [Madison: University of Wisconsin Press, 1987], 96).

    13. Quoted in Strouse, "Toni Morrison's Black Magic," 53.

    14. From a lecture given by Toni Morrison in São Paulo, Brazil, in
August 1990 see "Nobel de Literatura vai para escritora negra," *Folha de
São Paulo,* 8 Oct. 1993, 4.6.

    15. Bell-Villada, "García Márquez," 218. Hernández also places Gar-

cía Márquez within a Caribbean culture that is quite different from the "somber tones" of Hispanic or Andean areas that include Argentina, Chile, Peru, and Colombia's Andean region ("Seductive Life," 44).

16. Gabriel García Márquez, *El olor de la guayaba: Conversaciones con Plinio Apuleyo Mendoza* (Barcelona: Editorial Bruguera, 1982), 73; my translation. On his visit to Angola, García Márquez saw "popular forms of African art" very similar to "aesthetic manifestations" in the Caribbean area. He understood that "even without proposing it very clearly, [his] books contain very 'mestizo' elements" (interview with Manuel Osorio, "Poco cafe y mucha politica," in *García Márquez habla de García Márquez*, ed. Alfonso Rentería Mantilla [Bogota: Rentería Editores, 1979], 182; my translation). Vera M. Kutzinski argues that Latin American authors from the Caribbean differ from "mainstream" U.S. writers exactly because of their effective embrace of "Afro-American culture as a vital part of identity" ("Logic of Wings," 133–46).

17. García Márquez, *El olor de la guayaba*, 74.

18. In her hometown of Lorain, Ohio, poor Europeans, Mexicans, and U.S. blacks mixed in harmony. The steel-mill town had people from all over sharing similar poverty and working conditions. "We were all in one economic class and therefore mutually dependent upon one another. There was a great deal of sharing of food and services, and caring," Morrison remembers (interview with Rosemarie K. Lester for Hessian Radio Network, Frankfurt, Spring 1983; printed in *Critical Essays on Toni Morrison*, ed. Nellie McKay [Boston: G. K. Hall, 1988], 50). Her literary background is no less diversified: in adolescence she read and admired the specificity of the great Russian, French, and English novels. Later, she loved the same quality in Faulkner. She tries to be as specific and particular in her own stories of black culture. Faulkner and Virginia Woolf were the focus of Morrison's master's thesis at Cornell University. See Toni Morrison, interview with Nellie McKay, *Contemporary Literature* 24, 4 (Winter 1983): 414; and Morrison, interview with LeClair, 28.

19. I restrict myself to analogies between Morrison and García Márquez because of the limited scope of this chapter.

20. Earl Shorris speculates that, by being a Colombian, García Márquez is "culturally and perhaps genetically part Indian" ("Gabriel García Márquez: The Alchemy of History," *Harper's Magazine* [Feb. 1972]: 98).

21. The names of García Márquez's grandparents vary a little in different sources. I cite the names given in *Books Abroad* (Summer 1973): 501–4. The number of children in his family also varies. A really "Marquezian" confusion is the fact that though 1928 is usually cited as his birthdate, his father "revealed evidence that his son was born in 1927— so García Márquez admits that he is uncertain about the date of his birth" (George McMurray, *Spanish-American Writing since 1941* [New York: Ungar, 1987], 10).

22. Mario Vargas Llosa, *García Márquez: História de un deicídio* (Caracas: Monte Avila, 1971).

23. Quoted in Reid, "Basilisks' Eggs," 86, 195–96.

24. Gabriel García Márquez, interview with the Brazilian weekly *O Pasquim* (20 April 1979), reprinted in *Atlas: World Press Review* (July 1979): 50.

25. Robert L. Sims, "Matriarchal and Patriarchal Patterns in Gabriel García Márquez's *Leaf Storm*, 'Big Mama's Funeral' and *Hundred Years*," in *Critical Perspectives on Gabriel García Márquez*, ed. Bradley A. Shaw and Nora Vera-Godwin (Lincoln, Neb.: Society of Spanish and Spanish-American Studies, 1986), 33.

26. Reid, "Basilisks' Eggs," 192.

27. Morrison, interview with McKay, 413.

28. Ibid. Details of Morrison's life are based on this and other interviews.

29. Morrison, interview with LeClair, 27.

30. Toni Morrison, interview with Elsie B. Washington, "Toni Morrison Now," *Essence* 18, 6 (Oct. 1986): 134.

31. Morrison, interview with McKay, 415–21.

32. Quoted in Strouse, "Toni Morrison's Black Magic," 54.

33. Morrison, interview with McKay, 428.

34. Quoted in Strouse, "Toni Morrison's Black Magic," 52.

35. Washington, "Toni Morrison Now," 58.

36. Morrison, interview with McKay, 428.

37. References to pages in Toni Morrison's *Song of Solomon* are made in parentheses directly in the text. The novel's title may be simplified (revealingly!) as *SOS*. The book won the National Book Critics Award and the American Academy and Institute of Arts and Letters Award. Morrison later received the Pulitzer Prize for Fiction for *Beloved* in 1988.

38. Gabriel García Márquez, *One Hundred Years of Solitude*, trans. Gregory Rabassa (New York: Avon Books, 1970; © Harper & Row, 1970). Reference to pages of this book are made directly in the text; the novel's title may be abbreviated. I refer to the English translation; it was probably what Morrison read and allows meanings and connotations that may be absent in the original Spanish text.

39. Drake's attack is evoked in *Hundred Years* on pp. 19, 27, and 382.

40. Dorothy H. Lee reads the name Ruth employed here as an ironic play on the "ideal daughter and wife" of the Bible ("*Song of Solomon*," 66).

41. Macon's wife saw the new name optimistically: it suggested starting out a new life and wiping out the past (54). The wish to "wipe out the past" recurs in different instances in Gayl Jones's *Corregidora* and *Song for Anninho* and Marshall's *The Chosen Place, the Timeless People* and other novels.

42. Quoted in Strouse, "Toni Morrison's Black Magic," 55.

43. The critique of capitalism is valid but paradoxical; property is also synonymous with a long-sought freedom for those blacks whose memories of slavery and poverty are only too painful.

44. Strouse, "Toni Morrison's Black Magic," 55.

45. One is reminded of Frantz Fanon's concern with haste and widespread violence in wars of decolonization: "Racialism and hatred and resentment—'a legitimate desire for revenge'—cannot sustain a war of liberation" (*The Wretched of the Earth* [New York: Grove, 1963], 139).

46. Being on the move is, for Morrison, a "breaking ground" quality of black men. Her character Sula is "a masculine character" in the sense that she moves a lot and breaks barriers (Toni Morrison, interview with Robert Stepto, "Intimate Things in Place," in *The Third Woman*, ed. Dexter Fisher [Boston: Houghton Mifflin, 1980], 180). Pilate also shares that quality.

47. Morrison's Circe recalls Odysseus's mythical guide, who tells him how to reach the underworld—in Greek mythology, the "place of the departed spirits of the dead" (A. S. Hornby, E. V. Gatenby, and H. Wakefield, *The Advanced Learner's Dictionary of Current English* [London: Oxford University Press, 1963], 1098).

48. Aspects of Milkman's journey and self-discovery recall Avey Johnson's own quest in *Praisesong for the Widow*, by Paule Marshall, discussed in Chapter 2.

49. Walter Benjamin, "The Storyteller," in idem, *Illuminations: Essays and Reflections*, ed. Hannah Arendt, trans. Harry Zohn (New York: Schocken, 1968), 83–109.

50. Italo Calvino, "Myth in the Narrative," in *Surfiction: Fiction Now . . . and Tomorrow*, ed. Raymond Federman (Chicago: Swallow, 1975), 76, 79.

51. Similar points are made by Morrison (interview with LeClair, 26) and García Márquez (Reid, "Basilisks' Eggs," 195–96).

52. "Many people in Latin America live in both [traditional and modern worlds] at once." William Rowe and Vivian Schelling, *Memory and Modernity: Popular Culture in Latin America* (London and New York: Verso, 1991), 2.

53. For Morrison's African references, see Gay Wilentz, "Civilizations Underneath: African Heritage as Cultural Discourse in Toni Morrison's *Song of Solomon*," *African American Review* 26, 1 (1992): 61–76.

54. Written in 1961, it is the first story in the collection *La increíble y triste história de la candida Erendira y de su abuela desalmada: Siete cuentos* (Buenos Aires: Editorial Sudamericana, 1972); English translation, *Innocent Erendira and Other Stories*, trans. Gregory Rabassa (New York: Harper & Row, 1978).

55. Morrison, interview with LeClair, 26–27.

56. Dancing and singing in a ring are major characteristics of African folk ceremonies, usually evoking spirits and dead ancestors. See Sterling Stuckey, *Slave Culture: Nationalist Theory and the Foundations of Black America* (New York: Oxford University Press, 1987), 11–16. The traditional ring shout is danced in Paule Marshall's *Praisesong for the Widow.*

57. Aimé Césaire and Frantz Fanon are evoked in Milkman's brave feat. Commenting on Césaire's tragedy *Et les chiens se taisaient,* where the Negro, at "the limit of self-destruction . . . is about to leap . . . into the 'black hole' from which will come 'the great Negro cry with such force that the pillars of the world will be shaken by it,'" Fanon concludes "that the real *leap* consists in introducing invention into existence" (*Black Skin, White Masks* [New York: Grove, 1967], 199, 229).

58. Paul's First Epistle to the Corinthians attacks personal pride and vanity, exhorting people not to marry so that they may better prepare for Christ's Second Coming. See Lee, *"Song of Solomon,"* 66.

59. Toni Morrison, interview with Claudia Tate, in *Black Women Writers at Work* (New York: Continuum, 1986), 127.

60. García Márquez's grandfather killed a man when he was still very young; he moved far away to escape the possible revenge of the dead's family and there founded a village. See Gabriel García Márquez and Mario Vargas Llosa, *Dialogo sobre la novela Latinoamericana* (Lima: Editorial Peru Andino, 1988), 25.

61. Gabriel García Márquez, quoted in Robert Lewis Sims, *The Evolution of Myth in Gabriel García Márquez* (Miami: Ediciones Universal, 1981), 42. García Márquez rephrases the same idea in *El olor de la guayaba,* 24.

62. García Márquez believes that women sustain the world and the human species with "iron wrists," while men journey around the world in daring recklessness to push history forward (*El olor de la guayaba,* 109). Morrison has similarly contrasted her enduring and strong women with men who, like Milkman, must be on a constant journey, searching for adventure and meaning (interview with Watkins, 52).

63. Reid, "Basilisks' Eggs," 186.

64. D. P. Gallagher, "Gabriel García Márquez (Colombia 1928– )," in McMurray, *Critical Essays,* 115–16.

65. Morrison, interview with McKay, 426–27.

66. Quoted in Strouse, "Toni Morrison's Black Magic," 56.

67. George McMurray, "The Threat of 'La Violencia'," in McMurray, *Critical Essays,* 79.

68. García Márquez, *El olor de la guayaba,* 82–85.

69. Gabriel García Márquez, 1967 interview quoted by Susan Mott

Linker, "Myth and Legend in Two Prodigious Tales of García Márquez," *Hispanic Journal* 9, 1 (Fall 1987): 89.

70. Gabriel García Márquez, quoted in Wolfang A. Luchting, "Lampooning Literature: *La Mala Hora*," *Books Abroad* (Summer 1973): 472.

71. Morrison, interview with LeClair, 26.

72. Quoted in Strouse, "Toni Morrison's Black Magic," 56.

73. Toni Morrison, "Writers Together," *The Nation* (24 Oct. 1981): 396.

74. Toni Morrison, interview with Gloria Naylor, *Southern Review* 21, 2 (July 1985): 579.

75. In Toni Morrison's words, "The presence of Afro-American literature and the awareness of its culture both resuscitate the study of literature in the United States and raise that study's standards" ("Unspeakable Things Unspoken: The Afro-American Presence in American Literature," *Michigan Quarterly Review* 28, 1 [Winter 1989]: 3–4).

76. Not that the two novels have been unanimously acclaimed in that way: the magical style and apocalyptic ending in García Márquez's novel have been read as lip service paid to the status quo and the story itself as a liberal manifesto that dilutes other possible threats to the existing order within and outside of Colombia. For considerations of this position, see Hernán Vidal, *Literatura Hispano-Americana e ideologia liberal: Surgimento y crisis (Una problematica sobre la dependencia en torno a la narrativa del boom)* (Buenos Aires: Ediciones Hispamerica, 1976); and Brennan, "Cosmopolitans and Celebrities." Morrison's work has sometimes been accused of not reflecting the black experience and of echoing stereotypes of black life upheld by the white establishment. The problem became so critical after the publication of *Beloved* that a large group of influential black writers and critics was compelled to publish a statement of support: "Black Writers in Praise of Toni Morrison," *New York Times Book Review* (24 Jan. 1988): 36. For a review of the whole controversy, see Maria Diedrich, "'Things Fall Apart?' The Black Critical Controversy over Toni Morrison's *Beloved*," *American Studies/Amerika Studien* 34, 2 (1989): 175–86.

77. References to pages of Toni Morrison's *Tar Baby* are made directly in the text.

78. Quoted in Eric Williams, *From Columbus to Castro: The History of the Caribbean 1492–1969* (New York: Vintage, 1970), 81. The description is from the 1697 Treaty of Ryswick, which established French dominion over its settlement on the Spanish island of Hispaniola and named it Saint Domingue.

79. Morrison and other women writers have emphasized the supernatural powers and wisdom of members of their families and communities. The notion of a third eye goes back to ancient cultures in Africa,

India, and Greece. The third eye has been traditionally understood as "an invisible organ of spiritual perception and second sight . . . the channel of supreme wisdom and sublime intuition," conferring "almost divine knowledge." The pineal gland is believed by some to be "the seat of the third eye." (Benjamin Walker, *Man and the Beasts Within: The Encyclopedia of the Occult, the Esoteric, and the Supernatural* [New York: Stein and Day, 1977], 95, 216).

80. His act evokes the jumping ship of slaves who tried to escape slavery, even if that meant finding death in the waters of the Atlantic. However, his encounter with African myth happens almost against his wish, much like Milkman's in *Song of Solomon*.

81. In the title of "the Principal Beauty of Maine" given to Margaret, Susan Willis sees a possible literary allusion to "the most beautiful woman in the world," Fernanda del Carpio, in García Márquez's *Hundred Years*. Both Margaret and Fernanda (Aureliano Segundo's wife) are "beauty contest winners, beheld by future husbands in a parade, and neither is originally from the bourgeois class." The two women also share a hysteria developed "as result of the discontinuity between their pasts and presents," which is the cost of their "assimilation to bourgeois culture" (Willis, *Specifying*, 177).

82. Exhaustion of the soil and lack of jobs in overcrowded Port-au-Prince have pushed Haitians in large numbers out of their country to try to survive and improve their lot abroad. Many are so desperate that they are not afraid to dare risky boat crossings between Haiti and Florida. Besides poverty, people on the island must still cope with frequent hurricanes and storms.

83. His seven selves remind the reader of the reckless violence of the Seven Days in *Song of Solomon*.

84. Angry at her country's injustices, Morrison announced in the 1986 PEN Conference that "she had never considered herself American," to the outrage of conservative critics such as Stanley Crouch ("Aunt Medea," *New Republic* [19 Oct. 1987]: 43). In a 1977 interview, she declared that she had "never felt like a citizen," be it "an American or an Ohioan or even a Lorainite." Writing her novels gave her "a very strong sense of place, not in terms of the country or the state, but in terms of the details, the feelings, the moods of the community, of the town" (Morrison, interview with Stepto, 167).

85. Evelyn Hawthorne translates it as "King's Backyard" in "On Gaining the Double-Vision: *Tar Baby* as Diasporean Novel," *Black American Literature Forum* 22, 1 (Spring 1988): 100. Jadine's boyfriend, Ryk, is also Nordic.

86. The novel recalls "tar baby" folk stories told by slaves in the United States, in the title and in references about Jadine, Son (who is deep black and smells of tar), and the African woman in yellow (she has

"skin like tar" and "tar-black fingers"). The folktale tells of a black doll made of tar and set in the farmer's patch to trick and catch Brer Rabbit, who nevertheless outsmarts the farmer. Morrison plays with meanings of tar and possible nuances of that story.

87. Thérèse's role in inspiring and guiding a young man back to his African roots recalls Pilate's significance in *Song of Solomon*.

88. Toni Morrison, interview with Bill Moyers, in *A World of Ideas,* vol. 2: Public Opinions from Private Citizens (New York: Doubleday, 1990), 59.

89. Like Paule Marshall, Morrison does not idealize West Indians as being above the delusions and weaknesses of U.S. blacks or whites. In *The Bluest Eye,* Soaphead Church is a fake spiritualist from "an island of the archipelago in the South Atlantic between North and South America," who transmits to the protagonist Pecola the sense of inadequacy and struggle within his black skin (137–43). In *Tar Baby,* islanders may be poorer and closer to slave memories (the peasant world that Morrison would like to preserve), but they are not "pure" and uncontaminated.

90. Elliott Butler-Evans, *Race, Gender and Desire: Narrative Strategies in the Fiction of Toni Cade Bambara, Toni Morrison, and Alice Walker* (Philadelphia: Temple University Press, 1989) 156. I am very much in agreement with his analysis of *Tar Baby.*

91. Renato Rosaldo, *Culture and Truth: The Remaking of Social Analysis* (Boston: Beacon, 1989), 31, 42.

## CHAPTER 4
### The Dry Wombs of Black Women: Memories of Brazilian Slavery in *Corregidora* and *Song for Anninho*

1. Gayl Jones, *Corregidora* (Boston: Beacon, 1975) and *Song for Anninho* (Detroit: Lotus, 1981). References to pages of these two works are made in parentheses in the text. Gayl Jones has several other works with some connection with Brazil, such as *Xarque and Other Poems* (Detroit: Lotus Press, 1981), some narrative poems in *The Hermit Woman* (Detroit: Lotus Press, 1983); and the novel *Die Vogelfängerin* [The Birdcatcher] (Hamburg, Germany: Rowohlt, 1986), only available in German and the short story "Ensinanca" in *Confirmation: An Anthology of African American Women,* ed. Amiri Baraka and Amina Baraka (New York: Quill, 1983), 74–76. In a 1982 interview, she mentioned an unpublished novel, inspired by a Brazilian folktale, about a U.S. woman named Jaboti "after the Brazilian trickster turtle," as well as a short story in which "two contemporary Brazilians" visit a friend in Kentucky, "mingling place and historical moment" (Gayl Jones, interview with Charles H. Rowell, *Callaloo* 5 [Oct. 1982]: 34, 40). The small *jaboti* was already in her mind when she wrote *Song for Anninho;* the wise woman Zibatra

compares Almeyda to one: "You like fish and wild honey,/ to hide in your shell— / OK, little turtle,/ OK, little Jaboti, come out!" (13).

2. Jones, interview with Rowell, 40–41.

3. Gayl Jones, interview with Michael Harper, *Chant of Saints: A Gathering of Afro-American Literature, Art, and Scholarship*, ed. Michael Harper and Robert B. Stepto (Chicago: University of Illinois Press, 1979) 365–67. Gayl Jones praises the oral power and diverse narrative techniques of "African, African American, Native American, and other Third World literatures" in her essay book *Liberating Voices: Oral Tradition in African American Literature* ([Harmondsworth, England: Penguin, 1992], 1), in which she cites Ralph Ellison, N. Scott Momaday, Carlos Fuentes, Gabriel García Márquez, and Amos Tutuola among those who recreate "sustaining mythologies and culture heroes through oral tradition" (8). Gayl Jones has also referred to her mother and to her teachers Michael Harper and William Meredith as "the most important influences" on her writing (interview with Claudia C. Tate, *Black American Literature Forum* 13 [Winter 1979]: 144).

4. Jones, interview with Tate, 145. Jones's critical reviews in *Liberating Voices* avoid an exclusively black or African-American scope, noticing that themes such as liberation and self-affirmation exist in "all the world's literatures and criticism" (Jones, *Liberating Voices*, 192).

5. Comparing the slave histories of Brazil and North America, Gayl Jones concludes that "it's really difficult to say which was the most demanding" (interview with Roseann P. Bell, "Gayl Jones Takes a Look at *Corregidora*," in *Sturdy Black Bridges: Visions of Black Women in Literature*, ed. Roseann P. Bell, Bettye J. Parker, and Beverly Guys-Sheftall [Garden City, N.Y.: Doubleday, 1979], 283–84).

6. Both the English word *maroon* and the French *marron* come from the Spanish *cimarrón*, a term Spaniards used early in the *New World* to mean cattle disappeared in the hills of Hispaniola (today's Haiti and Dominican Republic) and extended to runaway Indian slaves. By the late 1530s, the word already referred primarily to African runaways, a "chronic plague" in all plantation societies (Richard Price, *Maroon Societies: Rebel Slave Communities in the Americas* [1973; 2d ed., Baltimore: Johns Hopkins University Press, 1979], 1–2).

7. Jones, interview with Tate, 146.

8. Frederick Douglas and other blacks praised the absence of color prejudice in Brazil even under slavery. Intellectual black leaders of the nineteenth century such as Martin Delany and Frank Webb had plans to move to Brazil. Ironically, the Brazilian government was interested in white European immigrants, not more blacks. Since then, interest in Brazil has remained a constant among black scholars and intellectuals, whether they admire or detest the Brazilian style of race relations as they perceive it. For more details, see David J. Hellwig, ed., *African-American*

*Reflections on Brazil's Racial Paradise* (Philadelphia: Temple University Press, 1992); and Teresa Meade and Gregory Pirio, "In Search of the Afro-American 'Eldorado': Attempts by North American Blacks to Enter Brazil in the 1920s," *Luso-Brazilian Review* 25, 1 (1988): 85–110.

9. Robert William Fogel, *Without Consent or Contract: The Rise and Fall of American Slavery* (New York: W. W. Norton, 1989), 18. The exact number of slaves is controversial. Fogel's estimate is similar to Katia M. de Queirós Mattoso's; she believes that "more than 9,500,000 Africans" were brought to the Americas between 1502 and 1860 (*To Be a Slave in Brazil, 1550–1888* [New Brunswick, N.J.: Rutgers University Press, 1986], 10). Earlier sources such as D. P. Mannix, David Brion Davis, Sidney Mintz, and Stanley Elkins tended to estimate a higher number, between fifteen and twenty million, usually based on the work of R. R. Kuczynski (*Population Movements*, 1936). Philip D. Curtin revised sources and came up with the estimate of 9,391,000, influencing subsequent historiography (*The Atlantic Slave Trade: A Census* [Madison: University of Wisconsin Press, 1969], 3–91).

10. Stanley L. Engerman, "A economia da escravidão," *Negros Brasileiros*, special ed. of *Ciência Hoje* 8 (Nov. 1988): 5.

11. The 1872 census in Brazil classified 15.2 percent of the population as slave and 42.7 percent as "free people of color." See Pierre L. van den Berghe, *Race and Racism: A Comparative Perspective* (New York: John Wiley & Sons, 1967), 62.

12. Early travelers, visitors, and historians tended to remark on the mestizo-mulatto look of the population in general and the familiarity between people of different colors, contrasting the Portuguese with the harsher British and North American planters. Robert E. Park went so far as to say that Brazilians seemed to have "regained that paradisaic innocence, with respect to difference of race, which the people of the United States have somehow lost" ("Introduction," in Donald Pierson, *Negroes in Brazil* [Chicago: University of Chicago Press, 1942], xii–xiv). The idea of a Brazilian social and racial democracy reached through miscegenation was particularly fostered by Gilberto Freyre's *Casa grande e senzala* (1933; published in English as *The Masters and the Slaves: A Study in the Development of Brazilian Civilization* [1946; reprint, Berkeley: University of California Press, 1986]) and by Frank Tannenbaum's *Slave and Citizen* (New York: Alfred A. Knopf, 1947).

13. In the 1970s, Brazilian historians, sociologists, and economists, such as Octavio Ianni, Fernando Henrique Cardoso, and Florestan Fernandes, sided with Eric Williams in their systematic critique of capitalism and colonialism, tending to place high emphasis on class conflict.

14. Marvin Harris, *Patterns of Race in the Americas* (New York: Walker, 1964), 64; Carl Degler, *Neither Black nor White: Slavery and Race Relations in Brazil and the United States* (New York: Macmillan, 1971),

101–2. Stanley Elkins had earlier attributed to the U.S. South "the most implacable race-consciousness yet observed in virtually any society" (*Slavery: A Problem in American Institutional and Intellectual Life* [Chicago: University of Chicago Press, 1959], 61).

15. Clovis Moura, *Sociologia do negro brasileiro* (São Paulo: Atica, 1988), 64.

16. Freyre, *Masters and Slaves*, xi–xii, 4–9, 13, 185–87, 279.

17. Ibid., 30, 85, 395.

18. Ibid., 74.

19. Sonia Maria Giacomini, *Mulher e escrava: Uma introdução histórica ao estudo da mulher negra no Brasil* (Petrópolis, Brazil: Vozes, 1988), 71.

20. Jones, interview with Harper, 356.

21. Freyre, *Masters and Slaves*, 74.

22. Slavery abolition was declared in 1888, and Brazil officially became a republic the next year. The government argued that the burning of slavery records had been a necessary purifying act for the newborn republic and a demonstration of racial union and fraternal respect to those ex-slaves joining "the Brazilian communion." See Thales de Azevedo, *Democracia racial: Ideologia e realidade* (Petrópolis, Brazil: Vozes, 1975), 12. Freyre and Azevedo, among other historians, believe the destruction of documents was meant to save the government from paying compensation to slaveholders after abolition.

23. Isabella, the name given in the novel to Princess Isabel of Portugal, "the Redemptress," is coincidentally the name of the Spanish queen who was instrumental in Christopher Columbus's voyages and in early explorations of the American continent. The glorification of Princess Isabel in official history (and in the memory of former slaves, for she represented their salvation) and the moral or economic justifications for the burning of the slavery papers have been under much dispute in recent historiography. For some, the burning of slavery documents was meant to "eliminate the stain" of blackness in Brazilian society and culture, promoting the national whitening long desired by the elites. See Clovis Moura, *Brasil: As raízes do protesto negro* (São Paulo: Global, 1983), 30. Other historians have questioned the idea of the slave as a passive, masochistic victim, thereby revising records and interpretations and overriding myths of all kinds. Besides, Rui Barbosa's fire *did not* erase slavery history, since "there are more than 1,500 deposits of documents, between public institutions and private archives, in about 300 cities" (Marília Martins, "Preto no branco," *Isto É* [20 April 1988]: 41; my translation).

24. In West Africa, the union between a man and a woman is formalized only after a child is born, a custom persisting among South Carolina descendants of Africans in the eighteenth and nineteenth centuries. See Herbert G. Gutman, *The Black Family in Slavery and Freedom 1750–1925* (New York: Vintage, 1976), 45–88. For African peoples like the

Hausa in Nigeria, it was "a religious duty to ensure the continuation of the family line established by one's ancestors. Barrenness was a calamity in Africa" (John Blassingame, *The Slave Community: Plantation Life in the Ante-bellum South* [1972; rev. ed., New York: Oxford University Press, 1979], 161).

25. Gilberto Freyre, among other historians, contrasts the vigor of Africans with the weak energy of the Portuguese planter class, those who held power but were ill fed and ill prepared to succeed in the tropics (*Masters and Slaves,* 18).

26. Portuguese masters resorted to witchcraft for virility, and some did die from poison put in "aphrodisiac beverages prepared by the black love sorceress" (Freyre, *Masters and Slaves,* 374).

27. Freyre says that the color line was not clear on Brazilian plantations, even if the social distance was enormous. He believes that before their experience in Brazil, the Portuguese were already "predisposed" to hybridity due to the Moor domination of Portugal and their influence on the culture and society. The Portuguese themselves have "doubtful ethnic purity"; with their usual brown skin and dark hair, they are "anthropologically and culturally a mixed people." The master may often be a mulatto (Freyre, *Masters and Slaves,* xiii, 4, 17, 202).

28. French anthropologist Roger Bastide notes that slave women provoked abortion or preferred that their children died, for painfully logical reasons: "What was the good of asking the gods to make women fruitful when they could bear nothing but infant slaves? Better to pray that their wombs might be sterile" (*The African Religions of Brazil* [Baltimore: Johns Hopkins University Press, 1960], 60). The conflict of motherhood under slavery is dramatically invoked by Toni Morrison in *Beloved.*

29. Jones, interview with Harper, 373–74. Several black women writers reacted against the traditional control of a woman's reproductive rights during the 1970s, when the care for the children and the charge of "saving the black race" was still on their shoulders. See Barbara Christian, "An Angle of Seeing: Motherhood in Buchi Emecheta's *The Joys of Motherhood* and Alice Walker's *Meridian,"* in *Black Feminist Criticism,* ed. Barbara Christian (New York: Pergamon, 1985), 223–24.

30. Freyre, *Masters and Slaves,* 438. Paule Marshall's Celestine voices the same idea in *Daughters.*

31. Elkins, *Slavery,* 137, 49, 74, 63; Degler, *Neither Black nor White,* 7.

32. Eugene Genovese, *Roll, Jordan, Roll* (New York: Pantheon, 1972), 414–31. Slave girls were often tempted or forced into intimate sexual acts with the master but more frequently with his sons, says Genovese.

33. Pierre L. van den Berghe, "The African Diaspora in Mexico, Bra-

zil, and the United States," in *Emerging Perspectives on the Black Diaspora,* ed. Aubrey W. Bonnett and G. Llewellyn Watson (Lanham, Md., New York, and London: University Press of America, 1990), 129. Winthrop D. Jordan also points out that "miscegenation was extensive in all English colonies" in spite of the "irreconcilable desire and aversion for interracial sexual union" among English colonials (*White over Black: American Attitudes toward the Negro, 1550–1812* [Chapel Hill: University of North Carolina Press, 1968], 137). The 1860 census data indicate that one out of every ten slave children in the U.S. South was a mulatto; the proportion was greater in smaller farms of border states or in cities. See Fogel, *Without Consent,* 182.

34. Jacqueline Jones, *Labor of Love, Labor of Sorrow: Black Women, Work, and the Family from Slavery to the Present* (New York: Vintage, 1985), 25–28. There is more on the topic in Deborah Gray White, *Ar'n't I a Woman?* (New York: Norton, 1985).

35. White, *Ar'n't I a Woman?* 29.

36. Ibid., 30–46. Richard Sutch says southern slaveowners often "fostered polygamy and promiscuity among their slaves" in order to increase breeding rates and profit from the sale of young slaves ("The Breeding of Slaves for Sale and the Westward Expansion of Slavery, 1850–1860," in *Race and Slavery in the Western Hemisphere,* ed. Stanley L. Engerman and Eugene D. Genovese [Princeton, N.J.: Princeton University Press, 1975], 198). Fogel argues that slave breeding was not a widespread policy or a "major source of profit," as studies developed in the 1960s indicated. Mistreatment and violence were also "more selective" than he and others had previously assumed (Fogel, *Without Consent,* 392). In 1974, Toni Morrison bitterly attacked Fogel and Engerman's mechanicist revision of slavery history in their work *Time on the Cross* and its argument that "the evils of slavery were not as terrible as historians have insisted" (Toni Morrison, "Rediscovering Black History," *New York Times Magazine* [11 Aug. 1974]: 20). Variations or differences in numbers and statistics certainly do not diminish the horrible violence of the slave past.

37. Sugarcane fields and mining were the main destination for slaves imported to Brazil. Sugar production centered in the northeastern states of Pernambuco and Bahia during the first two centuries of Brazilian history. The so-called gold cycle began around 1693 in Minas Gerais, when the discovery of gold and diamonds offered more promise. In the nineteenth century, the "coffee cycle" developed in the southeastern state of São Paulo. See Mattoso, *To Be a Slave,* 42–43.

38. Sonia M. Giacomini gives a documented account of facts that confirm the bleak story written by Gayl Jones. Brazilian slaveholders controlled the sexual lives of their slave women: with whom and with

how many they should sleep ("one Negro woman for four men"), whether they could marry, what to do with children. Acts of mutilation and torture were committed by the mistress on the slave woman, and the assassination of mulatto babies often occurred. The disruptive patriarchal system of slavery had drastic consequences on women of both races. See Giacomini, *Mulher e escrava,* 37–72, 79, 88.

39. Freyre, *Masters and Slaves,* 277.

40. According to Winthrop Jordan, the denial of mixed races in the United States is so ingrained that people "rarely pause to think about it or to question its logic and inevitability." In the social definition, mulattoes and Negroes are the same, and "white blood becomes socially advantageous only in overwhelming proportion" (Jordan, *White over Black,* 167). In Brazil, much of Latin America, and the Caribbean, offspring of mixed unions may find greater acceptance among whites and rise in the social scale. See Degler, *Neither Black nor White,* 107.

41. Bastide, *African Religions,* 79–80. He sees an "interiorization of the father" in Brazilian society, with ambivalent feelings usually displaced or sublimated among blacks.

42. *Corregidora* is concerned with slavery, racism, and sexism in the Americas. Africa is present in the history of slaves and their descendants and in the blues, but it is not directly evoked. The novel thus contrasts not only with *Song for Anninho* but also with Marshall's and Morrison's novels. This variety of points of view regarding origins well illustrates the lack of any unified and "correct" stance in relation to the process of formation of cultural identity.

43. Jones, interview with Harper, 360.

44. Jones, interview with Bell, 287.

45. Carlos Fuentes stresses the point: "No culture . . . retains its identity in isolation; identity is attained in contact, in contrast, in breakthrough" ("How I Started to Write," in *Multicultural Literacy,* ed. Rick Simonson and Scott Walker [St. Paul: Graywolf, 1988], 93).

46. Carlos Fuentes, *The Death of Artemio Cruz,* trans. Sam Hileman (1962; New York: Farrar, Straus & Giroux, 1964).

47. Jones, interview with Tate, 143.

48. Historical documents show Ganga Zumba as a powerful king who strengthened the Republic of Palmares during several decades. By 1678, however, his wife had been killed and his three male children arrested by Portuguese authorities. The Portuguese used the children as agents of an agreement for the end of Palmares in exchange for freedom, land, and privileges for Ganga Zumba and his family. The population of Palmares was divided; the majority stayed and resisted under the leadership of the brave general Zumbi. See Ivan Alves Filho, *Memorial dos Palmares* (Rio de Janeiro: Xenon, 1988), 85–92.

49. Fuentes has commented on how, since the Mexican Revolution, "heroic certitude becomes critical ambiguity, natural fatalism contradictory action, romantic idealism ironic dialectic" in Latin American fiction. The wealth of that literature lies in its ambiguous language, its "plurality of meanings" in a language of "openness" (Carlos Fuentes, *La nueva novela Hispanoamericana* [Mexico City: Joaquín Mortiz, 1969], 15, 31).

50. "Inventar un lenguaje es decir todo lo que la historia ha callado" (Fuentes, *La nueva novela*, 30; my translation).

51. Décio Freitas, *Palmares, a guerra dos escravos* (1971; 4th ed., Rio de Janeiro: Edições Graal, 1982), 13; my translation. Jones's book records the narrator, place, and date in the end: "*Almeyda, Barriga Mountains, 1697.*" The final destruction of Palmares took place with the killing of Zumbi on November 11, 1695, after almost a century of resistance.

52. Lois Parkinson Zamora argues that Fuentes rejects "progressive, dialectical historical models in favor of Vico's spiraling history" ("The Usable Past: The Idea of History in Modern U.S. and Latin American Fiction," in *Do the Americas Have a Common Literature?* ed. Gustavo Pérez Firmat [Durham, N.C.: Duke University Press, 1990], 31).

53. Freitas, *Palmares*, 30.

54. Jones, interview with Tate, 144.

55. Freitas, *Palmares*, 177. After one hundred years of resistance, expansion, and progress, the town of Macaco (where the Palmares government was centered) was successfully invaded and burned by the forces and cannons of the barbaric Domingos Jorge Velho on February 6, 1694. According to archives, thousands of men were beheaded and killed in Macaco and other villages of Palmares. Five hundred and ten men survived and were taken as prisoners; women and children were spared, but the women were so desperate at the thought of slavery that they chose to die of hunger or to kill their children. Velho was a violent mestizo adventurer from the *Capitania* of São Paulo, then a poor province. He and his band (later called *bandeirantes*) were known as barbarians for their savage atrocities in the repression and capture of Indians and Africans. Although Pernambuco authorities considered Velho's band "worse than the Negroes of Palmares," they hired them in a final attempt to destroy Zumbi. See Freitas, *Palmares*, 151–52.

56. Quoted in Freitas, *Palmares*, 181; my translation. The book also describes the violent tortures suffered by slaves, which often pushed them to escape: the flogging, beating, burning, decapitation, castration, hammering-out of teeth, breast amputation, eye perforation, hot-iron branding, drowning, strangling, and other forms of punishment and murder of slaves. Letters and records reveal that Negro women who did not breed as often as they should had breasts amputated or sexual organs mutilated; some foremen kicked the bellies of pregnant women and

hit men's heads again and again with heavy sticks. See Freitas, *Palmares*, 34–35.

57. For both quotes in the paragraph, see Freitas, *Palmares*, 181.

58. Ibid., 72. Most of the population of thirty thousand in the villages of Palmares was black, but there were "mameluc [mestizo Indian-white], mulatto, and white" people there too.

59. Ibid., 127.

60. Freyre, *Master and Slaves*, 12–14.

61. Alves Filho, *Memorial dos Palmares*, 169. The only Muslim reportedly living in Palmares was a Sudanese Moor, who supposedly suggested the plans for the palisade and the system of defense of Palmares. Sudanese Muslims led the repeated slave rebellions in the city of Salvador between 1805 and 1835, "the only urban insurrections in Brazil and the New World" (Décio Freitas, *Insurreições escravas* [Porto Alegre, Brazil: Movimento, 1976] 72).

62. Freitas, *Palmares*, 48.

63. Ibid., 125–26.

64. The Dutch attempted several incursions into the Portuguese colony of Brazil, the most successful being into Recife, Pernambuco, in 1630. They completely dominated the most profitable part of Brazil, controlled sugar production, and made allies among the plantation owners. Like the Portuguese, they tried in vain to destroy Palmares in several expeditions inland. After several wars against the Portuguese, they were forced to leave Brazil in 1654.

65. About the third eye, cf. n. 79 in Chapter 3, p. 200–201.

66. Freitas, *Insurreições escravas*, 163; and R. K. Kent, "Palmares: An African State in Brazil," in Price, *Maroon Societies*, 187. The episode happened in February 1694. Zumbi was said to have jumped and fled with his companions, but he had gone into hiding and was killed on November 20, 1695.

67. Jones, interview with Rowell, 40.

68. Aurelio Buarque de Holanda Ferreira, *Novo dicionário da língua portuguesa* (Rio de Janeiro: Nova Fronteira, 1986), 483; Real Academia Española, *Diccionario manual e ilustrado de la lengua española* (Madrid: Espasa-Calpe, 1989), 432. The powerful *"corregidors* of Indian towns" in Spanish America "regularly exploited their wards for personal gains" (Richard M. Morse, *New World Soundings* [Baltimore: Johns Hopkins University Press, 1989], 98). Jones's planter similarly exploited his slaves with the implicit approval of the law. According to Melvin Dixon, Gayl Jones used the female form "Corregidora" to designate Ursa as a "female judge" who "must bring justice to bear" upon the slavemaster's wrongs. Dixon, "Singing a Deep Song: Language as Evidence in the Novels of Gayl Jones," in *Black Women Writers (1950–1980): A Critical Evaluation*, ed. Mari Evans. New York: Anchor/Doubleday, 1984.

69. Jones, interview with Tate, 147.

70. Freitas, *Palmares*, 13.

71. The best known Brazilian work based on Palmares is the 1965 musical *Arena Conta Zumbi*, with text by Augusto Boal and Gianfrancesco Guarnieri and music by Edu Lobo (*Revista de teatro da SBAT* [Sociedade Brasileira de Autores Teatrais] 378, Rio de Janeiro [Nov.– Dec. 1970]). At a time of high political repression in the country, Zumbi is shown as the mythical hero whose dream of freedom and readiness for war are an inspiration for all Brazilians against imperialism and oppression. See also Claudia de Arruda Campos, *Zumbi, Tiradentes e outras histórias contadas pelo Teatro de Arena de São Paulo* (São Paulo: Perspectiva/ Universidade de São Paulo, 1988). In film, Palmares was immortalized by Carlos Diegues's *Quilombo* (1984).

72. Gloria Anzaldúa writes in bilingual form: "Caminante, no hay puentes, se hace puentes al andar" (Voyager, there are no bridges, one builds them as one walks) ("Foreword" to the 2d ed., *This Bridge Called My Back: Writings by Radical Women of Color*, ed. Cherríe Moraga and Gloria Anzaldúa [New York: Kitchen Table Women of Color, 1981]). Both Jones and Anzaldúa are intertextually connected to Spanish poet Antonio Machado (1865–1939), who wrote in his "Proverbios y cantares XXIX": "Caminante, no hay camino, se hace camino al andar" (Voyager, there is no road, one makes it as one walks) (in *Poesías completas* [1940; reprint, Madrid: Editorial Espasa Calpe, 1988], 239–40).

73. Carlos Fuentes, *El mundo de José Luis Cuevas* (Mexico City: Galería de Arte Misrachi, 1969), 9.

## CHAPTER 5
### No Final Chord:
### The Music of Morrison, Jones, and Marshall

1. Michelle Cliff, *No Telephone to Heaven* (New York: Vintage International, 1987), 87.

2. Toni Morrison, "Unspeakable Things Unspoken: The Afro-American Presence in American Literature," *Michigan Quarterly Review* 28, 1 (Winter 1989): 1. By associating with a hyphenated or "minority" category, any author tends to receive "less than full writer's status" in the United States and not a fair recognition of her or his talent (Tillie Olsen, "Foreword," in *Black Women Writers at Work*, ed. Claudia Tate [New York: Continuum, 1986], x).

3. Hortense J. Spillers includes works by Morrison, Marshall, and Jones in her list of fourteen major works of fiction published by black women between 1965 and 1983 in the United States ("Afterword," in *Conjuring: Black Women, Fictions, and Literary Tradition*, ed. Hortense J.

Spillers and Marjorie Pryse [Bloomington: Indiana University Press, 1985], 257).

4. Recent U.S. criticism still stresses opposition between North and South Americans when it focuses on the white "mainstream" literary tradition in the United States. Lois Parkinson Zamora, for instance, contrasts the sociopolitical and economic concerns in García Márquez and Fuentes with the subjectivism of U.S. writers. She argues that, except for the U.S. South, "the pressures of national identity and political self-definition in Latin America differ greatly from those in the United States." Due to their different "historical and cultural circumstances," their literatures contrast in the proportion of political to personal or subjective contents (Lois Parkinson Zamora, *Writing the Apocalypse: Historical Vision in Contemporary U.S. and Latin American Fiction* [Cambridge: Cambridge University Press, 1989], 179).

5. Carlos Fuentes argues that, especially in Latin America, "the fact of writing is always a revolutionary fact" that breaks "mental structures . . . mental habits" and the usual "silence" (interview with Herman P. Doezma, *Modern Fiction Studies* 18, 4 [Winter 1972–1973]: 499). Gabriel García Márquez believes that literature has a subversive function, always revolutionary and iconoclastic; see his statements in Susan Mott Linker, "Myth and Legend in Two Prodigious Tales of García Márquez," *Hispanic Journal* 9, 1 (Fall 1987): 89; and in Wolfang A. Luchting, "Lampooning Literature: *La Mala Hora*," *Books Abroad* (Summer 1973): 472. Toni Morrison wants to write a kind of "peasant literature" that is both "uncompromisingly beautiful and socially responsible" (interview with Jean Strouse, "Toni Morrison's Black Magic," *Newsweek* [30 March 1981]: 56). She believes novels must "confront important ideas," both political and historical (interview with Gloria Naylor, *Southern Review* 21, 2 [July 1985]: 579). Paule Marshall finds it important not only "to get the story of [her] community told" but also to insert it in a larger political meaning (interview with Sabine Bröck, "'Talk as a Form of Action,'" in *History and Tradition in Afro-American Culture*, ed. Günther H. Lenz [Frankfurt: Campus-Verlag, 1984], 204). Gayl Jones blends the erotic and the social, in the manner of Fuentes, and avoids "direct political statements" to concentrate more on "history as a motivating force in personality" (interview with Charles H. Rowell, *Callaloo* 5 [Oct. 1982]: 42–43). Jones feels kin to responsible Latin American writers who focus on "the particular historical and contemporary nightmares" (interview with Michael Harper, *Chant of Saints: A Gathering of Afro-American Literature, Art, and Scholarship*, ed. Michael Harper and Robert B. Stepto [Chicago: University of Illinois Press, 1979], 366).

6. The "tragic mulatta" and the "Aunt Jemima" (or "Black Mammy") figures emerged from "white southern mythology." They

were two of the most common stereotypical representations of black women in writings by both black and white authors, including slave narratives, during U.S. slavery and Reconstruction, and they persisted in early twentieth-century writings. According to Barbara Christian, the mulatta figure only went beyond the stereotype in novels by Zora Neale Hurston and Ann Petry, before the mid-twentieth century; recent black women writers have created more diverse and complex types. See Barbara Christian, "Images of Black Women in Afro-American Literature: From Stereotype to Character," in *Black Feminist Criticism*, ed. Barbara Christian (New York: Pergamon, 1985), 2–30. Paule Marshall commented on the stereotypes in the 1965 panel "The Negro Woman in American Literature" and selected her own *Brown Girl, Brownstones* and Gwendolyn Brooks's *Maud Martha* as examples of fiction with "fully realized" women characters (in Pat Crutchfield Exum, ed., *Keeping the Faith: Writings by Contemporary Black American Women* [Greenwich, Conn.: Fawcett, 1974], 33–40).

7. The word "mestizo(a)" usually describes individuals of mixed white and Indian blood. I use it more broadly to indicate any hybridity and also to recall Ursa's identification as "Spanish" in Gayl Jones's novel *Corregidora*.

8. Jones, in interview with Harper, 358.

9. Toni Morrison, interview with Robert Stepto, "Intimate Things in Place," in *The Third Woman*, ed. Dexter Fisher (Boston: Houghton Mifflin, 1980), 179–82.

10. Ibid., 172–73; and Keith Byerman, *Fingering the Jagged Grain* (Athens and London: University of Georgia Press, 1985), 171–216.

11. "My writing expects, demands participatory reading. . . . My language has to have holes and spaces so the reader can come into it" (Toni Morrison, interview with Claudia Tate, in *Black Women Writers*, ed. Tate, 125).

12. Toni Morrison, interview with Nellie McKay, *Contemporary Literature* 24, 4 (Winter 1983): 429.

13. Robert Stam applies the Bakhtinian notions of polyphony, dialogism, and heteroglossia to the analysis of ethnic representations in his "Bakhtin, Polyphony, and Ethnic/Racial Representation," in *Unspeakable Images: Ethnicity and the American Cinema*, ed. Lester D. Friedman (Urbana: University of Illinois Press, 1991), 251–76.

14. One should remember, however, that Morrison's Milkman descends from African Solomon and Indian Sing, so he is a hybrid American.

15. Toni Morrison, interview with Rosemarie K. Lester for Hessian Radio Network in Frankfurt, Spring 1983; printed in *Critical Essays on Toni Morrison*, ed. Nellie McKay (Boston: G. K. Hall, 1988), 53.

16. Jones, interview with Harper, 364.

17. García Márquez's work has been persistently compared to Faulkner's; he personally sees the connections as more geographical than literary. He found the small, decadent southern towns that inspired Faulkner's literary world, "dusty towns inhabited by hopeless people," very similar to places of his own memory and creation. See *Gabriel García Márquez habla de Gabriel García Márquez*, ed. Alfonso Rentería Mantilla (Bogota: Rentería, 1979), 145. Fuentes believes that Faulkner stands out among U.S. writers because he "is the only novelist of defeat in a country that basically has been a nation of optimism and success." A sense of loss connects Yoknapatawpha County to the Mexican experience of defeat and the writing of post-revolution authors. Carlos Fuentes sees the Faulknerian inclusion of all times in the present as another characteristic in common with Mexican culture (see Joseph Sommers, "The Present Moment in the Mexican Novel," *Books Abroad* 40 [Summer 1966]: 261–66; and in Luis Harss and Barbara Dohmann, "Carlos Fuentes, or the New Heresy," in *Into the Mainstream: Conversations with Latin American Writers* [New York: Harper & Row, 1967], 294).

18. Although Marshall shows the persistence of the past in present time and creates specific people and places modeled after her beloved Barbados, she assumes a less "realist" style and a stronger touch of magic and dream, other Faulknerian and Marquezian traits, in *Praisesong for the Widow*.

19. Paule Marshall, *Praisesong for the Widow* (New York: G. P. Putnam's Sons, 1983), 166–68.

20. Paule Marshall, among other black activists and writers, has stated that "though there are points of convergence sometimes, Black people in this country really do constitute a nation apart" (interview with Bröck, 205).

21. Cultural resistance through the creative "re-Africanization" of a nation's texts and rituals is a major theme in African struggles for liberation, although Frantz Fanon and others, such as Amilcar Cabral, leader for the independence of Guinea and Cape Verde who was assassinated in 1973, warned against the idealization of a pure "African" source. Peasant masses have "no need to assert or reassert their identity" because they are less affected by the influence of the colonizer than the bourgeoisie. They "keep intact the sense of their individual and collective dignity" in spite of the oppression (Amilcar Cabral, "Identity and Dignity in the Context of the National Liberation Struggle," in idem, *Return to the Source: Selected Speeches* [New York and London: Monthly Review, 1974], 61–69). Paule Marshall's *The Chosen Place, the Timeless People* and Toni Morrison's *Song of Solomon* show the poor rural folk as a reservoir of culture and resistance.

22. Amilcar Cabral, "National Liberation and Culture," in idem, *Return to the Source*, 43. The use of novels as cultural texts underlining specificities of a nation and drawing alliances with neighboring peoples in grievances against the oppressors recalls Benedict Anderson's view of print as a major element in the process of nation formation; see Benedict Anderson, *Imagined Communities* (London: Verso, 1983).

23. Barbara Christian, "Trajectories of Self-Definition: Placing Contemporary Afro-American Women's Fiction," in *Black Feminist Criticism*, ed. Christian, 185.

24. I echo contemporary issues of national or collective identity discussed in Homi K. Bhabha, *Nation and Narration* (New York and London: Routledge, 1990).

25. The blues does not simply tell what happened to you, says John Lee Hooker; "it's what happened to your foreparents and other people. And that's what makes the blues" (quoted in Lawrence W. Levine, *Black Culture and Black Consciousness* [Oxford: Oxford University Press, 1977], 237).

26. Barbara Christian, "The Race for Theory," *Cultural Critique* 6 (Spring 1987): 63.

# INDEX

abortion: in black women's literature, 192n.57; in Marshall's *Daughters*, 68–69, 192n.57; as practiced by Brazilian slave women, 131–32, 151–52, 154, 206n.28

African American: origin of as ethnic-racial category, 8–9; U.S. stereotypes of, 5

African diaspora: history of, 21–22, 171–73; role of, in Brazilian history, 122–25

African roots: in *Brown Girl, Brownstones*, 59–65; in *The Chosen Place, the Timeless People*, 34–35, 52–59, 189n.35; Jones' disregard of, in *Corregidora*, 140, 208n.42; Jones' use of, in *Song for Anninho*, 140, 208n.42; in *Praisesong for the Widow*, 61–65, 191n.51; return to, in black women's literature, ix–x, 24–26, 165–73, 214n.21

Afroamerica concept: intercontinental aspects of, 3, 176n.6; Jones' interpretation of, 121–25, 203n.4

Allende, Isabel, 195n.9

Allende, Salvador, 181n.55

America: cultural definitions of, 4–9, 120–21; exclusionary concepts of, 175n.1; U.S.-Caribbean-Latin American interconnections in, 1, 175n.1

American Dream, illusory nature of, in *Daughters*, 74–75

American Writers Congress, 106

ancestral figures, portrayal of, in *Daughters*, 73–74. *See also* African roots

Anderson, Benedict, 215n.22

Anglo-America, Latino writers' perception of, 7–8

*Anglo-African Magazine, The*, 183n.67

anti-imperialism: ideology of, with racial integration, 7–8

anti-Semitism: in black women's literature, 29–30; in *The Chosen Place, the Timeless People*, 36–37, 46–47, 55–56, 189n.36

anti-slavery movements: mestizo ideology and, 6–7

antiwar movement: impact on black women writers of, 20; portrayal of, in Marshall's *Daughters*, 77

Anzaldúa, Gloria, 13, 162, 180n.41, 211n.72

Arada tribe, 191n.51

*Arena Conta Zumbi*, 211n.71

Astúrias, Miguel Angel, 181n.55, 195n.9

autobiographical fiction: black women writers' use of, 176n.7; Jones' *Corregidora* as, 131–32; Morrison and García Márquez's work as example of, 102–103

avatar, symbolism of, in *Praisesong for the Widow*, 63

Azevedo, on destruction of slave documents, 205n.22

backras, role of, in *The Chosen Place, the Timeless People,* 51, 188n.33

Bajan culture: influence of, in Barbados, 187n.25; links with, in *Brown Girl, Brownstones,* 60, 170

Bakhtin, Mikhail: on Carnival imagery, 40–41; intertextuality and, 82, 213n.13

Bambara, Toni Cade, 13, 15, 171; assessment of Morrison's work, 88; "cultural workers" concept of, 20

"banana fever," of Colombian economic development, 86–87

Bantus: influence of, in Palmares Republic, 158; role of, in *The Chosen Place, the Timeless People,* 55, 189n.35

Barbados: economic structure of, 185n.13; English rule in, 186n.23; geographic description of, 185n.11; links with, in *Brown Girl, Brownstones,* 60; Marshall's depiction of, 28; politics of, 185n.12; symbolic importance of, in *The Chosen Place, the Timeless People,* 34–35

Barbosa, Rui, 129, 205n.23

Bastide, Roger, 139, 206n.28, 208n.41

*Beloved:* motherhood in, 192n.57; slavery records as source for, 81, 193n.2

Benjamin, Walter, 14–15, 98

Bhabha, Homi K., 215n.24

biblical imagery, in Morrison's *Song of Solomon,* 90–91, 101–102, 199n.58

Bight of Benin, roots of black Americans and, 191n.51

bird imagery, Morrison's and García Márquez's use of, 99–101. *See also* flying imagery

black community in U.S.: black women's writers' perspective on, 2, 168–73; Morrison's roots in, 84–85, 93–94, 118–19, 196n.18; separateness of, with nation, 21, 182n.61

Black Nationalist movement, 172: attitude towards Cuba of, 178n.30; maternal image of U.S. culture, 177n.19; Muslim orientation of, 158; (un)naming practiced by, 129

Black Power movement: Morrison's use of, in *Song of Solomon,* 95; portrayal of, in Marshall's *Daughters,* 76–77

black women writers: interconnections with Latin American and Caribbean culture, 168; political consequences in literature of, 106, 200n.75; renaissance of, in American literature, ix, 2, 22–23, 165–73, 195n.8, 211n.3

*Blake, or the Huts of America,* 25, 183n.67

blindness, as motif in Morrison's *Tar Baby,* 108, 115–16

*Bluest Eye, The,* 202n.89

Bo Diddley, 103

bodies, as motif in Jones' fiction, 154–55

Bolívar, Simon, 6–7

border imagery, in black and Latina literature, 13

*Borderlands,* 180n.41

Borges, Jorges Luis, 181n.50

Brathwaite, Edward, 184n.9, 187n.25

Brazil: Dutch presence in, 159, 210n.64; interconnections with, in Jones' *Corregidora,* 125–46; in Jones' fiction, 120–63, 202n.1; links with, in Morrison's *Tar Baby,* 193n.2; National Day of Negro Conscience, 161; role of Carnival in, 41–42, 187n.24; as setting in black women's literature, 1–2; in *Soul Clap Hands and Sing,* 31–34; slavery in, 23; statistical data on, 204n.11; symbolic importance of, in *The Chosen Place, the Timeless People,* 34–35

Brennan, Tim, 194n.8

Brooks, Gwendolyn, 213n.6

*Brown Girl, Brownstones,* 59–65, 213n.6

Byerman, Keith, 168

Cabral, Amilcar, 214n.21, 215n.22

Caliban image: in *Soul Clap Hands and Sing,* 31–34, 184nn.8–9; in Caribbean-Latin American stories, 6, 12

Calvino, Italo, 98, 195n.12

Campos, Héctor, 194n.8

"cannibal" image of Caribbean culture, 6–7, 177n.13

capitalism: Brazilian patterns of, 124–25, 204n.13; images of in Morrison's criticism of, 93–95, 111–12, 198n.43, 201nn.82, 84

Cardoso, Fernando Henrique, 204n.13

Caribbean region: African diaspora in, 21–22; black writers' links to, 1–2, 25–26; Carnival's symbolism in, 39–42; in *The Chosen Place, the Timeless People*, 34–35; "classic" narratives of, 186n.18; in *Daughters*, 66–79; federation politics in, 66; historical role of, 7–8; influence of, on Morrison and García Márquez, 84, 196n.16; linguistic variety in, 66–67, 191n.53; migration patterns in, 190n.43; as origin of Americas, 3; slavery in, 23; in *Soul Clap Hands and Sing*, 28–34; in *Tar Baby*, 106–18

CARICOM (Caribbean Common Market and Community), 189n.37

CARIFTA (Caribbean Free Trade Association), 189n.37

Carnival: on Barbados, 186n.23; celebration of Brazilian emancipation with, 129; of, in *The Chosen Place, the Timeless People*, 42–50, 57–59; cultural and symbolic importance of, 24, 39–59; images of in Morrison's *Tar Baby*, 114–15; in *Praisesong for the Widow*, 62; on Trinidad, 41–42, 44, 187n.24; role U.S. and European media's portrayal of, 40–41, 186n.18

Carpentier, Alejo, 103, 181n.55, 195n.9

Carriacou Island, 63–65, 191n.50

castration, images of, in Jones' *Corregidora*, 140

Castro, Fidel, racial concepts of, 11, 178n.30

Castro-Klarén, Sara, 194n.8

Catholic Church: presence of, in Brazil, 127, 158–59

Cervantes, Miguel de, 122

Césaire, Aimé, 17, 184n.9, 199n.57

Charles, Ray, 144

*Chosen Place, the Timeless People, The*: Caribbean and Brazil as reference points in, 1, 3; as ethnographic narrative, 28, 34–59; inter-American characteristics of, ix, 167–68; oblit-

eration of past in, 197n.41; parallels with *Daughters* in, 71–72, 169; storytelling as device in, 14

Christian, Barbara, 8, 171, 213n.6

civil rights movement: in *Daughters*, 76–77; emergence of black women writers and, 9, 20; inter-American relations and, 9–13; in *Song of Solomon*, 94–95

Civil War: Brazilian emancipation compared with, 129; in *Daughters*, 75

class: aspects of in Carnival celebrations, 43, 187n.24; in *The Chosen Place, the Timeless People*, 35, 55–59; mestizo ideology and, 7; in *Soul Clap Hands and Sing*, 28–34; in *Tar Baby*, 107–18

Cleaver, Eldridge, 178n.30

Cliff, Michelle, 164, 188n.33, 190n.45

Clytus, John, 178n.30

coalition politics, inter-American links in feminist movement and, 10, 178n.29

coffee cycle (Brazil), 207n.37

Colombia: Great Strike of 1928 in, 104–105; "La Violencia," 105; roots of García Márquez in, 85–86; War of a Thousand Days in, 86

colonialism: African diaspora in, 6, 22; Brazilian history and, 122–25, 162, 204n.13; in *The Chosen Place, the Timeless People*, 35–59, 188n.34; Latino writers' resistance to, 16–18; in *Soul Clap Hands and Sing*, 30–31; in *Tar Baby*, 110–11, 117–18

color hierarchy: in *The Chosen Place, the Timeless People*, 35, 51, 185n.13, 188n.32; inter-American concepts of, 166–67, 212n.6

communists, McCarthy era persecution of, 28–30

constellation imagery, in *Daughters*, 67–68, 192n.56

consumerism, portrayal of in *The Chosen Place, the Timeless People*, 51–52

cooperative action, patterns of, in Caribbean, 56–57, 189n.37

Coover, Robert, 195n.12

*Corregidora*: Brazilian master-slave relationships in, 122–26, 139–40, 142–44, 167; Brazilian-U.S. interconnectivity in, ix, 1, 125–46;

*Corregidora* (*cont.*)
extended Caribbean islands as reference point, 1–3; linguistic origins
of title, 160, 210n.68; Morrison's
assessment of, 168; motherhood in,
192n.57; obliteration of past in,
197n.41
Cortázar, Julio, 103, 181n.55, 195n.9
Crouch, Stanley, 201n.84
Cuba: African-Spanish synthesis in,
10–12, 178n.30; anti-imperialism
in, 7; Revolution as influence on
black and Latino writers, 7, 20,
181n.55; War of Independence in,
25
Cuffy (slave leader), 38–39, 186n.16
culture: as resource for black women
writers, 16–26, 170–73, 183n.65,
214n.21, 215n.22; Brazilian history
in context of, 121–25; crisscrossing
of, in Latin and Caribbean Carnival
festivals, 39–41; in *Praisesong for the
Widow*, 61–65; in *Song for Anninho*,
147, 208n.45
Curtin, Philip D., 204n.9

"dark" image of Latin America, Euro-
pean embrace of, 6–7, 177n.13
*Daughters*, 50, 167–69; constellation
imagery in, 67–68, 192n.56; U.S.-
Caribbean links in, 66–79
Davis, Angela, 192n.55
Davis, Arthur P., 195n.8
*Death of Artemio Cruz, The*, 148–49
Degler, Carl, 124, 133
Delany, Martin, 203n.8
de Musset, Alfred, 17–18
*Die Vogelsangerin*, 202n.1
Dixon, Melvin, 210n.68
Dominican Republic, Marshall's roots
in, 191n.54
Douglas, Frederick, 203n.8
Drake, Sir Francis, García Márquez re-
visionist view of, 104–105
DuBois, W.E.B., 17, 182n.61,
189n.36, 192n.62
Dunbar, Paul Laurence, 27

Eco, Umberto, 82
Eligio García, Eligio, 85
Elkins, Stanley, 133
Ellison, Ralph, 203n.3

Epstein, Joseph, 83
ethnicity, in *Daughters*, 78–79; inter-
American characteristics of, 2–3;
inter-American relations and, 10.
*See also* race and racism
ethnography: bifocal aspects of,
187n.28; defined, 183n.1; in *The
Chosen Place, the Timeless People*, 34–
59; culture defined in, 183n.65; influence on black American women
writers, 4, 15–16, 23–24, 176n.7;
in Marshall's novels, 27–28; in *Soul
Clap Hands and Sing*, 28–34
*Et les chiens se taisaient*, 199n.57
*Eva's Man*, 148, 154
"extended Caribbean" concept, ix, 3,
166, 172–73. *See also* Caribbean region

family: destruction of slave families by
Brazilian planters, 135; use of ties
to, in black women's literature, 15
Fanon, Frantz: on cultural resistance,
16–18, 178n.30, 214n.21; Jones influenced by, 135–36; Morrison influenced by, 199n.57; Pan-African
resistance and, 17–19; on racism in
white society, 11; on identity as
transformative, creative process,
189n.40; use of Shakespeare's *Tempest* by, 184n.9
Faulkner, William: Jones influenced
by, 148, 170; Morrison influenced
by, 89, 170, 196n.18
Federman, Raymond, 195n.12
feminist movement: coalition of wom-
en of color in, 9–10, 178n.10;
emergence of black women writers
and, 9, 169–73; inter-American relations and, 9–13; portrayal of, in
*Daughters*, 77
Fernandes, Florestan, 204n.13
Fernández Retamar, 34, 184n.9
fertility: in Jones' fiction, 120–21,
130–32, 135–36, 151–52, 205n.24,
206nn.28–29; stereotypes of slave
women regarding, 134, 207n.36. *See
also* abortion; pregnancy; sterility
Fischer, Michael, 176n.7, 184n.2,
187n.28
*Flying Down to Rio*, 6, 176n.11
flying imagery: in Jones' *Song for Anninho*, 160; in Morrison's *Tar Baby*,

115; Morrison's and García Márquez's use of, 99–100

Fogel, Robert William, 204n.9, 207n.36

folklore: Morrison's and García Márquez's use of, 99–100; rejection of, in Jones' fiction, 162–63, 202n.1; role of, in black women's literature, 19; use of in Morrison's *Tar Baby*, 115–16, 201n.86

folk medicine: in black women's fiction, 159–60

Foucault, Michel, 17

freedom, reality of, for blacks in Jones' fiction, 142–43

Freitas, Décio, 150, 209n.51

French culture: in *Praisésong for the Widow*, 62, 190n.47; in *Tar Baby*, 109–10

Freyre, Gilberto: on Brazilian miscegenation and socialization patterns, 124, 127–29, 132–33, 140, 156; on destruction of Brazilian slave documents, 205n.22; on Portuguese culture and racial characteristics, 131, 205nn.26–27

Fuentes, Carlos, ix; American perceptions of, 212n.4; antipathy to Anglo-America of, 8; on culture, 208n.45; distrust of folklore, 162–63; Faulkner's influence on, 170, 214n.17; García Márquez influenced by, 103; Jones influenced by, 2, 14, 120–22, 145, 148–49, 164, 168, 203n.3; on Mexican Revolution, 209n.49; mixing of literary genres by, 148–51, 176n.7, 209n.52; Morrison's novels influenced by, 164, 194n.3; popularity of, in Latin American "boom," 181n.55, 195n.9; storytelling used by, 14; on subversiveness of art, 166, 212n.5; "Third Cinema" and, 181n.50

Gaines, Ernest, 122

Ganga Zumba (slave leader), 149, 152–53, 208n.48

García Márquez, Gabriel, ix; African roots in work of, 15, 180n.47; Angolan visit of, 196n.16; antipathy to Anglo-America of, 8, 176n.8; critical appraisal of, 82–83, 194n.8,

195n.9, 212n.4; on Cuban culture, 11; family origins of, 85–86, 102–103, 196n.21, 199n.60; Faulkner's influence on, 170, 214n.17; fiction as social transformation, 16–18, 166, 181n.50, 212n.5; images of white women in fiction of, 201n.81; influences on work of, 83–84, 195n.12, 196n.16; Jones influenced by, 14, 121–22, 145, 149–50, 160, 163, 203n.3; Morrison's intertextual dialogue with, in *Song of Solomon*, 2, 81–106, 119, 164, 168; revolutionary aspects of literature, 16–18, 105–106, 166, 181n.50, 212n.5; popularity of, in Latin American "boom," 19, 83, 181n.55, 194n.6; storytelling techniques used by, 14, 98–99

Garvey, Marcus, 60

Gates, Henry Louis Jr., 8

Gaye, Marvin, 77

gender: inter-American characteristics of, 2–3, 171; issues of, in *The Chosen Place, the Timeless People*, 50–51, 57–59; Morrison's views on, 104–105; role of, in Jones' *Corregidora*, 126–46; role of, in Jones' fiction, 123–25

Genovese, Eugene, 133, 206n.32

Giacomini, Sonia, 128, 207n.38

gold cycle (Brazil), 207n.37

Gramsci, Antonio, 182n.60

Grenada: role of, in black women's literature, 191n.50

Guillén, Nicolás, 179n.36, 192n.62

Gutierrez, Gustavo, 182n.58

Haiti, 12; Marshall's roots in, 191n.54; multinational development projects in, 185n.14; revolution in, 25, 106–107, 200n.78

Hall, Stuart, 189n.40

Harlem Renaissance, 9, 11–12

Harper, Michael, 122, 203n.3

Harris, Marvin, 124

Hemingway, Ernest, 122

*Hermit Woman, The*, 202n.1

Hernández, Enrique, 194n.6

Herskovits, Melville, 8

historiography: black women writers and, 23–26; destruction of Brazilian slave papers and, 205n.23; of Bra-

historiography (*cont.*)
zilian race relations, 120; on interracial relations, 133; statistical information on slavery and, 204n.9
history: confluence with myth, in
black women's fiction, 150, 165–
66; cycle of, in *Song for Anninho*,
150–62; image of strong black
women in, 60, 67, 94–95, 191n.55;
intertextuality as key to, in Morrison's *Song of Solomon*, 82–106;
Jones' use of in *Corregidora*, 121–
25, 144–46; Marshall's use of, in
*The Chosen Place, the Timeless People*,
55; redefinition of, in Morrison's
fiction, 81–119; rewriting and reinvention of, in *Daughters*, 70–79;
role of, in work of black women
writers, 16–26, 182n.58; in *Tar
Baby*, 107–18
Holiday, Billie, 144
Holocaust, in black literature, 46–47,
189n.36
homosexuality: in Jones' *Corregidora*,
139; in *The Chosen Place, the Timeless
People*, 50, 188n.30
Hooker, John Lee, 215n.75
Hooks, Bell, 195n.8
Hughes, Langston, 9; on racism in
Latin America, 11–12, 179n.36
Hurston, Zora Neale, 14, 121–22,
213n.6

Ianni, Octavio, 204n.13
identity: black women writers' search
for collective, 170–73, 214n.21,
215n.24; discovery of, in *Chosen
Place, Timeless People*, 56–59,
189n.40; in *Soul Clap Hands and
Sing*, 33–34
Iguarán Cotes, Tranquilina, 85
immigration, portrayal of, in black
women's literature, 45, 61–65,
190n.43; images of in *Tar Baby*,
111, 201n.82. *See also* Migration
Immigration and Naturalization Act of
1965, 190n.43
incest, in Jones' fiction, 128–29, 156;
in Morrison's fiction, 89–90
Indians. *See* East Indians; Native
Americans; West Indians
inter-American connectivity: of black
women writers, ix, 2–3, 8–13;

Morrison, Jones, and Marshall and,
14–26, 180n.43
intertextuality: between *Song of Solomon* and *One Hundred Years of Solitude*, 82–106; in Jones' fiction,
121–25, 161–62, 168, 211n.72; inter-American links in literature and,
ix; in *Tar Baby*, 107–18, 168
Ivask, Ivan, 195n.9

Jackson, Jesse, 8
Jamaica, Carnival in, 41; Maroon settlements in, 67, 191n.55
Jameson, Fredric, 179n.38
Jews: as portrayed by black women
writers, 29–30; in *The Chosen Place,
the Timeless People*, 36–37, 46–47,
55–56, 189n.36. *See also* anti-Semitism
Jones, Gayl: Brazil as reference point
for, 1; extended Caribbean in literature of, 1, 3, 172; family roots of,
131–32; Fuentes' influence on, 2,
14, 120–22, 145, 148–49, 163,
168, 203n.3; on fiction as agent for
change, 16, 166, 212n.5; García
Márquez's influence on, 14, 121–
22, 145, 149–50, 160, 163, 203n.3;
inter-American connections in work
of, 14–26, 164–73; Morrison's
novels assessed by, 194n.3; Morrison's assessment of, 168; prominence of, 9, 165–73; reconciliation
with slave past in work of, 25; rejection of feminist category, 169–
70; storytelling techniques used by,
98; (un)naming concept and, 129,
177n.20. *See also Song for Anninho*;
specific works, e.g., *Corregidora*
Jones, Jacqueline, 133
Jones, LeRoi, 177n.20
Jordan, Winthrop, 208n.40
Joyce, James, 122

Kenyatta, Jomo, 192n.62
Kerouac, Jack, 179n.35
Kincaid, Jamaica, 190n.45
Kristeva, Julia, 82
Kuczynski, R. R., 204n.9
Kutzinski, Vera M., 194n.3, 196n.16

Lamming, George, 184n.9
language: as vehicle in *Song for An-*

*ninho*, 146–48, 160–62; plurality of, in Latin American fiction, 150, 209n.49; role of, in Marshall's *Daughters*, 66–67, 191n.53

Latin America: black writers' links with, 25–26; cultural meaning of term America in, 5–8; stereotyping of, by U.S. culture, 5–6, 176n.11

Latin American writers: "boom" in popularity of, 2, 8, 18–21, 83, 122, 181n.55, 194n.6, 195n.9; Jones influenced by, 121–22, 203n.3; Morrison influenced by, 82–83, 194n.4; U.S. perceptions of, 165, 181n.50, 212n.4

Lead-belly, 103

LeClair, Thomas, 193n.3

Lee, Dorothy H., 193n.3, 197n.40

Leonard, John, 193n.3

Lewis, Gordon K., 3, 186n.18

literary gaze, of black women writers, 2

literary genres: crossover of, by black American women writers, 4, 148–49, mixing of by Latin American writers, genres by, 148–51, 176n.7, 209n.52

literary inter-space (*entre-lugar*), 2, 175n.2

Lorde, Audre, 137; on cultural identity, 11–12; family of, 179n.34; Grenadan roots of, 191n.50; inter-American connectivity in work of, 15; (un)naming concept and, 177n.20

L'Ouverture, Toussaint, 106–107

Machado, Antonio, 211n.72

Mair, Lucille, 192n.55

manumission, Brazilian slaveowners' use of, 123–24

Maroon settlements: defined, 187n.27; in Brazil, 122–23, 153, 203n.6; in Jamaica, 67, 191n.55. *See also* Palmares (Brazilian Maroon settlement)

Márquez Iguarán Maria, 85

Márquez Iguarán, Nicolas Ricardo, 85

Marshall, Paule: Brazil as reference point for, 11; ethnographic elements in work of, 15–16, 27–28; extended Caribbean in literature of, 3,

7, 11, 84, 172; on fiction as agent for change, 166, 212n.5; inter-American connections in work of, 14–26, 164–73; list of works, in order of publication, 184n.3; literary influences on, 170, 214n.17; positive aspects in work of, 59, 189n.41; prominence of, 9, 165–73; on stereotype of black women in literature, 213n.6; storytelling techniques used by, 98. *See also* specific works

Martí, José: anti-imperialist ideology of, 7–8; nationalism and resistance in ideology of, 17–19; "Nuestra America" concept of, x, 7–8

Martins, Silveira, 136

Marxism, influence of, on Latin American writers, 181n.50

*Masters and the Slaves, The,* 127

*Maud Martha,* 213n.6

Meredith, William, 203n.3

mestizo culture: aspects of, in Brazilian Portuguese planters, 124–25, 131, 204n.12, 206n.27; defined, 213n.7; emergence of, 6–7; influence of, in Morrison and García Márquez, 84, 196n.16; myths of, in Latin American literature, 11, 166–67, 212n.6; racism in Cuba and, 179n.36. *See also* mulattoes

Mexico: history of, as depicted by Fuentes, 148–49, 209n.49; racial identity in, 11, 179n.35; stereotyping of, in movies, 6

Mighty Sparrow, 41

migration: in *Brown Girl, Brownstones,* 60, 190n.43; in *Corregidora,* 141–42; in *The Chosen Place, the Timeless People,* 50–51, 188n.31; in *Daughters,* 74–75; in Morrison's work, 95–96, 198n.46. *See also* immigration

Miller, Floyd, 183n.67

Minas Gerais (Brazil), 207n.37

miscegenation: in Palmares Maroon settlement, 155–56, 210n.58; patterns of, in Brazil, 124–25, 127–29, 132–34, 156–57, 204n.12, 206nn.32–33, 208n.40. *See also* mulattoes

Momaday, N. Scott, 121–22, 203n.3

Monk, Thelonius, 144

Montserrat: Carnival celebrations on, 44, 187n.25

Morrison, Toni: (un)naming concept and, 177n.20; black writers' appraisal of, 106, 200n.76; historiography of slavery criticized by, 207n.36; family roots of, 84–88, 102–103; on fiction as agent social transformation, 16–17, 166, 212n.5; inter-American connections in work of, 1, 14–26, 164–73; intertextual dialogue with García Márquez, 81–106, 119, 164, 168; Jones assessed by, 168; list of books in order of publication, 193n.1; on participatory reading, 169, 213n.11; prominence of, 9, 165–73; redefinition of history and geography by, 81–119; resistance to categorization of black writers, 84, 165, 169–70, 211n.2; storytelling techniques used by, 98–99; Vargas Llosa's work linked with, 181n.55

motherhood: African traditions regarding, 130–31, 205n.24; in black women's literature, 169, 192n.57. See also fertility; pregnancy; sterility

"mothers' gardens" motif in black women's literature, 26

Moura, Clovis, 205n.23

movies, stereotype of Latin America in, 5–6

Muddy Waters, 103

mulattoes: in Brazilian culture, 124–25, 139, 156–57, 204n.12, 207n.38; census data on, 207n.33; in Jones' Corregidora, 125, 137–38; Portuguese planters as, 130–31, 206n.27; white stereotypes of, 166–67, 212n.6

multinational companies, development projects in Caribbean and Latin American countries, 185n.14

music: black women writers' use of, 164–73, 215n.25; in Jones' Corregidora, 138–39, 144; Morrison's use of, 103–104, 169–73

Muslims, in Palmares maroon settlement, 156–58, 210n.61

mythology: in Morrison's Tar Baby, 107–109, 108n.80; Morrison's and García Márquez's use of, 96, 99–100, 198n.47

Nascimento, Elisa Larkin, 8–9

nationalism, Latino writers embrace of, 181n.50

Native Americans: as ancestors of black Americans, 78; U.S. stereotypes of, 5; writers, Jones influenced by, 121–22, 203n.3

neocolonialism: African diaspora and, 21–22; in in The Chosen Place, the Timeless People, 36–37, 47–59; Morrison's Tar Baby, 107–18

Neruda, Pablo, 192n.62

New World concept. See inter-American links; neocolonialism

Nichols, John, 195n.12

Nobel Prize: Morrison and García Márquez as recipients of, 82–83; prestige of, as agent for social transformation, 17

Nobel, David W., 4, 176n.8

"Nuestra America" concept, x, 7–8, 12

Nuno, Juan, 177n.19

O'Connor, Flannery, 169

Old Gringo, The, 149

One Hundred Years of Solitude: critical appraisal of, 82–83, 106, 194n.8, 195n.9, 200n.76; intertextual dialogue with, in Morrison's Song of Solomon, 2, 81–106

Palmares, Republic of (Brazilian Maroon settlement), 55, 140–41, 150–62, 209n.51; historic importance of, 161–62, 211n.71

Pan-Africanism: writers of color and, 17–19

Park, Robert E., 204n.12

patriarchal structure: of Brazil's slave-master relationships, 133–34, 208n.41; in Jones' Corregidora, 125–26, 139–40, 142–44

Paz, Octavio, 5, 9

Petry, Ann, 213n.6

Pleasures of Exile, The, 184n.9

politics: Morrison's views on literature and, 106, 200n.75; portrayal of, in Daughters, 70–79

popular culture, politicization of, 44

Portuguese: as Brazilian slaveowners, 124–25, 127–31, 156–57, 204n.12, 206nn.25–27

*Praisesong for the Widow*, 59–65, 167–68, 170; parallels with *Daughters*, 74; storytelling as device in, 14

pregnancy: in black women's literature, 192n.57; in Marshall's *Daughters*, 68–69, 192n.57. *See also* abortion; fertility; motherhood

Princess Isabel of Portugal ("The Redemptress"), 129, 205n.23

property: black ownership of, in Jones' fiction, 143; women as, in Jones' *Corregidora*, 126–27

prostitution, in Jones' *Corregidora*, 135–37, 207n.38

Puig, Manuel, 195n.9

quest motif: in work of Morrison and García Márquez, 91–92

*quilombos*, 140, 150–51, 155, 187n.27

race and racism: anti-imperialist ideology and, 7–8; Brazilian patterns of, 123–25, 203n.8, 204n.12; inter-American characteristics of, 2–3, 169–73; in Jones' fiction, 123–25; mestizo ideology and, 6–7; Morrison's views on, 104–105, 107–18; separatist notions of propriety in *Soul Clap Hands and Sing*, 32, 184n.8. *See also* color hierarchy

rape: images of, in Morrison's *Tar Baby*, 113–14; in Jones' fiction, 134–36, 154, 157–58

Reed, Ishmael, (un)naming concept and, 177n.20

Reid, Alastair, 103, 195n.9

ring shouts (ring dancing and singing) (African ritual), 24, 65, 100, 191n.51, 199n.56

rituals: in black women's literature, 23–24, 183n.64; in Morrison's *Tar Baby*, 114–15; in *Praisesong for the Widow*, 64–65, 191n.51

Robeson, Paul, 192n.62

Rodrigues, Ana Maria, 187n.24

Roosevelt, Franklin Delano, 19

Rosaldo, Renato, 183n.65

Rout, Leslie B., Jr., 178n.30

Rulfo, Juan, 195n.9

sadism, against Brazilian slave women, 136–38, 207n.38

sadomasochism, in Jones' fiction, 128–29

"Sailing to Byzantium," 184n.4

Saldívar, José David, 193n.3

*Salt Eaters, The*, 13

samba parades, during Brazil's Carnival, 187n.24

Sangari, Kumkum, 182n.55

self-affirmation: cultural and political resources for, 17, 203n.4; in Morrison's *Song of Solomon*, 96–97

self-determination, Caribbean movement for, 28–31

self-segregation, limits of, 9

sexual abuse, in Jones' fiction, 132–46, 154, 207n.38

sexual orientation: in black and Latina literature, 180n.41

sexuality: in *The Chosen Place, the Timeless People*, 50–51; in *Corregidora*, 125–46, 161–62, 169; in *Song of Solomon*, 101–102, 169

Shakespeare, William, Caribbean and African appropriations of *The Tempest* by, 33–34, 184n.9

Shange, Ntozake, 12–13, 15, 171

Shapiro, Karl, 181n.50

Shorris, Earl, 181n.50

slave narratives: role of, in Brazilian revisionist history, 122–24, 203n.5; stereotyping in, 212n.6

slave rebellions: history of, in Brazil, 140–41; in Barbados, 38–39, 185n.16; Jones' research into, 122–25, 203n.5; Muslim influence on, 210n.61; re-enactment of, in Carnival, 42–45, 187n.27; role of women in, 67, 191n.55; in *Song for Anninho*, 146–62. *See also* Maroon settlements

slavery: in Barbados, 38–39, 185n.16; in black women's literature, 22–23, 25, 167–73; in Caribbean islands, 3; Carnival depiction of, 44–45; Brazilian system of, 122–63; burning of Brazilian documents related to, 129–30, 205n.22; emancipation in Brazil, 129–30; in Jones' fiction, 128–63; records of, as source for Morrison's work, 81, 193n.2; statistical data on, 11, 124, 204n.9

Smith, Barbara, 10, 178n.29

Soares, Antonio, 155

social dramas, in black women's literature, 23–24, 183n.64

social transformation, black women's literature as agent for, 2, 22–23, 15–16, 166–73

*Song for Anninho*, 67; as epic of Palmares slave rebellion, 140, 146–62, 167; Brazilian history in, 1, 3, 122, 124–25; Caribbean islands as reference point in, 1, 3; motherhood imagery in, 192n.57; obliteration of past in, 197n.41; storytelling as device in, 14

*Song of Solomon*: awards received by, 197n.37; Caribbean imagery in, 81; Colombian geography and history in, 81; comparisons with *Tar Baby*, 202n.87; critical appraisal of, 106, 193n.3, 200n.76; inter-American characteristics of, ix, 167; intertextual dialogue with *One Hundred Years of Solitude*, 2, 81–106; storytelling as device in, 14

*Soul Clap Hands and Sing*: as ethnographic narrative, 28–34

Spillers, Hortense J., 182n.59, 188n.30

spirit possession: in *Praisesong for the Widow*, 63–65, 190n.49; in *Tar Baby*, 108. *See also* witchcraft

spirituals, Morrison's work influenced by, 103–104

Spivak, Gayatri, 13, 17, 182n.60

Stam, Robert, 213n.13

Stepto, Robert, 168

stereotypes: dominance of U.S. culture in shaping, 5–6; of fertility in slave women, 134, 139, 207n.36; of mulattoes by whites, 166–67, 212n.6; in slave narratives, 212n.6

sterility: in *Corregidora*, 126–27, 130–32, 135–36, 145–46, 205n.24, 206nn.28–29; as motif in Jones' fiction, 120–21, 151–52, 154

storytelling: Jones' use of, in *Corregidora*, 141–42; in Latin American novels, 19; in Morrison's fiction, 88, 98–99; in *Praisesong for the Widow*, 62–65; use of, in black women's literature, 14–15

Strouse, Jean, 193n.3

sugar production, Brazilian slave labor in, 207n.37

Sutch, Richard, 207n.36

syncretism: in Cuban culture, 10–11

*Tar Baby*: Brazil as reference point in, 1, 3; color hierarchy in, 167; extended Caribbean as bridge in, 1, 81, 106–18; storytelling as device in, 14

Taylor, Patrick, 44

*Tempest, The*, 6; Caribbean and African appropriations of, 33–34, 184n.9

*Temple of My Familiar*, 180n.43

"Third Cinema," 181n.50

third eye, African cultural concept of: in Jones' *Song for Anninho*, 159–60; in Morrison's *Tar Baby*, 108, 200n.79

Third World, terminology regarding, 12–13, 179n.38

*This Bridge Called My Back*, 180n.41

tidal patterns, as motif in *The Chosen Place, the Timeless People*, 53–54

time as literary device, Morrison's and García Márquez's use of, 99

Toomer, Jean, 122

tourism industry, as portrayed in Morrison's *Tar Baby*, 107

trade unionism, portrayal of, in *The Chosen Place, the Timeless People*, 51–52

Treaty of Ryswick, 200n.78

Trilling, Lionel, 83

Trinidad: role of Carnival in, 41–42, 44, 187nn.24–25

Turner, Victor, 187n.24

Tutuola, Amos, 203n.3

UNIA (Universal Negro Improvement Association), 60

United Fruit Company, 86–87

United States: as portrayed in Morrison's *Tar Baby*, 112–13, 201n.84; Brazil compared with, 123–24; Caribbean migration patterns in, 190n.43; criticism of, in *The Chosen Place, the Timeless People*, 47–49, 71–72, 188n.29; cultural appropriation of concept of America by, 4–5, 176n.8; Morrison's roots in, 84–85, 196n.18; portrayal of, in *Daughters*, 67–79; reinvigoration and subver-

sion literature of, by black writers, 2–3

(un)naming, practice of, by African Americans, 8, 129, 177n.20

van den Berghe, Pierre L., 133

Vargas Llosa, Mario, 181n.55; international popularity of, 195n.9; Morrison's work compared with, 193n.3; on influences on García Márquez, 85–86

Velho, Domingos Jorge, 153–55, 209n.55

"Very Old Man with Enormous Wings, A," 99–100

Vidal, Hernán, 200n.76

Wagley, Charles, 5, 176n.6

Walker, Alice: "womanist" literature of, 10–11, 122, 178n.30; inter-American connectivity in work of, 15, 171; (un)naming concept and, 177n.20

Waller, Fats, 103

Wallerstein, Immanuel, ix, 3, 172

Webb, Frank, 203n.8

Weekly Anglo-African, The, 183n.67

Welty, Eudora, 169

West Indians, comparisons with U.S. blacks and whites, 202n.89

Western civilization and culture: in The Chosen Place, the Timeless People, 47–48, 54–59; concept of America shaped by, 5; Morrison's concern with, in Tar Baby, 108–109; in

Praisesong for the Widow, 61–65, 190n.47

White, Deborah Gray, 134

Williams, Eric, 17, 204n.13

Willis, Susan, 19, 181n.55, 193n.3, 195n.12, 201n.81

witchcraft, practice of, in Brazil, 130–31, 206n.26

Wofford, Chloe Anthony. See Morrison, Toni

women: strong images of, 60, 67, 94–95, 102–104, 116–17, 191n.55, 199n.62; images of white women in Morrison's fiction, 109, 136–37, 201n.81; role of, in Palmares Maroon settlement, 157–58; violence of white women against Brazilian slave women, 133–34

Woolf, Virginia: Morrison's thesis on, 196n.18

Wright, John, 8

Xarque and Other Poems, 202n.1

Yeats, W. B., 184n.4

Zamora, Lois Parkinson, 209n.52, 212n.4

Zumbi (slave leader), 149, 152–53, 158, 160, 208n.48, 210n.66; as mythical hero, 211n.71; killing of, 55, 154–55, 209n.51; marriage to white woman, 156–57, 160

43/64
75800011